Race and College Admissions

Race and College Admissions

A Case for Affirmative Action

JAMILLAH MOORE

McFarland & Company, Inc., Publishers

Jefferson, North Carolina, and London

LIBRARY OF CONGRESS CATALOGUING-IN-PUBLICATION DATA

Moore, Jamillah.
    Race and college admissions : a case for affirmative action /
Jamillah Moore.
       p.   cm.
    Includes bibliographical references and index.

    ISBN 0-7864-1984-9 (softcover : 50# alkaline paper)

    1. Discrimination in higher education — United States.
    2. Affirmative action programs in education — United States.
    3. Universities and colleges— United States— Admission.   I. Title.
LC212.42.M66   2005
378.1'61— dc22   2004025786

British Library cataloguing data are available

Cover illustration: ©2005 Artville.

Manufactured in the United States of America

*McFarland & Company, Inc., Publishers
  Box 611, Jefferson, North Carolina 28640
  www.mcfarlandpub.com*

Acknowledgments

This book came out of three years of research and work with the California State Senate Select Committee on College and University Admissions and Outreach. The chair of the committee, Senator Teresa P. Hughes has been instrumental in my political and academic career. I can't thank her enough for selecting me to take on such a large task. Without her support this book would not be possible. Senator Richard Alarcon and his staff were instrumental in assisting me with data and giving me the opportunity to continue to work with the committee.

I would like to give special thanks to my mother, Velma, for her guidance, faith, wisdom and support. Without her I would not be the person I am today. Special thanks to the University of California and former president Dr. Richard Atkinson for their support and research assistance with the book. Special thanks also goes to those from the university community who took time out to verify and provide important data.

I must thank Dr. Anita DeFrantz: Her guidance as my graduate advisor and encouragement to move forward with this project is appreciated. Special thanks to Andro Rios, Dr. Charles Ratliff, Anne Garcia, Dara Fong, Barbara Randall, and Duane and Karen Newcomb. The time, energy and assistance they provided were priceless.

Contents

Preface

Until the late 1990s, underrepresented students of color were beginning to make gains in college admissions. Now all minority students are facing a real setback. Why? Because blacks, especially, are being denied admission to colleges that can't consider race as an admissions criterion. Other colleges are so intimidated by the courts and opponents of affirmative action that they have begun to alter their admissions policies drastically. The cry is, "We're going to level the playing field." Fair enough, if this were true.

But as the California Senate Select Committee on College and University, Admissions and Outreach discovered, nobody has leveled the playing field. Yes, some colleges and states have dropped preferences based on race. But many colleges still blatantly use unfair preferences so established that they've become almost invisible to the public and especially to the college admissions officials making the decisions.

The University of Virginia, for instance, gives preference to the sons or daughters of alumni or to students from wealthy families who might give generously to the school. John A. Blackburn, the dean of admissions, said (in *The Wall Street Journal*, February 2003), "The university will admit a student from a wealthy family if it looks like that family will give a significant gift to the school, even if that student isn't eligible otherwise." A number of other similar criteria used by colleges and universities nationwide are simply swept under the rug.

Race and College Admissions shows readers why the effort to create a color-blind society by denying the use of race as a criteria for admission has created complete chaos for underrepresented students of color hoping to enter selective and elite colleges and universities.

The efforts to substitute percentage plans for race haven't worked, and the courts have created a hodgepodge of rules that have left admissions policies without guidelines. Colleges, many without realizing it, are condoning far more unfair admission preferences that have nothing to do with affirmative action.

And inner-city schools aren't offering a quality of education that would allow their students of color to compete for admission to top universities.

Race and College Admissions looks at all of these problems in detail. It then offers comprehensive recommendations aimed at correcting the problems that are now standing in the way of underprivileged quality underrepresented students who want and desperately need a college education to be able to compete in America's future.

I was inspired to write this book by my experience as the former senior consultant to the California State Senate Select Committee on College and University Admission and Outreach. In my work and research, I have found that a majority of students and parents do not have a working knowledge or understanding of the admissions process and its connection to affirmative action. Individuals must be educated beyond the 30-second sound bite on what affirmative action is, and they must understand its importance and purpose in higher education. My intention in this book is to present the goal and purpose of affirmative action and dispel the misconceptions, articulate the continued need for affirmative action at elite and selective institutions, and explain the role race plays in higher education.

Frustrating and controversial are the definitions of preferences and merit. The university can admit a student under any preference it chooses without adhering to any requirement (through a process called admission by exception). It is deemed unfair, however, to admit on the basis of race.

Race and College Admissions sorts out the preference questions, examining a wide range of unfair admissions practices. It also questions what is meant by merit, a term which many universities fall back on to justify their preferences, and asks that merit for inner-city disadvantaged students be looked at in a light different from merit for students from affluent high schools. A single mom with two children, for instance, who is supporting her children and still going to high school and making good grades, is showing as much merit as the student supported by his or her parents and whose merit is defined as being the editor of the high school newspaper.

In conducting research for the committee, I discovered that while underrepresented students of color make up a large proportion of the student demographics, they continue to decline as a proportion of college enrollment.

This decline is a direct result of barriers these students encounter as they progress through the educational pipeline. The attack on the use of race in college admissions decisions is an obstruction of equal access to selective and elite institutions for underrepresented students of color. The practice of considering race along with many other factors presented by college applicants has too frequently been misconstrued as students of color taking a given "right" away from students who have been identified as worthy based on academic merit.

Race and College Admissions will carefully examine all aspects of the admission problem for underrepresented students of color and offer solutions that will begin to create a level playing field for everyone.

Introduction

The vestiges of racial discrimination still exist in almost every aspect of American life, even after the passage of civil rights laws. In the 21st century the issues of race and equity are still as controversial and divisive as they were in the 17th century. Numerous studies demonstrate that race is still an issue in this country, finding that in health care, bank loans, employment, housing, social services and business, most people of color encounter discrimination. Affirmative action is a policy designed to redress the vestiges of discrimination and exclusion.

Discrimination is a two-way street, as it gives a preference to one while it makes disadvantages for another. This preference is often invisible to those who benefit the most. In our society the benefits go largely to white people, called the "privileged." They garner access to opportunities frequently out of reach for nonwhites. Peggy McIntosh, a researcher and professor at Wellesley College, was the first to define "white privilege" as an invisible package of unearned assets that whites can cash in on every day, all the while remaining oblivious to their own privileged state. This obliviousness drives the color-blind movement and critics of affirmative action.

Affirmative action is not a policy geared toward race or a discriminatory practice against whites. However, race comes into the picture based upon the history of the United States and the power of the dominant group. Affirmative action attempts to redress inequities, providing opportunities and access for underrepresented groups who more often than not are nonwhite.

Education is the gateway to opportunity, and many students compete to gain admission to selective and elite institutions every year throughout the United States. As the population increases and access to resources, employment and education become increasingly limited, competitive poli-

1

cies like that of affirmative action will continue to come under attack. And when a student gets denied admission from the college of his choice, affirmative action and underrepresented students of color become the scapegoats.*

The 2003 U.S. Supreme Court decisions in the Grutter and Gratz cases have once again sustained affirmative action in college admissions. The Court has acknowledged diversity as a compelling interest. Colleges and universities have an established set of goals and values. These issues are outlined in their mission statements, and they all share the same goal of ensuring a diverse learning environment that prepares students to work in a democratic society. In the belief that academic excellence is fostered when students have the opportunity to learn from each other, institutions strive to provide classrooms that offer perspectives from diverse cultures and ethnicities. Educational opportunities are drastically limited without diversity, and that compromises the institution's ability to maintain its own mission and goals.

Diversity characterizes and intellectually embraces excellence on college campuses. As the American Association of University Professors asserts, institutions must have the authority to establish policies and implement practices that will attract students who will contribute to the shared values of the academic community and who will collectively create an environment conducive to accomplishing the institutions' missions. Admitting a diverse student body means an extensive admissions process must look at all aspects of diversity: geography, economic background, special talents, students' home languages, and a student's ability to overcome hardship.

The use of race in college admission becomes controversial at elite and selective institutions because they have many more qualified applicants than there are spaces available. Underrepresented students of color who gain admission to selective institutions must be eligible to compete in the process. Affirmative action does not mandate that a school provide access to unqualified students. All applicants must be qualified before they can even enter the admission process. There is a misconception that applicants with high test scores and GPAs are the only type of student entitled to admission into a selective institution and that underrepresented students hinder the admission process. This misconception runs counter to an institution's ability to make sound decisions in choosing among well-qualified applicants. A comprehensive admission process examines characteristics of individual applicants and the total applicant pool in an effort to compose a quality, diverse student body. Institutions are responsible to make sure that all applicants are evaluated fairly. In *The Chronicle of Higher Education* (Feb. 7, 2003), Lee Bollinger, former president of the University of Michigan and the current president of Columbia University, said. "there is no right to be admitted to a university without regard to how the overall makeup of the student body will affect the educational process or without regard to the needs of the society." Merit does not mean admitting all 4.0 GPA students who apply or those with high test scores.

While some campuses are making claims that affirmative action is no longer needed in college admission, this is not the case for selective and elite institutions that are struggling to attract and enroll underrepresented students. In addition, while admissions numbers may go up at some of these selective institutions, their enrollments may continue to decline. With the controversy centered on the term "race," the issue of race and its role in college admission, there is a belief that race dominates the college admissions process. Most individuals believe that racial preference is synonymous with affirmative action. In addition, few understand the difference between eligibility and admission. To be eligible means you are qualified to participate in the process; eligibility alone is not a guarantee of admission.

There is a misconception in the public that underrepresented students of color are gaining admission based solely on skin color. This is not the case. Another misconception is that race-conscious admission policies somehow shame or harm underrepresented students of color. Race-conscious admission policies do not harm or stigmatize underrepresented students of color. Race is one of many factors institutions use in composing a student body.

There are race-neutral alternatives, like percentage plans, but they are not as effective as affirmative action and are simply another form of quotas. Also, they do not apply to professional and graduate schools. Percentage plans are too dependent on segregation at the secondary school level in order to increase access for minority students.

Unfortunately, for most underrepresented students of color, college admissions problems start in high school. Even when a student graduates from high school with a straight A average he has no chance of getting into many of the nation's selective and elite colleges. Faten Abushaer, a graduate of Balboa High School in Los Angeles, complains, "I wanted to be the first in my family to go to college, but my high school didn't offer the courses I needed to compete for admission."

The University of California, like many other universities, gives an admissions edge based on grade point average. But students taking Advanced Placement courses who get an A receive an extra point — 5 instead of 4. It is perfectly possible for outstanding students in some high schools to wind up with a 4.5 GPA. But many inner-city high schools like Balboa can't afford to offer these classes.

This means that a student just entering one of these poorer high schools will be denied college admission even before he takes one high school course. The solution seems simple: go back to the old system where an A, any A, is rated at 4.0. But affirmative action critics like Ward Connerly, a University of California regent who led the 1996 campaign to ban racial preferences in California, says admission to elite campuses must remain merit-based. That's fine, but you must allow all students to play the game in the first place.

There is a difference between the use of race to exclude individuals and the use of race to enhance awareness through education and learning. Enhancement of learning is the mission of colleges and universities. A study by William Bowen and Derek Bok (whose results were published in 1998 as *The Shape of the River*) indicated that underrepresented students of color admitted to elite and selective institutions since the 1970s have been successful in matriculating and participating in their communities. Underrepresented students of color should have access to elite and selective institutions if we are to become an inclusive society by which all members can participate at the same level.

There never was in the world two opinions alike, no more than two hairs or two grains. The most universal quality is diversity.

— Michel De Montaigne

1. The Grim Reality

My journey toward understanding the controversy regarding race and college admissions began in Sacramento, California, in 1997. I had just been appointed the consultant to the California State Senate Select Committee on College and University Admissions and Outreach. The committee was established as a direct result of the University of California's ban on race with the passage of the regents referendum Special Proposal One (SP-1) in July 1995. The ban prohibited the consideration of race or national origin as criteria that could be used in admitting students into the university. As the university began to resegregate college admissions, I was working in the California Legislature as an educational consultant. The new policy was slated for implementation in 1997 and at that time I took on the role as a liaison between the legislature and the institution in educating members on the importance of affirmative action.

The chair of the committee was Senator Teresa P. Hughes, a former educator and at the time one of only three African American members of the California State Senate. Senator Hughes created the committee to show members that this new attack on affirmative action would curtail access to elite institutions for students of color. My first responsibility was to pull together research to help educate legislative members and the educational community about admissions. Our goal was to show the impact this ban would have on access to higher education for various student groups.

The mission of the committee was to examine historical inequalities and current disparities regarding access to public universities. The function of the committee was to explore and develop policy and to make recommendations for redefining college admissions, at the California State University and at the University of California. The emphasis was to ensure that broad-based higher education opportunities would be available to all Californians.

5

This chapter looks at the misconceptions of race and college admissions through the eyes of a beneficiary of affirmative action. The author focuses specifically on elite and selective institutions because enrollment of underrepresented students of color at these institutions has stagnated.* The story begins in California and expands across the country with an examination of the impact that the growing opposition and challenges to the consideration of race in college admissions is having at the national level at selective institutions. The author will show the impact that eliminating race in admissions has had on underrepresented students of color seeking access to college.

Historical Background

Our country's racist past brought about a need for policies like that of affirmative action. Historically, access to the most prestigious educational institutions was restricted to whites, more particularly white males.† During the segregationist days of Jim Crow laws, most universities chose not to admit any students of color. Many of the universities that did applied separate admission criteria. Some universities, for instance, required students to attach a picture to their application. This allowed college admissions officials to screen out students of color. In the nineteenth and early twentieth centuries this was common practice for such Ivy League campuses as Princeton and Stanford. Rice University, a private institution in Texas, had a specific clause in its charter that restricted admission to whites only. At Cornell University Sara Brown was the first African American to graduate from the school, in 1897. Yet the university remained primarily white. In 1932, more than a quarter century later, Margaret Morgan Lawrence was admitted to Cornell. She was the only Black student in the College of Arts and Sciences. Because of her race she was not permitted to live on campus and during her four years at the university there was only one other black student.

The University of Georgia did not admit any black students for the first 175 years of its existence until a court order in 1961 allowed two blacks to enroll. When Bob Jones University opened in 1927, classes were restricted to whites only and that policy remained in place until 1975. The university also prohibited interracial dating because of its position on

---

*Underrepresented students of color are defined as Latinos, African Americans and Native Americans. The term Latinos includes Mexican and Puerto Rican Americans and the term black means African Americans.

†White refers to Caucasian European students.

interracial marriage: "It breaks down the barriers of God as he has separated people for his own purposes." The university kept this ban in place until 2000. These exclusionary tactics have perpetuated more than 332 years of racial segregation. During this time most states in the nation had separate public colleges to accommodate black students. There were almost no selective campuses in the country that had significant enrollments of Latinos, African Americans or Native Americans.

Affirmative action policies and programs were brought about through the civil rights movement of the 1960s. It was through this movement that laws regarding civil rights and equal opportunity were put in place. Simply put, affirmative action supported race-conscious policies and practices as a necessary means to address embedded racial inequalities and to preserve the civil rights of all Americans. After years of blatant policies of discrimination, judges and agencies realized that the only way to effectively provide equal opportunity was to consider race when necessary to eliminate segregation and exclusion.

With the enactment of the 1964 Civil Rights Act, federal guidelines that require race to be taken into account to break the effects of segregation became the law of the land. School desegregation plans and other programs were put into place with explicit goals of developing desegregated schools and equalizing educational opportunity. Affirmative action in college admissions is a part of this effort. Without explicit plans, almost no integration existed on selective and elite college and university campuses.

According to Orfield and Whitla (2001), "Elite campuses outside of the South went into the civil rights period with no significant integration. The basic idea of the new policies was that the effects of a history of racial exclusion were deeply embedded and could not be altered without a serious plan to change them."[1] Such plans required affirmative efforts to identify, recruit and select students from underrepresented racial and ethnic groups. It was not until 1978 that the federal government began to enforce the Civil Rights Act and required historically segregated colleges and universities to develop plans for integration. This is discussed in greater detail in Chapter Three.

When the wall of segregation began to fall, underrepresented students of color started to enter colleges and universities in record numbers. This resulted in the graduation of several thousand students of color from America's most prestigious universities. Affirmative action policies gave access to many more students of color than otherwise would have been able to attend. Between 1972 and 1996 the percentage of underrepresented students enrolling in college rose fairly steadily, approaching the 50th percentile. The increased access began to attract attention to affirmative action programs and prompted opponents to challenge its legality all the way to the U.S. Supreme Court. In 1978 a divided Supreme Court ruled that universities could not use quotas based upon race, but they could consider race as a factor in admissions to maintain a diverse student body. This ruling established that under law the government has a compelling interest in maintaining racial and ethnic diversity on campuses.

In the University of California *Regents v. Bakke* decision this is exactly what Justice Lewis F. Powell, Jr., held in his opinion when he stated that colleges could give some consideration to race in an effort to attain a diverse student body. Many selective institutions like that of Harvard, Stanford and Yale have used this ruling as the basis for including race as a criterion for admission decisions. The continued inclusion of race as one of many factors considered by institutions in selecting its student body has assisted them in expanding access to underrepresented students of color. The legal aspects of college admissions will be discussed in greater detail in Chapter Four.

Not until the 1980s and early 1990s did underrepresented students of color begin to make real gains in college admissions. For example, at Harvard University more than 4,000 underrepresented students have graduated with the help of affirmative action. More specifically, Harvard's School of Law has graduated 2,000 highly qualified African American lawyers, all of whom were admitted under affirmative action policies. Harvard's policy on diversity is centered on the diverse background of classmates who contribute to the learning environment. Specifically, it suggested that "the measure of a class consists largely in how much its members are likely to learn from each other, which is the real beginning of learning, both intellectually and emotionally."[2]

Benefits of Diversity

Educational diversity is the main reason why those in the higher education community want to maintain the use of race in admission. A former president of Harvard, Neil Rudenstine, described diversity as "an educational resource comparable in importance to the faculty, library or science lab. Diversity is not an end in itself, or a pleasure but dispensable accessory. It is the substance from which much human learning, understanding, and wisdom derive. It offers one of the most powerful ways of creating the intellectual energy and robustness that lead to greater knowledge."[3] Gerhard Casper, former president of Stanford, followed and defended the university's admissions policy by stating, "We do not admit minorities to do them a favor. We want students from a variety of backgrounds to help fulfill our educational responsibilities."[4] John DiBiaggio, president of Tufts University, asserted, "I believe that there is a genuine misunderstanding of what is meant by affirmative action. In essence, affirmative action has taken us beyond the passivity of 'equal opportunity' and engaged us in the active and creative seeking of qualified, underrepresented candidates."[5]

In the mission statements of several colleges and universities a diverse student population is clearly pinpointed as a main goal. For example, the University of Georgia "endeavors to prepare the university community and the state for full participation in the global society of the 21st century. It seeks to foster the understanding of, and respect for, cultural differences necessary for an enlightened and educated citizenry."[6] Mission statements also assert the role diversity has in enhancing learning in higher education. Diversity enriches the educational experience. We learn from those whose experiences, beliefs and perspectives are different from our own, and these lessons can be taught best in a richly diverse intellectual and social environment. Some students experience diversity for the first time on a college campus.

Research shows that students who are educated in a diverse environment can enhance their racial understanding, cultural awareness and appreciation of differences. When this interaction is reduced or in some cases eliminated the quality of education at the institution is diminished. Forty years ago diversity in college admissions meant students from different states, cities and farms. Now that diversity also encompasses racial background it is a controversy. The benefit of diversity is that it allows students the opportunity to learn to understand how others think and develop the ability to interact and function across racial divides. In order for students to experience and have an appreciation of diversity requires interaction with diverse peers.

Achieving diversity requires a commitment to examining and making an assessment of the broad background that all students applying to the university bring to the table. Students benefit significantly from diversity, and institutions should be allowed to maintain it.[7] Maintaining diversity requires a commitment of access to higher education for all qualified students, especially those who historically have been denied equal postsecondary opportunities. In the affirmative action debate, the need to ensure diversity constitutes a compelling government interest. Thus, admission policies that guarantee diversity are vital. Social science research asserts that racism, historic racial segregation and separation in our society are patterns that can be broken through higher education with diverse experiences. Institutions that are composed of racially diverse students are critical to the intellectual viability of students as well as the long term foundation of democracy.

Diversity is important to the function of education. If colleges and universities are designed to provide a higher quality of education then it is essential that students be exposed to individuals from a wide variety of different backgrounds. For some students college is the first time to experience situations outside of their home environments. Higher education thus becomes influential in shaping students' experiences and attitudes that last beyond college classrooms. If those experiences involve diverse interactions students will learn and think more across diverse educational lines and will be better prepared to work and interact in broader diverse communities. Racial diverse college campuses are important in assisting students in becoming conscious, critical learners and thinkers. Astin (1993) refers to this important function of diversity as "informal interactional diversity," an opportunity for students to interact with individuals from diverse backgrounds. It is the interaction with a student's peer group that becomes one of the most vital aspects of the college experience, and most college alumni agree that this enhanced their educational careers. Students who experience racial diversity in education increase their understanding of and exposure to different perspectives, exhibit tolerance and have a greater appreciation of the uniqueness of diversity.

Diversity is critical to the development of identity. Psychologist Erik Erickson (1946) discussed the concept of identity and its effect among young adults. According to Erickson, identity develops when students are provided with a time and place to experiment with different social roles, which leads to an establishment of commitments to relationships, occupations, social groups, communities and a philosophy of life.

Colleges and universities provide a stage upon which this type of development can take shape. For most students, attending college is the transition from a secondary educational past into experiences with new relationships and social roles. If students who make that transition interact with individuals from diverse racial and geographic backgrounds that challenge them, then social identity, development and intellectual experimentation will flourish.

Professor Patricia Gurin (1999) asserts that diversity enriches learning outcomes: "Students learn more and think in deeper, more complex ways in a diverse educational environment. A curriculum that deals explicitly with social and cultural diversity, and a learning environment in which diverse students interact frequently with each other, naturally will affect the content of what it is learned. In education the notion that students' mode of thought is affected by features of the learning environment, and that diversity is a feature that produces deeper and more complex thinking. I refer generally to these mode-of-thought benefits of diversity as learning outcomes."[8]

Diversity in higher education prepares students for a democratic society and the changing workforce. Higher education that provides students with the opportunity to interact with a diverse student population plays a fundamental role in preparing students to live and participate in a democracy. Students in a diverse population are obtaining the foundations to interact in a pluralistic society. Democracy is founded and thrives on an educated citizenry. Students educated in diverse settings are better equipped to engage in the process.

According to Aristotle, what makes democracy work is "equality among citizens who are peers but who hold diverse perspectives, and whose relationships are governed by freedom and rules of civil discourse. It is discourse over conflict, not unanimity, that helps democracy thrive."[9] Corporations and employers value diversity as a critical tool to increase competitiveness in the economy. They expect higher education to provide an environment as well as prepare students for the diverse work environment they will inherit upon graduation. That preparation requires institutions to produce students who have the ability to work in groups with individuals from diverse backgrounds and the ability to see others as peers and work effectively in groups.

Jean Piaget articulated the theory of perspective taking. His theory asserts intellectual and moral development. According to Piaget, "Children and adolescents can best develop a capacity to understand the ideas and feelings of others and to move to a more advanced stage of moral reasoning when they interact with diverse peers who are also equals."[10]

The National Association for College Admission Counseling conducted a study on diversity. It found that colleges and universities across the nation were committed to diversity and those that conduct race-conscious admission found it helpful in maintaining a diverse student body:

• Seventy-four percent of colleges and universities include in their mission statement a commitment to diversity of some form.
• Sixty-eight percent of colleges are guided by mission statements that encourage a racial and ethnic mix of students on campus.
• Sixty-four percent said those mission statements also included a commitment to increasing diversity in other student populations.
• Among those who consider race/ethnicity as a factor in the admission decision, a sizable 82 percent credited this policy with boosting the

number of racial/ethnic minority students represented in the student body.

　　• Seventy-four percent of institutions use specific recruitment activities including programs, Web sites, print, or other publications to increase underrepresented racial and ethnic populations in the student body.

Source: Diversity and College Admission NACAC (2003)

　　The mission of higher education is an obligation to create a pluralistic educational environment for all students. We are preparing future leaders of tomorrow, and the main focus of that preparation is to make diversity work in everyday life. According to the Association of American Colleges and Universities (1995), higher education is:

> Uniquely positioned, by its mission, values, and dedication to learning, to foster and nourish the habits of heart and mind that Americans need to make diversity work in daily life. We have the opportunity to help our campuses experience engagement across differences as a value and a public good. Our nation's campuses have become a highly visible stage on which the most fundamental questions about difference, equality, and community are being enacted. The academy brings indispensable resource: its commitments to the advancement of knowledge and its traditions of dialogue and deliberation across difference as keys to the increase of insight and understanding.[11]

　　A racially diverse university has significant benefits for all students, underrepresented as well as whites. Diversity provides a better learning environment, enhances students' ability to participate in a pluralistic society, and the democratic process and can produce increased interaction among diverse groups after graduation.

　　To legally remove the use of race as a tool puts the majority as well as minority students at risk. The risks it presents are that of fostering of racism, continued inequity, America's economic competitiveness and value change.

Fostering Racism

　　Students who do not gain exposure to other races, ethnicities, and cultures are unable to learn how to respect and appreciate differences and will have more difficulty interacting in a multicultural society. Experience with diversity requires interaction with peers from a diverse background. Students unable to interact effectively are more prone to be less tolerant, to foster stereotypes and to use limited thinking that increase self-segregation. These students are at an increased risk of becoming aversive racists.

Aversive racism (Gaertner and Dovidio, 1986) is a theory that refers to the unintentional expression of anti-color or anti-black feelings by people who sincerely endorse, on a conscious level, values and principles of equality. Rather than reflecting bigotry or hatred, the anti-color feelings held by aversive racists reflect fear and discomfort. Their discriminatory behavior toward individuals of color is characterized more by avoidance than by intentional hostility. This creates an excuse for a continued lack of awareness. Consider the following:

Justine, a white freshman at an East Coast university, moved into the dorms and to her surprise discovered that her roommate, Kelly, was African American. Justine came from a community in which she had no contact with any African Americans and felt very intimidated by Kelly. While Justine did not come out and express her discomfort, she and her parents requested that she be moved. When they could not provide a valid reason to the housing office, Justine was informed that her request would not be honored and she would have to make other arrangements off campus. Kelly, sensing Justine's discomfort, politely let her know that she had never lived with a white person before so they should take it one day at a time. During the course of the semester they realized through communication that they had a lot in common. Justine and Kelly played the same sports in high school, and both had an older brother. By the end of the semester Justine found that Kelly was more than a roommate, she had become a good friend, and they ended up remaining roommates throughout their college careers.[12]

Heather Johnson, an English major at North Carolina State University who is white, said that the diverse mix of her classmates introduced her to new ideas and people she had never known at her high school in coastal Brunswick County. "There are things I don't support," she said, "but even if I don't support them, it's important to be around it to grow into who you are."[13]

Christoph Guttentag, Duke University's undergraduate admissions director, says "If you had two students whose profile was exactly the same except for race, the chances are excellent that the two of them would bring different perspectives to the classroom, sometimes dramatically different perspectives. Building a student body with different perspectives is a big part of what we are about."[14]

Continued Inequities

The 2000 Census has indicated that people of color are growing at a faster pace than European Americans and that in some parts of the country will make up the majority. California, for example, is one of the most diverse states, where the total number of people of color comprise 53.47 percent of the population. However, students of color are still underrepresented in the enrollment of public colleges and universities. For example, in Texas, the proportion of white student enrollment in college remains higher than their proportion of the general state population. In 2000, whites comprised 53 percent of the general state population yet represented 56 percent of public university enrollment in Texas. Specifically, at Texas A&M University, white students made up 78 percent of the fall 2000 class and 76 percent of the fall 2002 class. Education is an important, if not crucial, first step toward providing equity.[15] Acceptance of the status quo will continue the historical pattern of differential access to post-secondary education and frustrate reform efforts aimed at eliminating the achievement gap between students of color and their white peers.

Impeding Economic Competitiveness

The world has become increasingly global and for our nation to maintain its prosperity in the 21st century, students will need to communicate and interact competently in the multiracial society. To compete effectively, it is vital that America develops and uses the talents of all its citizens. Students who are unable to function effectively in multicultural settings will lose out in today's workplace. Ensuring that students learn about and acquire the skills to respectfully interact with individuals from diverse backgrounds is essential to maintaining America's competitiveness. Institutions must provide educational environments by which students can communicate and interact across racial communities on a regular basis. These types of interactions are essential to global skills that corporations look for. Corporations will begin to increasingly seek international students who have been educated in U.S. institutions as employees who can effectively work in a global economy.

Value Change

Access to diversity can contribute to changing the values that shape individual perceptions about civil rights and issues of equity. The Bowen and Bok survey (1998) found that the "majority believed that going to college with a diverse body of students made a valuable contribution to their education and personal development."[16]

Specifically, 80 percent of white university graduates surveyed feel that their university should continue to place an emphasis on achieving a diverse student body. A Gallup poll survey taken from Harvard and the University of Michigan Law Schools examined students' perspectives on diversity. Eighty-one percent of the students enrolled in these two law schools participated in the survey. The survey revealed that whites were less likely to interact with people of color on a regular or frequent basis while growing up. In the results there were no Latino or African American students who attended the law schools that came from highly segregated educational backgrounds, but almost half of the white students did.[17]

Most whites attend segregated schools. According to Orfield and Whitla (2001), "a national study of school segregation patterns in 1996–97 showed that whites were by far the most segregated ethnic group in U.S. schools and that they were remaining highly isolated even as the nation's diverse school enrollments reached 36 percent." Diversity, they found, enhanced their ability to look at problems differently. When students were asked what the impact of racial and ethnic diversity is on "your ability to work more effectively or get along better with members of other races," 39 percent of Harvard students and 47.8 percent of Michigan students who participated said it increased their ability.[18] Very few students, only one in 16 surveyed, saw a negative impact from having a diverse student body. Most of the students surveyed indicated that the informal discussions in classes were more or less beneficial based upon the diversity of their schools. These interactions resulted in a value change regarding civil rights. Interactions with students from different backgrounds have led to extraordinary educational experiences for many students on issues of race.

Eligibility v. Admission

The primary misconception of affirmative action is the belief that unqualified students are admitted over more deserving students. This belief is the misunderstanding of eligibility versus admission. The first step in the admissions process is determining the eligibility of applicants. Virtually all students must be eligible to be considered for admission, meaning they must meet all of the quantitative university requirements before they can apply. Specifically, in college admissions, eligibility is synonymous with qualified. Eligibility is almost always left out of the equation in the affirmative action debate because so many people automatically assume that students of color are admitted simply because of their race.

For example, if a university's requirement for admission is a 3.0 GPA,

1000 SAT score, and completion of college preparatory courses, all students who meet or exceed those requirements are "eligible" for admission. What this means is that the student is qualified and the university will accept his application for consideration. Eligibility and admission are two different things. A student can apply and not be eligible, but meeting eligibility requirements does not mean an applicant will automatically be admitted.

The difference between eligibility and admission is a set of criteria the university will employ in making its decision on which students will get through the door. Not all institutions use the same set of criteria in selecting eligible students. These include such things as the extent to which GPA and test scores exceed minimum requirements, state or country of permanent residence, special talents and abilities, earned honors, civic involvement, geographic location, family background, income level, and personal characteristics. So, when critics of affirmative action argue that too many underrepresented students of color are getting accepted with scores that are less than white students, the critics are assuming that admissions decisions are made largely on the basis of race and that unqualified students of color are being admitted over qualified whites.

Selective colleges and universities seek first to acquire a pool of eligible applicants and then from among that pool use multiple criteria (including special talents, race, geography, etc.) to assemble a diverse student body. The institutions fail to acknowledge that admissions decisions to enhance diversity are being made from among eligible applicants, not between qualified and unqualified applicants. It is very possible to have a diverse freshmen class academically as well as ethnically students with a 4.0 GPA as well as those with a 2.9 or 3.5, students from Kansas and students from Ghana, promising musicians and physicians.

The misconception can even be found among those within the education community and at one of the most elitist college institutions. For example, University of California Regent John Moores produced a confidential report that somewhat "analyzed" admission at the University of California, Berkeley, one of the most selective institutions in the UC system. The Moores report, which was leaked to newspapers across the state, focused on SAT scores and the admission of some applicants with scores lower than other applicants rejected by the institution. Moores' report found that of the "36,472 applicants, 374 applicants were admitted to Berkeley with SATs under 1000 while 3,218 applicants with 1400+ SAT scores were denied admission."[19] Moores asserted that the report showed that students with SAT scores lower than 1000 had no business attending Berkeley. Moores' report and comments created a firestorm at the University of California, in the media and especially the campus at which the report was focused. The UC president called for an investigation into all undergraduate admissions practices. The chancellor of UC, Berkeley, Robert Berdahl, in a letter to Moores, made this statement about the report: "It has done singular damage to the Berkeley campus. By saying 'They don't have any business going to Berkeley' you have attacked the small percentage of high-achieving freshmen (5 percent) who have overcome substantial economic, social, and educational disadvantages to come to Berkeley. They deserve more than derision from the chair of the Board of Regents."[20]

Under eligibility and UC's comprehensive review, Moores' report was flawed. For example, all of the Berkeley applicants rejected with SAT scores higher than 1400 had already withdrawn their applications, applied to extremely competitive engineering programs or encountered intense competition because they were not residents of the state. Of the 374 applicants admitted to Berkeley in 2002, half of them graduated in the top 4 percent of their class, were all qualified and talented, and displayed other qualities like that of leadership, community service, athletics, etc., all qualitative attributes the institution looks for. What Moores failed to realize is that under the institution's comprehensive review, the SAT is not the sole predictor of admission to the university. In addition, his report focused attention on a small proportion of the admissions decisions at UC, Berkeley. For example, a closer look at the results of the study revealed that out of 10,859 applicants, Berkeley offered admission to 264 applicants with 900–1000 SAT scores while only 3.5 percent of total admissions offers were provided to students with SATs of 1000 and only 1.1 percent of offers went to students with SATs below 900.

According to the *Los Angeles Times* (2003), "All told, the groups underrepresented on UC campuses—African Americans, Latinos and Native Americans—are admitted with below average SAT scores at the same rates as whites and Asians."[21] At the end of the day, Moores, while involved in admissions as a UC regent, did not himself understand eligibility versus admission and like so many others viewed the process as one of numbers, not of the total quality of qualified applicants within the system.

What matters is that all applicants who are offered admissions are qualified and have the potential to be successful. While critics view the use of race as the wrong "preference" even if used among qualified applicants, they fail to acknowledge the real preferences that still persist to exclude underrepresented students of color such as admission by exception (open enrollment), alumni legacies, affluent family admissions, and the sacred cow of special athletic admissions. These preferences do not always employ the use of eligible students, yet they equate more privileges to the haves while continuing to exclude the have-nots. However, these preferences are rarely part of the national debate. These types of preferences will be discussed in Chapter Five.

Michael Adams, president of the University of Georgia, defends the typical admissions process with his forceful articulation that a quantifiable structure is not the only fair way to assess a candidate. According to Adams, "True fairness also includes a professional assessment of unique family situations, the schools the student has attended, the community he or she came from, and whether the applicant had to overcome economic hardships to build a record of academic achievement. These items are important indicators of that applicant's chances for success."[22]

The challenge for most underrepresented students of color seeking access to colleges is the uphill battle they must make on the road to higher education. The K-12 path most of these students have taken has not been easy. Underrepresented students of color are concentrated in schools that do not prepare them for college success. They are far more likely to attend schools where as many as two of every five teachers are underqualified, where insufficient numbers of textbooks are available and many of them are outdated, where the physical plant is in poor repair, and where learning supports are few or non-existent. In addition, poor and underrepresented students have access to fewer advanced placement and honors courses and systematically are taught that less is expected of them. This issue will be discussed in more detail in Chapter Three.

The issue of race has become so controversial in our country that its use in any form is now synonymous with discrimination or inequality. When college officials admit students based on a set of criteria and one of those criteria is race, they are automatically criticized for giving an unfair preference to students of color or accused of being racists.

Those who do not have a working knowledge of the admissions process will always flood the debate with misinformation. To claim that underrepresented students of color are admitted based solely on the color of their skin is an inaccurate assertion. Case in point: the University of North Carolina at Chapel Hill is an elite institution with an extensive admission process. According to the director of undergraduate admissions, Jerry Lucidio, "race is one of many things we consider, and it's never the first criterion. The admissions process is far more complex than just ranking students by their race and their test scores."[23] The primary criterion is to find students who will be successful. For example, in 2002, the National Collegiate Athletic Association stated that graduation rates were higher for African American students than for whites at eight University of North Carolina campuses. The controversy is the reality that universities, parents, and students do not all agree on what constitutes a "qualified" applicant. However, it is an institution's academic freedom to elect the criteria by which it selects a diverse student body. Institutions have a level of deference and essential freedoms such as the ability to determine on academic grounds what can be taught, who may teach it, how it shall be taught, and who may be admitted to study.[24]

Basing admission decisions solely on test scores and grades means that white students, who tend to earn higher scores than African American, Latino and Native American students on tests like the SAT, will have a competitive advantage. However, SAT scores do not reliably predict who will successfully complete a college education. So, according to admissions officers, you must look at the total package and consider all of the qualities and qualifications of eligible students in making a decision on who gets in. There are some institutions that examine the whole applicant without reference to test scores. There are 700 four-year U.S. colleges and universities that admit students without the SAT or ACT. With the competitive nature of admissions, many institutions cannot afford to rely solely on test scores. According to Bob Schaeffer of FairTest, "College and universities eliminate test score requirements for many reasons. Many are concerned about the negative impact on race and gender equity that results from relying on test scores."[25]

Elite institutions struggle to maintain diversity because they always have a pool of eligible applicants larger than available space will accommodate. George Dixon, North Carolina State University's undergraduate admissions director, states: "Most freshmen [have] SAT scores ... [of] at least 1100, have earned 3.74 GPAs and finished in the top 20 percent of their high school classes. Admission would be very easy if we just ranked everyone from first to last based on an SAT score, but a big part of our job is to ensure a rich environment in which students bring with them varied backgrounds. At competitive colleges where diversity is a goal, those criteria are just the beginning of the process."[26]

Prior to women or minorities having access to college campuses, education was for white males only, and even then colleges had their own style of affirmative action. Affirmative action at that time focused on the children of wealthy families and alumni. As time pressed on it became available for poor white farm boys. True access for all means accepting new circumstances that are not confined to test scores, such as life experiences, admission by exception, and athletic or musical ability. Let's look at it from the gender perspective. For example, teaching and nursing are female-dominated careers, and many colleges and universities will include a preference for men in their admissions process to credential or nursing programs.

The case is the same for engineering and architecture schools. In some instances female law school applicants outnumber males 2 to 1. To create a balance, males have a greater chance of gaining admission than females. This is done in an attempt to create a diverse student body. So race is not the only affirmative action criterion that exists. In college admissions, not everyone who applies gets in. The reality is that well-qualified students from all backgrounds get rejected every year by their institution of first choice; it does not mean they were excluded based upon their race. Critics won't touch this because there are no scapegoats to single out.

Look at it from a numbers perspective. Let's say that the admission criteria for the University of Texas require students to have an 1100 SAT score and a 3.0 GPA to be eligible. In comparing white to Native American applicants, there are many more white applicants who meet this criteria than Native Americans. The university has a very low Native American population, 1.5 percent in comparison to 64 percent white, and there are 1,200 white applicants and only 250 Native American applicants that meet the admission criteria. In this case, like that of the male to female ratio, it is appropriate for the dean of admissions to admit more Native Americans than whites. There are far too many people who do not understand the broad range of the admissions process that exist at universities and those people will make the assumption that if the population of underrepresented students of color rises by more than 5 percent then whites are facing discrimination or being misplaced.

What has been left out of the debate on race and admissions is that whites have not been displaced by affirmative action. They have suffered very little in comparison to underrepresented students of color. Whites are admitted into universities at three times the rate of minorities, a rate equivalent to their overall population in the United States. At the University of Michigan, white plaintiffs charged that the university's undergraduate admissions policy was discriminatory toward whites even though they make up 65 percent of the entering class and African Americans 8.9 percent, Latinos 6.1 percent, and Native Americans 1.1 percent. Some officials at the University of Michigan assert that eliminating affirmative action will drop the admissions rate for students of color without a policy that allows for the consideration of race.

With the end of the 20th century came the elimination of race-conscious admissions for some states. California was first to eliminate the use of race and few other states, like Washington, Texas and Georgia, have followed. Now underrepresented students of color face a real setback. Why?

Because African Americans, especially, are being denied admission to colleges that can't consider race as a factor in the decision process. In states where a race-neutral admissions policy has been implemented, a new segregation for students of color has developed. We will examine some of the selective institutions in the states with a prohibition in place in an effort to demonstrate the disparity in access for underrepresented students of color.

The dismantling of affirmative action has all but abolished access for underrepresented students of color to highly selective "flagship" colleges and universities. For it is these institutions that have come under attack over the attempts to give underrepresented students of color a place among their student bodies. While this issue is centered on the use of race it is important for us to define it in the context of admission.

Race Defined

The reality of the issue is that you cannot have racial diversity without the use of race. The term race is often confused with culture, which is a shared set of beliefs or values. Campbell (2003) says you learn culture, but you inherit race. Race is used to describe groups with similar biogenetic inheritances. Yet race is primarily a social category, not a biological classification. It is a social concept that changes over time and according to the American Sociological Association it is important to study the social consequences of the categorization of race, for it allows us to document how race is used in providing access to resources. The study of race and racial categories allows us to identify and track the disparities that exist in an effort to achieve social justice and equity. These categories have been used to describe groups of similar make-up. In this material the term race is connected to people of color, who are "Groups in the United States and other nations who have experienced discrimination historically because of their unique biological characteristics that enabled potential discriminators to identify them easily."[27] African Americans, Latinos, Asians and Native Americans are groups in the United States that are referred to as people of color. A detailed definition of affirmative action can be found in Chapter Three. Unfortunately, race in this country is still widely used to identify an individual's ability to succeed in education. But this is not reality when it comes to admitting someone into college.

Undergraduate Admissions

Gaining access to postsecondary education is the gateway to opportunity, economic prosperity, and opportunities to assume positions of civic leadership for many people. This is particularly the case for people of color who have been historically underrepresented in colleges and universities, as well as in the upper echelons of business and commerce. This relationship was explicitly recognized by former President Lyndon Johnson and spurred his "war on poverty" in the mid-1960s. He reasoned that if the poor were not provided further education, including access to higher education, the government would be saddled with high costs of caring for or incarcerating them. The war on poverty initiative prompted substantial federal and state investment in education, particularly outreach programs to encourage underrepresented students of color to pursue postsecondary education and compensatory programs to support them once they arrived on college campuses.

For nearly 40 years, states have supported creative efforts to attract students from underrepresented groups and enroll them at college and university campuses. Within the past decade, however, there has been a growing tide of concern about the combined impact of population growth, limited capacity at the more selective universities, and grade inflation in access to preferred university campuses. This concern has pitted values of diversity against merit and prompted challenges and intense scrutiny of admissions policies and practices.

Debates about whether efforts to achieve diversity deprive students with high academic marks from access to selective universities have prompted legal challenges and lawsuits, even constitutional amendments in some states, to bar consideration of racial and ethnic diversity in college admission decisions. It is important to keep track of how these challenges and changes play out over time because the nation's teachers, doctors, and industry leaders are all products of a successful undergraduate education. Failure to maintain and expand access for people from underrepresented groups will have a profound impact on the economic foundation and social cohesiveness of the nation.

University of California

The University of California was the first public institution in the mid-1990s to eliminate consideration of race, ethnicity, gender, and national origin in admissions decisions prior to a statewide initiative or executive order. In the fall of 1995, the University of California had one of the most diverse student populations in the country, with 21 percent of its incoming freshmen comprised of underrepresented students of color. From 1980 to 1993, the University of California, Berkeley, had a 50 percent increase in African American student enrollment. The freshmen enrollment was 12 percent Latinos in 1993, while Latinos represented 29 percent of the state population. The university at that time expected that minority enrollment would continue to increase. SP-1 was the foundation of Proposition 209, inaccurately termed the California Civil Rights initiative, which eliminated the use of race, ethnicity and gender in hiring, public education and contracting in public institutions statewide. When the institution implemented race-blind admissions in 1998 for undergraduates the number of minorities declined.

Today, systemwide the university has over 160,000 students and operates in a state in which more than 50 percent of the population are people of color, yet very few students of color have access to the flagship institutions. Let's look at undergraduate figures for one of the selective campuses. In 1995, 566 African Americans, 118 Native Americans and 1,434 Latinos were admitted to UC, Berkeley. In 1998, those numbers dropped to 216 African Americans, 27 Native Americans, and 619 Latinos. Underrepresented students continue to see declines at the selective campuses. For example, at Berkeley in 1997, African American admittance was at 7.3 percent but in 2001 that percentage dropped to 3.4 and in 2003 that percentage remained virtually unchanged at 3.9.

The devastation began in 1997, when graduate programs saw a 50 to 60 percent decline in admission of underrepresented students of color. In 1998, the case was the same for underrepresented students entering undergraduate programs. Since eliminating the prohibition on the use of race, California has created a crisis and caused elite universities to search frantically for alternate ways to continue diversity on campuses.

In California the selective campuses of Berkeley and Los Angeles have struggled to increase representation for incoming freshmen. In 1998, at UC Berkeley, admittance plunged 66 percent for African Americans and 38 percent for Native Americans. At UCLA, African American admission also dropped 43 percent and 53 percent for Native Americans. For Latinos, the decline was 53 percent at Berkeley and 33 percent at UCLA, even though Latinos at the time were 32 percent of the state population. Combined, UCLA's offers to Latino and African American students dropped from 27 percent in 1995 to 13 percent in 1998. Since the decline was so drastic there was a concern that blatant discrimination was taking place against students of color. As a result the American Civil Liberties Union filed a lawsuit against UC Berkeley and the regents after 800 underrepresented students of color with 4.0 GPAs were denied admission to the campus.

In 2001, the University of California regents repealed SP-1, but it was largely symbolic, as Proposition 209 remains in effect statewide. The desirability of enrollment at the Berkeley and Los Angeles campuses has generated intense competition and distress for both students (and their parents) who have their heart set on getting into a major California university. One father explained the problem of gaining access to flagship campuses this way: "Instead of skiing like his friends or hanging out at the mall, my son took advanced classes, volunteered in the community, served on a board and was captain of a sport team, He earned a 3.9 GPA — and so far hasn't been accepted at any University of California school."

A mother adds: "My daughter is one of those unfortunate high-achieving students who has now been turned down for all but three of the UC campuses she applied to. We haven't heard from the other three. She has a 3.95 GPA. Her SAT scores were 1200. She has been involved in varsity volleyball and community service. Now she asks why? She fulfilled her end of the bargain."

This has been a shock to students who expected to get into the college of their choice. One honors student with a 3.9 GPA didn't get into any of the five University of California campuses to which he applied. Says Julie Flathmann, head counselor at Folsom High School in California: "These are students with straight As and impressive SAT scores. I hate to think about what must be happening to the unfortunate B+ student."

Not much has changed, even though in April of 2002, the University of California boasted that for the first time since the elimination of race-sensitive admissions policies it has admitted more underrepresented students. The Los Angeles Times reported that "Minority Levels Rebound at UC." All the major newspapers reported that for the first time in five years, underrepresented students at UC had surpassed the pre-ban level in systemwide admission, growing from 18.8 percent to 19.1 percent, without affirmative action. However, this does not surpass the 1995 systemwide percentage. Yet critics of affirmative action claimed that diversity could now be reached without the consideration of race.

Let's take a close look at this so-called increase at the University of California. The drop in undergraduate admissions around the nine UC campuses was most dramatic for the two selective campuses, UCLA and UC Berkeley. The other campuses only had an 11 percent decline in comparison to UCLA's 45 percent and Berkeley's 55 percent plunge for underrepresented students. Yet, Berkeley and UCLA still lag behind their 1997 levels of underrepresented students, and a majority of the UC campuses lag behind their 1995 levels. For example, in 1997, UCLA's freshmen class was 21.8 percent underrepresented minorities and for 2003 only 18.2 percent. So, to claim that the entire UC system has returned to the 1997 levels of diversity is inaccurate, and Bob Laird, former admissions director at Berkeley, agrees. He says: "I think the university is distorting what's happening. I think they're doing everything they can to put things selectively and carefully in the best possible light. My sense is that there's really a crisis. For African-American students at Berkeley, UCLA and San Diego, I think the situation is extremely serious. I don't see the longer-term prospect of repairing that. I don't think it's an accurate reflection of what's really going on."[28]

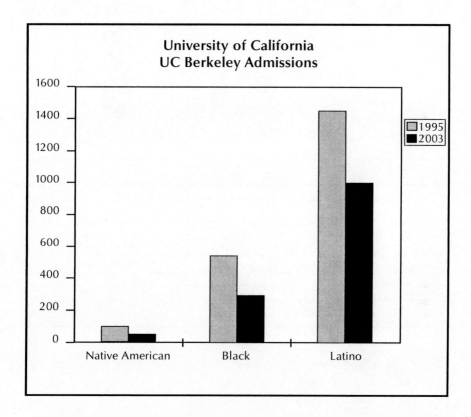

Two reasons UC systemwide admissions have made a partial recovery may include a change in the admission policy and changes in California high school graduates. In an attempt to address the dwindling numbers of students of color in November of 2001, the university altered its admission process. The old criteria, requiring 50 to 75 percent of first selection students (Tier I) admission based solely on academic factors, such as grades and test scores, were thrown out. It was replaced with a "comprehensive" plan that allows all applicants to be judged based on a single set of criteria that includes academic as well as personal attributes. According to for-

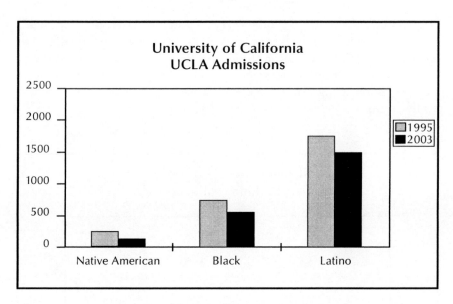

	UNIVERSITY OF CALIFORNIA UC BERKELEY ADMISSIONS UNDERREPRESENTED STUDENTS			UNIVERSITY OF CALIFORNIA UCLA ADMISSIONS UNDERREPRESENTED STUDENTS		
	1995	*2003*	*% Change*	*1995*	*2003*	*% Change*
Native American	118	45	-62%	105	33	-69%
Black	566	302	-47%	661	267	-60%
Latino	1,434	998	-30%	1,993	1,303	-35%
Source: University of California Office of President						

mer UC President Richard Atkinson, the new admissions plan puts the university in sync with other institutions: "We're not doing anything creative, we are simply moving in the direction in which every other competitive university is."[29]

The comprehensive plan has contributed to some of the increases in the admission of applicants from underrepresented groups in that it changed the criteria considered (GPA, standardized test scores, college preparatory course work, honors courses, applicant may be in top four percent of the class, educational opportunities available in secondary school, performance in specific academic subject areas, special projects in academic field, marked improvement in academic performance, special talents, academic accomplishments in light of the applicant's life experiences, and location of the applicant's secondary school and residence) and in large part assisted in examining merit beyond the walls solely of academic criteria.

Not surprisingly, this opened the door to more students of color, but it did not assist much in the most selective campuses. Under the new plan UC, San Diego, admitted 32 percent more underrepresented students. Mae Brown, San Diego's assistant vice chancellor for enrollment, stated that this is not enough: "We certainly are not where we should be in terms of diversity, and we are not where we need to be in terms of underrepresented students. We were not there in 1997 or in 1995."[30] UC, Riverside, has the largest diverse entering class, with close to one-third Latino, Native American, and African American students. However, the comprehensive plan only applies to undergraduate admissions, not professional schools, which continue to see declines in access.

A study conducted by the Tomás Rivera Policy Institute (2003) asserts that while UC is claiming strong increases in admissions for underrepresented students of color, the increase is in the number of applications and that acceptance rates for these students has become a decreasing percentage of the overall UC freshmen student body. Whites and Asians have gained the most in UC admissions upon the implementation of SP-1. For example, "White freshmen accounted for 31 percent of all acceptances in 1997, growing to 33 percent in 2002, and Asian students grew from 35 percent to 40 percent during the same time period."[31] Overall, systemwide Latino acceptance rates have fallen from 64 percent to 47 percent and for African Americans, 57 percent to 36 percent.

The study provides evidence pertaining to the continued disparity in admissions for underrepresented students of color. Since the elimination of race-neutral admissions over 23,000 underrepresented freshmen applications have been denied by the University of California. For example, the increase in applications has not kept pace with acceptance rates. In 2001, UC Berkeley admitted 963 Latinos and in 2002, 964 Latinos. What is unique about 2002 is that the university had 300 additional applications from 2001 to 2002 yet only one additional student was admitted. At UCLA, African American admissions fell from 5.6 percent in 1997 to 3.4 percent while applications went from 1,272 to 1,757. The study confirms that while African American applications to the institution have increased by 55 percent and for Latinos 73 percent, African Americans have experienced a 36 percent declining acceptance rate and Latinos 47 percent systemwide.* In the end, while the media and the university tout admissions increases, acceptance rates for underrepresented students of color continue to decline

*Data on Native Americans not provided in the Tomas Rivera study (2003).

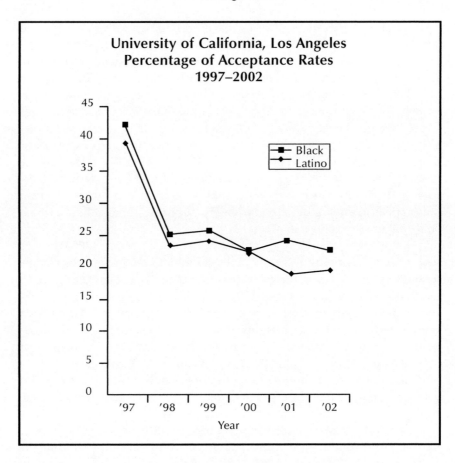

University of California, Los Angeles
Percentage of Acceptance Rates
1997–2002

	'97	'98	'99	'00	'01	'02	Rate Change
Black	38.4	23.6	24.0	22.0	18.1	19.0	-19%
Latino	40.8	24.5	25.2	22.3	23.6	22.4	-18%

Source: UC Office of the President, Tomas Rivera Policy Institute Report

at elite institutions while the rate of high school graduates who are UC-eligible increase. The chart above is an example of the declining acceptance rates.

Texas

The picture in Texas changed dramatically in 1996 when a three-judge panel of the U.S. Court of Appeals for the Fifth Circuit ruled (the Hopwood decision) that the use of race to admit students at the University of Texas Law School was unlawful. The University of Texas at Austin (UT) and Texas A&M University (TAMU) were the only two state institutions that used race as an admissions factor. Both institutions experienced declines in admissions of underrepresented students of color. In 1993, UT had its highest enrollment of underrepresented students with African Americans at 4.5 percent, Latinos at 15.6 percent, and Native Americans at .4 percent. In 1997, the first year of admissions under Hopwood, percentages dropped dramatically. African Americans at UT had declined to 2.5 percent, Latinos to 12.1 percent while Native Americans increased to a mere .5 percent. At TAMU in 1996, African Americans were 4 percent of the freshman class, Latinos 11 percent and Native Americans one percent. In 1998, while numbers were already low at TAMU, the prohibition on the use of race had an impact: African Americans fell to 3 percent and Latinos to 9 percent. Native Americans remained at one percent. The chart displays the enrollment numbers of students. While there have been some increases, the numbers of actual admissions still falls below the pre-Hopwood days.

Enrollment figures are different from admissions. While enrollment numbers have fluctuated, admission numbers have declined. For example, in 1995,* the University of Texas (UT) admitted 508 African Americans and 1,728 Latinos. In 1997, after the Hopwood decision, the University of Texas admitted only 419 African Americans and 1,592 Latinos, and in 2001, that number had dropped further to 380 African Americans, 1,513 Latinos, and 52 Native Americans.[34] Texas A&M admitted 654 African Americans in 1995 and 1,701 Latinos. In 1997, only 420 African Americans and 1,298 Latinos were admitted, and those numbers declined still further in 2001, with 193 African Americans, 652 Latinos, and 36 Native Americans. While applications are increasing, admissions and enrollments are not. For example, UT applications have increased since 1996, yet admissions and enrollment have not kept pace and in most cases are declining with the number of students enrolling. The enrollment figures for Native Americans and African Americans have declined over the past six years, while applications have remained steady or increased:

The Hopwood decision had a chilling effect on all of the top eight

---

Texas Higher Education Coordinating Board, Report on the Effects of the Hopwood Decision. Native Americans not included in the research.

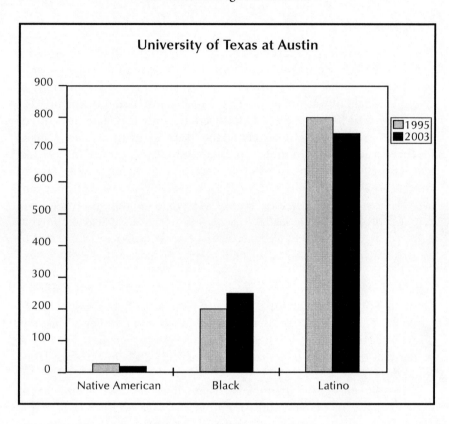

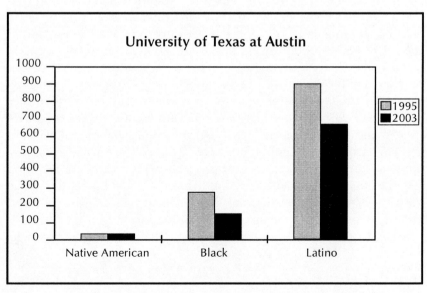

	UNIVERSITY OF TEXAS AT AUSTIN ENROLLMENT			TEXAS A&M UNIVERSITY ENROLLMENT		
	1995	*2003*	*% Change*	*1995*	*2003*	*% Change*
Native American	25	19	-0.24%	25	27	0.08%
Black	190	237	-0.24%	285	158	-44%
Latino	803	706	-12%	892	689	-77%

Source: Office of Institutional Research and Institutional Studies and Planning, University of Texas at Austin and Texas A&M University

UNIVERSITY OF TEXAS UT				
		APPLIED	ADMITTED	ENROLLED
1998	Native American	80	56	32
	Black	937	367	261
	Latino	2,042	1,396	762
1999	Native American	71	58	22
	Black	957	452	251
	Latino	2,615	1,498	861
2000	Native American	98	51	28
	Black	1,073	461	243
	Latino	2,763	1,518	877
2001	Native American	115	52	26
	Black	999	380	205
	Latino	2,998	1,513	832
2002	Native American	96	49	31
	Black	1,080	431	232
	Latino	3,165	1,654	935
2003	Native American	108	34	19
	Black	1,275	397	237
	Latino	3,822	1,572	926

Source: University of Texas UT, Office of Admissions and Texas Higher Education Coordinating Board.

Texas state institutions, ranging from small to profound. African-American enrollment dropped to 2.9 percent from 4 percent when affirmative action ended. For Latinos, freshman enrollments dropped from 15 percent

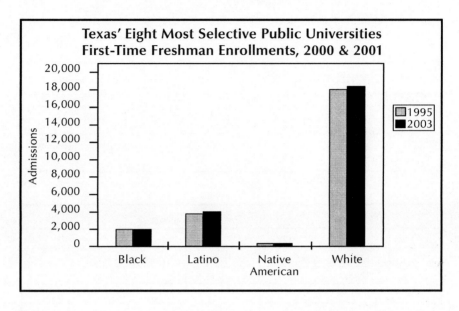

TEXAS' EIGHT MOST SELECTIVE PUBLIC UNIVERSITIES FIRST-TIME FRESHMAN ENROLLMENTS 2000 & 2001				
	ADMISSIONS		'00-'01 DIFFERENCE	
	2000	2001	NUMBER	PERCENT
Native American	138	130	-8	-6%
Black	1,646	1,610	-36	-2%
Latino	3,546	3,624	+78	2%
*White	18,247	18,452	+205	1%
Source: Texas Higher Education Coordinating Board				

to 12 percent. However, for whites, access improved. Enrollments have risen up to 67 percent for whites even though their population in the state was at 58 percent in 1995 and down to 52 percent in 2000.

Overall, in 1997, the eight most selective Texas public universities enrolled 1,442 African Americans and 3,102 Latinos. The data shows that certain institutions are more accessible to underrepresented students than others. For example, that same year The University of Texas at Dallas enrolled only 19 blacks; Texas A&M University-Corpus Christi enrolled 13 blacks and 58 Latinos. This compared to the 692 blacks and 58 Latinos that enrolled at the University of Houston during that same period.

Georgia

The University of Georgia (UGA) is the elite flagship institution in the University System of Georgia. Like most institutions in the South, its history is rooted in segregation. In 1961, Gov. Ernest Vandiver, citing a state law that refused funds to integrated institutions, closed the university instead of admitting two African American students, Charalyne Hunter and Hamilton Holmes. It was not until Judge William A. Bootle of the U.S. District Court forbade the university from refusing their applications that the university admitted them and Hunter and Holmes integrated UGA.

While segregation is not unique to the history of the United States, UGA did not have an approved desegregation plan until, after being ordered by the courts, the board of regents adopted a plan that went into effect in 1978. For about 15 years ending in 1987, the University System of Georgia institutions had been under a federal court order to diversify the racial composition of the student bodies. The University has used various strategies to redress its segregationist past where underrepresented students, primarily African Americans, were excluded on the basis of race. In the past decade the population and legal landscape has changed. With a growing number of applicants, about 14,000 seeking 4,000 slots, affirmative action has come under attack.

In 1997, three white students filed a reverse discrimination lawsuit against the UGA undergraduate admission policies after they were not granted admission. Two years later Judge B. Avant Edenfield dismissed those claims and ruled that race did not play a role in denying admission to the plaintiffs. However, he did offer an opinion on the legality of current UGA admission practices, which weights race in one stage of the admission process. This case is discussed in detail in Chapter Four.

The university has employed an admissions process that admits 90 percent of applicants solely on quantifiable means in establishing a "total student index," then the remaining 10 percent of freshmen are admitted on additional factors. These factors included race, state residency, extracurricular activities, employment while matriculating, and a relative of alumni and/or being among the first generation in their family to attend college.

According to Nancy McDuff, former admissions director, "By far the large majority of students are admitted solely on academic records. For the small percentage of students evaluated under the total student index, no single factor determines whether an applicant is admitted or denied."[35] The university stood by its process and continued to use race until 2000. President Adams along with the board of regents passionately defended the process and ensured that they would take affirmative steps to recruit "qualified minority students."[36] In the meantime, students of color on UGA's campus were feeling targeted as unqualified. Sherwood Thompson, UGA's director of the Office of Minority Services and Programs, stated, "Minority students, especially African Americans, have expressed displeasure with the fact that there are still debates about the issue of pursuing educational access for minority students, since society as a whole makes considerable gains from their inclusion."[37]

Many students look at UGA as an opportunity for success. Hilton Young, former president of the National Alumni Association and graduate of UGA, stated, "I lived in the projects in Athens, and it was my mom and dad who pointed me toward this institution as a lofty goal."[38] Professor Marie Cochran, graduate of the UGA class of 1985 and professor of art, stated: "I don't think there's enough discussion about the climate for minorities at UGA. We need a consistent and dedicated look at the issue of equity, which is how I think this should be framed, rather than talking about diversity. I was born in 1962, the year after the University of Georgia was integrated, so it's only within my lifetime that minorities have had access to this institution."[39] Mark Anthony Thomas, the first African-American editor-in-chief of the campus newspaper, opined: "Why are people concerned about using race as a factor but not legacy status? With the university not desegregating until 1961, that puts minority students at a disadvantage because we're far less likely to have a parent who is an alumnus. In 1999, it's still important to keep race as a criteria and to do everything we can both individually and as an institution to recruit minority students of all races."[40]

In 2000, Judge Edenfield ruled that the university cannot constitutionally justify the affirmative use of race in its admissions decisions. Glenn White, a member of the University System Board of Regents, said in a prepared statement "we respectfully disagreed with the decision,"[41] but vowed that the board was committed to ensuring that all students within the state have full access to an education. Despite the ruling, President Michael Adams stated, "I remain convinced that our students will be better prepared for the world if they have the opportunity on this campus to interact with people of different backgrounds and beliefs."[42]

While UGA stopped using race and gender as a factor in admissions, the university still has an array of support. Georgia's Gov. Barnes, a graduate of UGA and a supporter of affirmative action, stated, "given Georgia's history, it was necessary to continue to bring about some inclusion at the University of Georgia; things that go on for centuries just don't go away when a court says, 'that's gone.'"[43] UGA asserted that its process was designed with the specific goals and hopes of serving the needs of students, the University of Georgia, the state and society in general by attempting to create an academic community that reflects the world in everyday life.

According to the University System of Georgia, the percentage of African-American students at three of its premier public universities, the University of Georgia, Georgia Tech, and the Medical College of Georgia, continues to decrease. According to Georgia Sen. Charles Walker, "our society must make some fundamental decisions about diversity. Can we afford to revert back to a segregated society where access to a top university education will be restricted to the elite?"[44] This is exactly the case when you consider that virtually all increases in postsecondary education for African American students took place at the state's second-tier public institutions. The biggest increases in enrollment have been evident at Georgia State, Georgia Southern university campuses, and Clayton College and State University, in which more than a quarter of the student body is African American.

Of the nation's flagship institutions, the University of Georgia has struggled to maintain enrollment of underrepresented students of color, The 2003 enrollment percentage for University of Georgia first-time freshmen was 5.16 percent African American, 0.11 Native American, and 2.15 percent Latino. The percentage of underrepresented students of color enrolled at the University of Georgia does not come close to approximating their proportion of the state population. For example, 29 percent of the state is African American, yet they make up less than 6 percent of the students enrolled at the university. In 1996, the University of Georgia had its highest enrollment of African Americans, at 6.89 percent. That same year the white enrollment was 87.22 percent. While underrepresented student numbers were not large to begin with at the institution, they continue to decline for African American and Native American students since the court ruling.

Washington

Washington state voters approved Initiative 200 in 1998. Identical to California's Proposition 209, the initiative barred preferential treatment on the basis of race, gender, and national origin in the operation of public education. The impact this initiative has had on Washington has been similar to that of California, in which students of color are pushed out into less selective institutions. For example, the University of Washington (UW) has six campuses around the state. After the passage of I-200, UW saw declines in admission statewide, but this has had a profound impact on

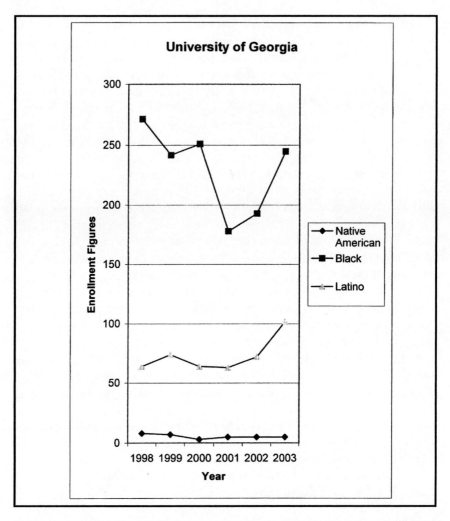

UNIVERSITY OF GEORGIA						
	1998	*1999*	*2000*	*2001*	*2002*	*2003*
Native American	8	7	3	5	5	5
Black	271	242	251	178	193	245
Latino	64	74	64	63	72	102
*White	3,710	3,671	3,345	3,555	3,369	4,025

Source: University System of Georgia, Office of Institutional Research

*White students were included in this chart to show the large disparities in enrollment in comparison to underrepresented students of color.

admission for underrepresented students of color at the state's flagship institution, the University of Washington in Seattle.

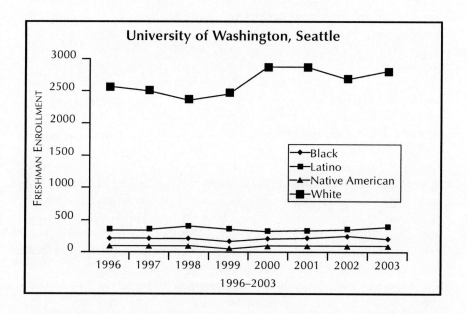

UNIVERSITY OF WASHINGTON, SEATTLE FRESHMAN ENROLLMENT								
	1996	*1997*	*1998*	*1999*	*2000*	*2001*	*2002*	*2003*
Native American	49	60	52	38	50	52	59	46
Black	116	107	124	83	122	120	138	142
Latino	169	168	196	131	123	193	178	216
*White	2,587	2,539	2,301	2,439	2,748	2,752	2,648	2,688

Source: University of Washington, Seattle

*White students were included in this chart to show the large disparities in enrollment in comparison to underrepresented students of color.

The Office of Minority Affairs at UW indicated that the number of African American, Native American and Latino students was gradually increasing since 1970. When the ban on race-sensitive policies went into effect, African Americans experienced the largest decline in enrollments. In 1998, 124 African American students enrolled, but in 1999, the number of new African American students enrolling at the university declined to 74, a 40 percent drop in one year. One year after the passage of I-200, UW saw a 23 percent drop in Native Americans, a 33 percent drop in Latinos, and a 40 percent decline in African Americans. Tim Washburn, UW director of admissions, observed: "The numbers are disappointing but anticipated. We hope to turn it around. This is just the first impact; the trend will be reflected in the classes three to four years from now if we do not reverse it."[45] Part of the reason the numbers were so low in 1999 was the overall drop in numbers of applicants. African American freshman applicants to UW dropped by 20 percent, Native Americans decreased 14 percent, and Latinos dropped by 8 percent. With the passage of I-200, Karen Copetas, director of admissions for Western Washington University, had this to say, "I wonder if the perception is that they may not be admitted elsewhere."[46] Students declined to even apply based upon the perception given by I-200 and the University of Washington. All of this had a powerful impact upon admissions numbers, especially those of Native American and Latino applicants.

However, the figures show since enactment of Initiative 200, the university is struggling to maintain admission of underrepresented students of color. In an address to the university, former President McCormick expressed his concern: "The decline of diversity in the freshmen class is deeply disappointing. Diversity is a critically important value to the educational mission of the University of Washington."[47] The average freshman admitted to UW has a 3.63 GPA and 1158 SAT score. UW has begun seeking more diversity through outreach with the assistance of its diversity advisory committee, which was established as a result of I-200. The university's goal is to communicate to the students in the community that opportunities are still available at UW.

Washington's Higher Education Coordinating Board adopted Resolution No. 96–06 aimed at increasing and monitoring minority enrollment at colleges and universities throughout the state. While the board acknowledges that African American enrollments declined, its research indicates that fluctuations in admissions make it unclear if diversity goals have been reached for underrepresented students. Myron Apildao, the former vice president for minority affairs at UW, stated, "One thing is certain, this is going to have a very big effect on this campus."[48]

In September of 2000 UW admitted its largest freshman class ever, with over 4,000 new students. With the increase, however, enrollment of underrepresented students of color still did not rebound to pre-I-200 figures. African Americans were up 47 percent, Native Americans up 22 percent, and Latinos went down 6 percent. The percentage of underrepresented students of color enrolled at the university dropped from 9 percent in 1998 to 6 percent in 2000.

The admission director admitted that I-200 was still having an impact. Charles Hirschman, UW sociology professor, conducted a study which concluded that the largest declines in minority enrollment were at the flagship campus of UW, the state's largest educational institution. According to Hirschman, "These declines were in stark contrast to a substantial rise in non-Hispanic white freshman enrollments."[49] Asian American enrollments went up 15 percent and white enrollment 13 percent. Part of the problem at UW was the continued decline in minority applications and the impact I-200 had on the perceptions of students of color.

Affirmative action plays more than one role in the admission process. First, it allows the university to take extra steps to attract and take a close look at candidates from underrepresented groups. It also sends a message to underrepresented students of color that they will be in an open environment and that they are welcomed. When affirmative action goes away, the procedure as well as the symbolism of what it means also disappears. That loss of symbolism has a profound impact on underrepresented students of color as well as the high school counselors who advise them. The downside for flagship institutions like UW is that a drop in applications from underrepresented students also means that many of them are seeking access to other selective institutions like Harvard and Stanford, completely bypassing Washington state.

In the fall of 2003, first-time freshmen enrollment increased by 2.7 percent at UW, and enrollment of underrepresented freshmen increased by 12 percent. African American enrollment was unchanged at 2.85 percent (142), Native Americans declined from 1.2 to 0.92 percent (46), Latinos increased from 3.67 to 4.34. percent (216).

Florida

In 1999, Gov. Jeb Bush introduced a plan to end affirmative action in college admissions to the state's 10 public universities. To ward off a statewide initiative that was in the works, Florida was the first state to voluntarily ban the use of race in college admissions as a political step without the passage of an initiative, resolution or legislative action. Bush's "One Florida Plan" eliminates the use of race or ethnicity in undergraduate or graduate admissions to universities. Instead, race is replaced with other factors like that of student's socioeconomic background, geographical diversity, first generation admission, or whether the student comes from a low-performing school. Bush also instituted his "Talented 20" program, which guarantees that the top 20 percent of graduates of every high school in the state are eligible to be admitted to a public university. Percentage plans are discussed in greater detail in Chapter Six.

According to Bush, affirmative action in admissions was no longer necessary because the university system had "significantly increased minority student enrollment."[50] It was Bush's aides who claimed at the time that the plan would increase minority eligibility by an additional 1,200 students as a result of the high concentration of minority students located at specific high schools in the state. Charles E. Young, president of the University of Florida, was the loudest dissenting voice to Bush's plan. Young stated, "The governor's plan was a capitulation to anti-affirmative action forces and could hurt minority enrollments at the university."[51] Young believed the policy was being imposed for entirely political reasons and was developed rapidly without involvement from those in the education community.

In 2000, the Florida regents adopted the governor's race-neutral plan. In September of that same year while Florida's universities claimed minority enrollments were on the rise despite the prohibition on race, the raw numbers for the flagship campus told a different story for undergraduates. In examining the impact to African Americans, the Journal of Blacks in Higher Education (JBHE) assert the flagship campus of the University of Florida (UF) was severely impacted. In 2001, 1,046 African American students were accepted to the University of Florida (UF) for admission. This was down by more than 600 students since the university admitted 1,671 African Americans in 2000. The first year race-neutral admissions were in place, African American enrollments dropped 44.4 percent. Latino students were not as severely impacted by the plan, in large part due to their overall population in Florida. Native American access decreased as well. In 2000, 140 Native Americans were admitted to the University of Florida and 80 enrolled. In 2001, that number was reduced by more than half when only 35 were admitted and 20 enrolled, a decline of 75 percent in one year. In 2002, the underrepresented population was 23 percent of the UF student body, with 7.2 percent African American and 9.6 percent Latino. African Americans are still 21 percent below the pre-affirmative action levels of 1999 when race-conscious admissions were still in place. While Latinos have begun to bounce back in college enrollments, African Americans and Native Americans have not returned to the pre-affirmative action ban since the prohibition began in 2000.

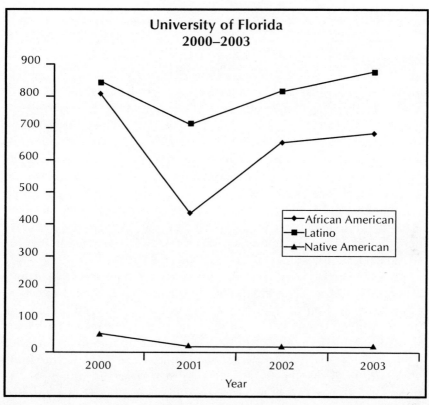

University of Florida 2000–2003

Legend:
- ◆ African American
- ■ Latino
- ▲ Native American

X-axis: Year (2000, 2001, 2002, 2003)

UNIVERSITY OF FLORIDA
FRESHMAN ENROLLMENT

	2000	2001	2002	2003
Native American	80	22	24	29
Black	829	460	659	676
Latino	847	716	817	851

Source: Governor Bush One Florida Plan Figures

While Bush totes the plan as a success, there are those who have continued concerns. Kweisi Mfume, president of the NAACP, said that Bush's plan is "misleading and will not increase access."[52] The Rev. Jesse Jackson stated: "Maybe those sons who inherit without effort can't hear the sons and daughters of denial. It's not about African American and white, it's about wrong and right."[53]

Nationwide

In examining the issue nationwide the author derives research from the U.S. Department of Education along with the Office of Minorities in Higher Education of the American Council on Education. ACE compiles an annual report that details the progress of racial and ethnic groups in postsecondary education. For the past 20 years underrepresented students of color have made gains in college participation. However, they still trail whites. Underrepresented enrollment jumped by "122 percent, from 2 million in 1980–81 to 4.3 million in 2000–01."[54] While the growth in enrollment is promising, where the disparity exists is that of college participation for recent high school graduates. The college participation rate for high school graduates has widened between whites, Latinos and African Americans.* "From 1978–80 to 1998–2000, the college participation rate increased by 14 percentage points for whites, 11 percentage points for African Americans, and 5 percentage points for Latinos." [55]

In 1978–80 the college participatory rate for Whites was 31.4 percent, 29 percent for African Americans and 29.1 percent for Latinos. In 1998–00 college participation rates rose to 45 percent for whites; 40 percent for African Americans and 34 percent for Latinos. Rates increased for whites and African Americans while Latinos saw a decline. In addition, a majority of the growth for African Americans and Latinos came in the early to mid-1990s prior to the nationwide attack on affirmative action. Latino participation rates declined for 18 to 24-year-old high school graduates enrolled in higher education from 35.4 percent in 1995–97 to 34 percent in 1998–2000.

African Americans have experienced some of the largest drops in admission to the nation's highest-ranked colleges and universities. In the early to mid-1990s, African Americans were making gains in college enrollments. But after the elimination of the use of race in college admissions in the late 1990s, according to *U.S. News & World Report*, those gains were significantly reduced.

For some of these universities the college president has led the charge for increased diversity. For example, Yale University President Kingman Brewster stated that "Yale will become a place that better reflects the demographic and regional composition of the country at large."[56] According to the U.S. Department of Education, the liberal arts colleges have had some of the largest increased enrollment of African Americans since the 1980s. From 1980 to 1993, the percentage of African Americans had increased at 14 of the nation's most selective liberal arts colleges.

Data is not collected on a regular basis regarding college participation for Native Americans. Therefore, the data was not provided in the study.

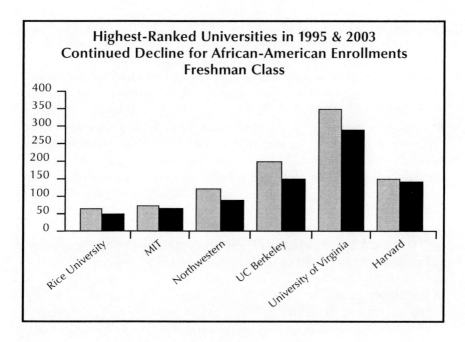

Highest-Ranked Universities in 1995 & 2003
Continued Decline for African-American Enrollments
Freshman Class

	HIGHEST-RANKED UNIVERSITIES IN 1995 & 2003 CONTINUED DECLINE FOR AFRICAN AMERICAN ADMITS FRESHMAN CLASS		
Institution	*1995*	*2003*	*% Change*
Rice University	64	35	-45%
MIT	69	62	-10%
Northwestern	126	90	-29%
UC Berkeley	202	149	-26%
University of Virginia	350	290	-17%
Harvard	149	140	-0.06%

Source: Journal of Blacks in Higher Education

In 1996, some of the institutions that showed large gains reported larger declines in African American enrollments. The largest decline came from Northwestern University, where only 80 black students enrolled, compared to 126 the previous year. The University of Michigan enrolled 470, down from 602, a 21.9 percent drop; at the University of Pennsylvania 124 enrolled, a 20 percent drop from 155 the year before. Significant

declines also occurred at Rice University, down by 18 percent; Georgetown, 17.5 percent; Dartmouth, 14.9 percent; Emory, 12 percent; Notre
Dame, 9.7 percent. Harvard experienced a 6.7 percent decline.

For some of these institutions the African American student acceptance rate was higher than the acceptance rate of white students. According to the Journal of Blacks in Higher Education, at Dartmouth College
in 1996, 42.6 percent of all African-American applicants were accepted
compared to only 19.3 percent of white applicants. This does not mean that
unqualified African Americans were gaining admission over whites; what
it meant was that some admission officers accepted more students in one
category to ensure they have a larger number of students who will matric-
ulate. In addition, these same students met all of the academic requirements for the institution.

When JBHE conducted its 1997–98 survey, the declines in enrollment
outweighed the increases as anti-affirmative action policies were being
implemented. Once again, the numbers for African Americans admitted
to the highest ranked universities had declined. The University of California had the largest decline in 1998, the first year of the implementation
of race-blind admissions for its undergraduate programs. While the numbers in declining enrollment are larger for some universities, not all have
been impacted by race-blind admissions. Yet all institutions were reexamining their affirmative action policies in the wake of the outcomes in
California and Texas, and this contributed to the declines. Based upon the
institutions included in the survey in 2003, continued declines exist for
African Americans at selective and elite institutions.

Some of the highest ranked universities showed declines for African
Americans in 1995 through 2003. Caltech had the largest decline in 2002.
The institution admitted five African American freshmen in 2001 and three
in 2002, resulting in a 40 percent decline. Princeton University came in
second with a 12.5 percent decline from 2001–02. The University of Notre
Dame also took the prize with a 40 percent decline, with 86 African Americans admitted in 2000 and 61 in 2001.

The foregoing discussion provides evidence of a significant reduction
and stagnant growth in the diversity of new freshmen at selective colleges
and universities throughout the nation when race and ethnicity are
removed as admissions criteria. While affirmative action programs continue to exist, most have been stripped of the most effective means of
achieving racial and ethnic diversity in undergraduate student bodies.

There are three realities that must be present in the debate on racial
diversity in college admissions. First, you cannot have racial diversity on
a college campus without the use of race as criteria. Second, not everyone

who applies gets in, so colleges and universities will always have to use a set of preferences in choosing students to admit. Institutions not only need to acknowledge all of the preferences they use, but articulate the benefits the students admitted will bring to the institution. Third, not until individuals understand the difference between eligibility and admission there will always be an assumption that any student admitted over another student with higher scores was not qualified. Until Americans have a working knowledge of how college admissions processes work, there will always be one side to the story and the preservation of diversity on public college campuses will be allowed to diminish.

Failure to make the investments necessary to improve the preparation of underrepresented students of color will continue to constrain access to elite postsecondary institutions for these students. Inability to consider race and ethnicity among other criteria will further dampen access and significantly reduce the numbers of underrepresented students eligible to seek enrollment in graduate and professional schools.

For too long, diversity has been thought of as something that takes away from some to give to others, as if opportunity exists only in finite quantities. In reality, diversity gives to all.

— Dennis W. Archer, President,
American Bar Association (2003)

2. The Professional School Armageddon

Ensuring representation of underrepresented minority groups that is consistent or at parity with the demographics of the population has and continues to be one of the challenges to maintaining diversity in graduate programs. For example, "the legal profession is more than 90 percent white and less than 8 percent of color while the U.S. population is 70 percent white and 30 percent of color."[1]

In order to serve all Americans, diversity in the legal profession is a must, and fairness is developed in a system that is accessible to all. Alexis de Tocqueville's view of oppression details this need.* "If oppressed, blacks may bring an action at laws, but they will find none but whites among their judges; and although they may legally serve as jurors, prejudice repels them from that office."[2] Diversity is essential in the legal profession to improve public trust in the system of justice; many Americans, especially underrepresented minorities, view the legal system as biased and untrustworthy.

Lawyers are representatives of the Constitution in serving the legal rights and liberties of all people in society. In a diverse society that representation must be a reflection of all race, color, or creed in order for equity and democracy to prevail. Thurgood Marshall is a prime example of the importance of diversity. After being denied access to the University of Maryland because of segregation, he attended Howard University. After obtaining his degree he and other African American attorneys dedicated their careers to ending segregation in education. In 1954, Thurgood Marshall and Charles Hamilton Houston were the architects of the U.S.

Alexis de Tocqueville, Democracy in America, 1835.

46

Supreme Court decision in *Brown v. Board of Education*. Marshall went on to become the first African American appointed to the U.S. Supreme Court.

Nationwide organizations have recognized the need for diversity in the legal profession. The American Bar Association provides accreditation for American law schools. The ABA requires all law schools to demonstrate a commitment to diversity and opportunities for all fully qualified applicants in the study of law. In 1986 the ABA established the Commission on Racial and Ethnic Diversity in the Profession. Its primary goal is to promote "full and equal participation in the profession by minorities and women."

With the lack of diversity in the profession as well as on the bench, numerous studies indicate that justice is not blind and bias does exist, including the Michigan Supreme Court (1987), the New York Judicial Committee (1992), American Bar Association (1994, 1996, 1999) and the District of Columbia Circuit Study (1996). Specifically, in a report by the judicial committee of New York, attorneys witnessed judges making such comments as "there's another nigger in the woodpile" or "not having a Chinaman's chance."[3] The results of a 1998 survey of over 1,000 lawyers commissioned by both the National and American Bar Associations substantiated the perception that bias in the profession exists. Half of the minorities surveyed indicated that bias is predominant in the system. Fifty-two percent of African Americans asserted that bias runs the system. Only 39 percent of respondents indicated that the courts were not biased and that all racial groups were treated with equity.[4] Another study conducted by Carter (1999) found that 92 percent of African American lawyers believe the justice system is racially biased.

A study by Rattman and Tomkins (1999) revealed that underrepresented minorities, especially African Americans, do not receive equal treatment. Sixty-eight percent of African Americans indicate that people of color, especially African Americans, are treated worse in the court system than whites. Forty-three percent of whites and 42 percent of Latinos came to the same conclusion.[5] Perceptions of fairness are made through visibility. The makeup of the legal profession speaks to this reality. Individuals form their perceptions based upon what they see, and if they do not see anyone who reflects them, the perception is mistrust. It is that mistrust coupled with the segregated history of the system that leads most to believe that the justice system will not treat them fairly. "Trust is the foundation of the judicial system, and people must believe that the system is fair. But trust is difficult to obtain when there appears to be a systematic exclusion of certain races and ethnicities— the same groups who have historically borne the brunt of the system's punishment."[6] Two systems of justice exists: on one side whites and on the other side underrepresented minority groups and the poor. In light of the research there is validity to the perception that minority groups are not afforded equality in the courts. Therefore, the commonality shared by all the research was the need to increase racial diversity on the bench and in the legal profession.

Diversity in the legal profession would reduce the perception of racial bias and increase representation of low-income minority groups and individuals. For example, the Constitution does not guarantee legal representation for civil cases, putting people of color at risk of no representation, incompetent or ineffective representation for non-criminal disputes. It is in a state's best interest to ensure access to justice for minority groups. Otherwise, the cycle of oppression and bias will maintain the dichotomy in the legal profession and the courts, that of a system for whites and another system for everyone else. Therefore, we must take steps necessary to counter and change the perception of this continued dynamic with future representation of underrepresented groups in law schools and among law teachers, lawyers, and judges. It is the courts that therefore must protect the integrity of the judicial process. The Supreme Court has asserted the importance of inclusiveness in the perception of fairness for minority groups in the system (*Powers v. Ohio*, 499 U.S. 400, 406, 410 [1991]).

Justices based their decision for this need on two principles: (1) the harm minority groups of color experience when excluded from the process is an experience that is not only wrong but undermines impartiality of the system; and (2) the court must avoid the perception of unfairness. With a lack of participation in the process, the courts will continue to be viewed as inaccessible and unjust. A judicial system that excludes sections of the community is aggressively participating in a process that not only undermines the legal system but destroys confidence in it by the very people it is designed to protect.

Seeking equal justice is an element of democracy we all strive for, which is why it comes as no surprise that there is a need for improvement of legal services for people of color. Many underrepresented students of color demonstrate the drive for equal justice whereupon graduation they tend to provide assistance to underserved communities at a higher level than that of whites. This is due in large part because most underserved communities have a higher level of minority groups and because for some attorneys, they are returning home.[7] Minority attorneys are twice as likely to enter practice in the public sector in government work or public interest law.* It is harder for underrepresented attorneys to enter firms in private

---

Minority attorneys and underrepresented students of color are defined as Latinos, African Americans and Native Americans.

practice. "Non-whites are 7.5 percent less likely than whites to enter private practice, while the rate of non-whites practicing in the public interest considerably exceeds the rate of whites."[8] In addition, underrepresented minorities share an enhanced understanding of the culture of working with underprivileged individuals and for some, an understanding of the language also. This is not to imply that only underrepresented attorneys can work with poor and minority clients, but that they participate at higher levels working within their own community than whites. According to the National Hispanic Bar Association (2003), many Latino attorneys provide more than just legal representation by offering a connection to the process, the culture and the ability to assist those with a language barrier who often cannot participate in their own defense.

The continued use of race-conscious admission for qualified law applicants will not only increase the number of minority lawyers in the pipeline but also will assist in the amelioration of racial bias in the system. In addition, it will promote equal access to the legal system. The need to increase diversity within the legal profession is not just an idea, but a necessity for the administration of justice. As the population becomes increasingly diverse so to should professional schools, but they are not. According to the 2000 Census, while Latinos represent 12.5 percent of the nation's population they were only 5.5 percent of the 2000 graduating class in comparison to 81 percent non-minority graduates.[9]

The political arena tends to favor those with a legal education. Those who seek the opportunity to participate in elected office have a better chance with a legal education. For example, 23 of 50 governors, 52 of 100 senators, 159 of 435 congressional representatives and 26 of 43 presidents attended law school.[10] As a legal education has proven to be the gateway to political participation, a diverse representation of those on the bench and the Bar will improve public confidence in the government as a true representation of the population.

In the 1970s the number of underrepresented students of color entering law school began to increase, and in 1976 there were 9,500 students of color entered. By the late 1990s that number had grown to 25,000. This increase contributed to the number of qualified underrepresented students of color entering the legal profession.[11] However, the trend of continued increase from the 1970s no longer exists, and the number of underrepresented students of color is declining. If law schools are unable to maintain diversity among their student bodies and faculty, the goal of an equitable society will not be realized.

Unlike undergraduate programs, graduate schools do not have the luxury of percentage plans, leaving the admissions criteria solely to quantifiable criteria of grades and test scores. This has resulted in a serious problem across the country. While progress has been slow and in some cases nonexistent, let's look at the state of both the law and medical schools.

Law Schools

California

Minority enrollment at the University of California, Berkeley, law school (Boalt Hall) dropped precipitously in 1997 after race-sensitive affirmative action was thrown out. That year, 256 African Americans applied, 14 were accepted, and one enrolled. In comparison, 2,676 whites applied, and 608 were accepted.

The lone African American student, Eric Brooks, a graduate of Indiana University, was admitted to Boalt in 1996 when race-sensitive affirmative action was still in use. He deferred enrollment for one year, becoming the only African American in the 1997 entering class. Most of the African American students who were accepted decided to enroll in other universities. Why? Because of the lack of diversity and the fact that they believed they would be coming into a hostile environment. Brooks did reconsider and looked into other law schools in the San Francisco Bay Area for possible admittance, but in the end he decided that he would not let this situation set him back.

Eric Burton, on the other hand, was one of the 14 African American students accepted to Berkeley's law school in 1997 who decided to go elsewhere. Burton says his decision was further complicated after visiting the campus during "admit day." "I was the only African American there, and it was a really strange vibe. There were signs and placards saying, 'Welcome to Jim Crow Law School' and piñatas looking like Pete Wilson" (the former governor of California). Burton said most of the students and faculty he spoke with were supportive and concerned about the impact SP-1 would have on diversity at Boalt. "The dean said she was also concerned about the numbers but was quick to add that in this era of conservatism, they had to comply with the regents' decision and Prop 209."[12] Burton, who had also been accepted to UCLA, Stanford, Georgetown, the University of Pennsylvania and New York University, says he "agonized over the decision for a couple of months." Ultimately, Burton registered at UCLA, where he studied public interest law and policy.

The situation was not unique to Berkeley because in that same year, UCLA admitted only two African Americans. Says Crystal James, one of the two African American students admitted among 286 new students that fall, "There are times when I feel isolated and excluded, an outcast from my classmates."

The University of California has three law schools, at Berkeley, Los Angeles, and Davis. Since the mid–1990s there has been a decline in the number of underrepresented students admitted to these law schools. From fall 1994 to fall 2001, the number has declined over 50 percent under California's anti-affirmative action movement. During this time African Amer-

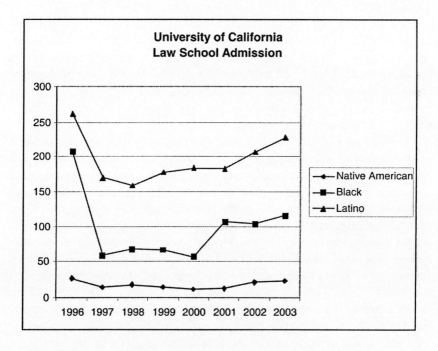

UNIVERSITY OF CALIFORNIA LAW SCHOOL ADMISSION								
	1996	*1997*	*1998*	*1999*	*2000*	*2001*	*2002*	*2003*
Native American	26	14	18	14	11	12	21	23
Black	208	59	68	67	57	107	104	116
Latino	262	170	159	177	184	183	207	228
Source: University of California, Office of the President								

The figures in all the graphs and charts represent full-time first-year students.

icans admitted to law schools at the University of California declined by
55 percent, from a total of 239 to 107, and their enrollment rate declined
68 percent, from 87 to 28. Latinos admitted to the law schools declined
33 percent, from 273 to 184, and the enrollment rate also declined 48 percent, from 110 to 57. For Native Americans, admission declined 65 percent, from a total of 34 to 12, and their enrollment rate declined by 58
percent, from 12 to five.

The California Senate Select Committee on College and University
Admissions and Outreach, formed to examine equity in those areas, held
its first public hearing at UC, Berkeley, on September 22, 1997. This was
an ideal location since the university was under criticism for its deplorable
decline in graduate admissions of underrepresented students. The goal of
this hearing was to try to understand why there was such a huge decline
for students of color admitted to the university. While most of the professional schools in California experienced a decline in minority enrollment, Boalt Law School was on the hot seat that day with the enrollment
of only one African American student.

In addition, it had become known that the university was using a
grade weighting scale that gave extra points to students dependent upon
their undergraduate school of study. For example, students who applied
from the Ivy League of Yale and Williams University received an additional
84 points added to their overall grade point average whereas students from
such universities as UC, Riverside or CSU, Chico, were given a mere 68
points and Howard University 57.5 points. There was no historical black
college that was ranked at the same level as Harvard, Duke or Stanford.
Former dean Herma Kay provided an explanation that she believed justified
the use of the scale. She explained that the scale was a formula based on
the number of students who take the LSAT at particular schools, corre-
lated with their grade point average, and that this produced a ranking.
This was a unique scale known only to those involved in the admission
process. Not surprisingly, after the scale was revealed, the university
claimed it stopped using it based on the concern about the scoring advantage it provided to certain institutions. The university has replaced this
process, but it is not clear or public what the new process is.

According to Dean Kay: "We are in the process of re-evaluating the
question of whether we should continue to weight the grades. But I point
out if we stop doing that, that will leave it up to other individuals who
may not weigh scores by an objective criteria."[13] Dean Kay did not understand at the time that the scale clearly favored students at the elite institutions while down rating those at other institutions.

When the controversial question of the admission of African Americans was posed to Dean Kay, her response was that it was the result of the changes the school made in the application forms. In 1997, in response to SP-1, the university removed the ethnicity boxes from the forms and put the information on an optional postcard, which could be returned to the university. Very few students returned those forms, or they declined to state their race or ethnicity. By the time applicants received the information from law school admission services on who those students were, all except two or three had chosen to go to other schools. This resulted in the university admitting only 14 African Americans, none of whom chose to attend Berkeley.

The only one who enrolled was the deferral from the previous year. All members of the committee found the information troubling and

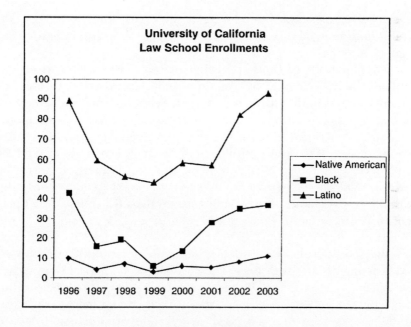

UNIVERSITY OF CALIFORNIA LAW SCHOOL ENROLLMENTS								
	1996	*1997*	*1998*	*1999*	*2000*	*2001*	*2002*	*2003*
Native American	10	4	7	3	6	5	8	11
Black	43	16	19	6	14	28	35	37
Latino	89	59	51	48	58	57	82	93
Source: University of California, Office of the President, www.ucop.com								

advised Berkeley to get its act together and come up with alternatives to increase diversity. It was clear that UC had a public relations problem. Many students did not bother to apply, assuming they would not be welcomed.

Texas

California, however, was just the beginning. After the Hopwood court decision of March 1996, minority enrollments for Texas public law schools declined across the board. Texas has four public law schools (Southern University, Texas Tech, University of Texas, and the University of Houston). In 1996, 207 African Americans were admitted in Texas, 163 Latinos, and 15 Native Americans. In 1997, 159 African Americans, 132 Latinos, and seven Native Americans were admitted. Native Americans experienced the largest decline in admissions, with a 53 percent drop from the previous year.

The University of Texas at Austin enrolled 67 African American students in the 1997–98 academic year, down 30 from the year before. The flagship campus of the University of Texas School of Law was hardest hit by the Hopwood decision. From 1954–74 the school had graduated only 22 African Americans. Then it implemented a race-sensitive affirmative action program. As a result, enrollment of students of color grew from 1986 to 1996. For example, in 1995, enrollment of African Americans was at 7.4 percent. After the university modified its admissions policies consistent with the Hopwood decision, enrollment numbers fell to less than 1 percent in 1997. For Latinos the number went from 12.5 percent in 1995 to 5.6 percent in 1997.

Previously, graduate programs saw increases for minorities in 1994–95 and remained constant in 1996. The post–Hopwood figures were so bad that in an effort to counter the negative publicity, law schools began running letters in student newspapers, stating their commitment to diversity. In addition, some programs devised "new avenues of admission" by establishing summer law school programs for students who did not meet admission requirements. Successful completion of the summer program provided an opportunity for the student to enroll. In an Amicus Brief filed by Texas law school deans in the Cheryl Hopwood case, Frank Newton, dean of Texas Tech School of Law, stressed that "Texas cannot prosper in the twenty-first century without reasonable representation on the bench and bar of all segments of society."

Realizing that diversity was continuing to decline in the professional and graduate schools, the Texas Legislature passed legislation aimed to

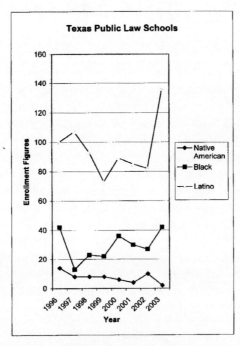

Texas Public Law Schools

TEXAS PUBLIC LAW UNIVERSITIES ENROLLMENT FIGURES								
	1996	*1997*	*1998*	*1999*	*2000*	*2001*	*2002*	*2003*
Native American	14	8	8	8	6	4	10	2
Black	42	13	23	22	36	30	27	42
Latino	100	107	93	73	89	85	82	136
Source: Texas Higher Education Coordinating Board								

broaden admission criteria. HB 1641 (2001) gave flexibility to universities in their use of standardized tests to admit students. The legislation required institutions to not use standardized test scores as the sole criterion for consideration of the applicant or as the "primary" criterion to exclude the applicant from consideration. At the University of Texas, Latino enrollment in 2001 rose to 7.1 percent and African American enrollment to 3.8 percent in 2001.

Rep. Irma Rangel, author of the legislation, stated that this policy is needed so that administrators will have an alternative without the fear of lawsuits. While university officials praised the increase in minority admissions for 2001, Rangel said, "I would not brag about the numbers that presently exist because they are not even reflective of the population of Texas." For example, Latinos are 33 percent of the population yet they are a mere 7 percent of the students enrolled at the institution.

Washington

The University of Washington School of Law has not always had large numbers of students of color, and since the ban on race their numbers have plummeted. In 1995, the school saw its highest number of minority enrollments at 36 for all three underrepresented groups combined. Since 1995, minority enrollments have declined. In 1996, only 19 underrepresented students enrolled, and that increased by a few in 1997 to 23 students. After Initiative 200 these small numbers went from bad to worse. While the institution received applications in the thousands, in 1998 it admitted eight African Americans (only one enrolled), seven Latinos, and zero Native Americans. In 1999, the school enrolled 11 underrepresented students of color. For 2000, the enrollment numbers were even worse, with one African American, three Latinos, and one Native American. However, in 2001 underrepresented admission increased to 19. While the numbers have grown they have not surpassed their 1995 high. In 2001, Latinos rebounded

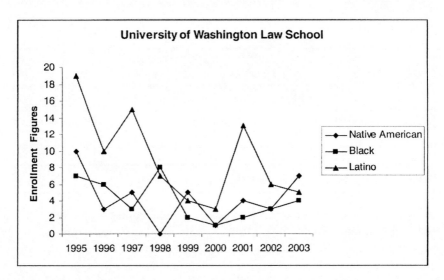

UNIVERSITY OF WASHINGTON LAW SCHOOL ENROLLMENT									
	1995	1996	1997	1998	1999	2000	2001	2002	2003
Native American	10	3	5	0	5	1	4	3	7
Black	7	6	3	8	2	1	2	3	4
Latino	19	10	15	7	4	3	13	6	5

Source: University of Washington, Office of Institutional Research

with a high of 13 admissions. For that same year the enrollment for African Americans was three and four for Native Americans—this clearly shows that underrepresented students' chances of getting a legal education are virtually non-existent in Washington.

Florida

At the flagship campus of the University of Florida Law School, underrepresented students of color have been affected by the prohibition of race consideration. In 1999, 80 African Americans, 108 Latinos, and 17 Native Americans were admitted. Those numbers increased in 2000 for two of the three groups, with 86 African Americans, 116 Latinos, and four Native Americans being admitted. In 2001, when the ban on race-conscious policies was implemented, 62 African Americans, 72 Latinos, and three Native

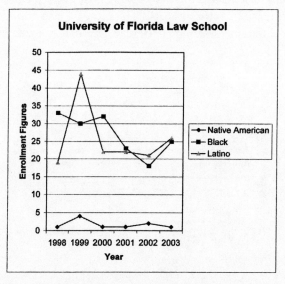

UNIVERSITY OF FLORIDA LAW SCHOOL						
	1998	*1999*	*2000*	*2001*	*2002*	*2003*
Native American	1	4	1	1	2	1
Black	33	30	32	23	18	25
Latino	19	44	22	22	21	26
Source: State University System of Florida						

2003 data for Florida not available for this material.

Americans were admitted. African Americans saw a 27 percent decline and Latinos 37 percent. There has been minimal change in Native American admissions. Enrollments are the other critical piece in the process. (Not every admitted student actually enrolls.)* According to the chart, under-represented student enrollments have primarily experienced declines since the late 1990s.

The situation is basically the same around the country, with Gov. Jeb Bush of Florida saying that "we've got enough lawyers; the problem is we don't have enough in 2001." U.S. law schools have experienced the largest increase in applicants since 1991, according to the Law School Admissions Council. Preliminary numbers show that approximately 78,724 persons applied to at least one American Bar Association-approved law school. The figure represents a 5.6 percent increase over the previous year. "The increase is good news for law schools that saw a nearly one-third decrease in the number of applicants during the '90s," says Philip D. Shelton, pres-ident and executive director of LSAC. The increase also allows law schools to be more selective and assemble better law school classes, he says. "Unfor-

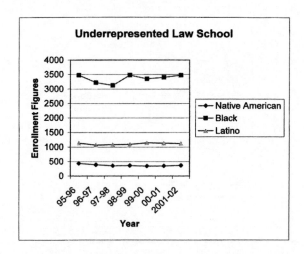

UNDERREPRESENTED LAW SCHOOL ENROLLMENT							
	95-96	96-97	97-98	98-99	99-00	00-01	2001-02
Native American	436	391	355	361	342	348	365
Black	3,474	3,223	3,126	3,478	3,353	3,402	3,474
Latino	1,132	1,067	1,083	1,091	1,144	1,132	1,117
Source: American Bar Association							

tunately for minorities, this increase in applications has not resulted in an increase in acceptance."

Figures from the American Bar Association confirm this decline for underrepresented students. African American enrollment in law school hit its peak in 1994 with 3,600. That number has steadily declined, and in 2001–02 the number of African Americans enrolled was 3,474, a 3 percent decline. In 1995–96 Native American enrollment was at an all-time high of 436. In 2001–02, that number had dropped to 365, a 16 percent decline. Latinos are broken into two groups (Mexican and Puerto Rican). Mexican American enrollments were the highest in 1994 at 902; in 2001–02 that number dropped to 896. For Puerto Ricans the peak was 275 enrolled in 1993–94, and it dropped to 221 in 2001–02, a 19 percent decline. This decline was evident in the number of degrees awarded. During an 11-year period (1990–2001) law degrees awarded to underrepresented students hit their peak in 1998 at 6,882; in 2002 that number dropped to 6,668.

Graduate school admissions, like those of undergraduate admissions, are warped with misconceptions on how race is used in the process. Admission committees are faced with challenging situations in the process of selecting a diverse student body. For example, when an elite institution is concluding its admission process it has two applicants, one Latino and the other white, both seeking the last seat available for law school. The Latino applicant is not fully eligible and the members of the admission committee do not find the student to be a strong candidate. While the white applicant is not an outstanding candidate, he is eligible for admission. Admission is offered to the white applicant because he is "qualified." Even if the institution has not enrolled any Latino students, affirmative action does not allow admission of "unqualified" applicants no matter what their racial background. Another common situation faced by admissions committees is when one applicant is African American and one is white. Both are eligible, but neither one is outstanding, and only one slot is available for admission. As African American applicants are severely underrepresented in the school, the committee offers admission to the African American applicant. As a qualified member of an underrepresented group the applicant gains access, and admitting the qualified African American applicant is the appropriate implementation of affirmative action.

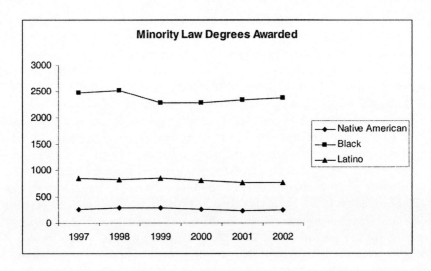

UNDERREPRESENTED LAW DEGREES AWARDED						
	1997	*1998*	*1999*	*2000*	*2001*	*2002*
Native American	263	298	293	264	242	251
Black	2,470	2,513	2,272	2,270	2,325	2,369
Latino	858	826	850	806	763	761
Source: American Bar Association						

Medical Schools

During the days of segregation, white doctors accepted only white patients, which created a need to train doctors of color. Had it not been for Historically Black Colleges and Universities like Howard University, students of color would not have been able to become doctors in the United States. Access to professional schools was not available to blacks until the mid–1800s. In 1868, Howard University opened a medical school and eight years later was followed by Meharry Medical College. These institutions were the first of their kind in providing access for blacks and students of color. For decades these were the only medical schools in the country for blacks, and the institutions combined were responsible for placing more than 80 percent of black graduates into the medical field. In the early 1990s, Howard University was responsible for training more than 25 percent of black physicians practicing in the United States.

The Association of American Medical Colleges in 1968 encouraged all medical schools to voluntarily admit increased numbers of students of color and students from diverse geographic areas and economic backgrounds. At that time about 130 African Americans were enrolled in white medical schools. Affirmative action goals were set to increase enrollment of minority groups to levels close to their parity in the population. In 1968 underrepresented students of color were a mere 2 percent of enrollment in U.S. medical schools. According to the *Journal of Blacks in Higher Education* (2003), from 1952 to 1972 only 12 blacks graduated from Harvard Medical School. By 1975 enrollment of underrepresented students in medical schools had grown to 10 percent.

After a half-century of progress, enrollments of students of color peaked in the 1990s. In 1995, the number of underrepresented students of color in U.S. medical schools was at an all-time high of 8,254 in comparison to whites at 43,894. It was during this time that the University of California's five medical schools ranked among the top eight schools for graduating doctors of color. These doctors and those from other schools across the U.S. have since become leaders in their fields. Before looking at what has happened since admissions to some medical schools have become "color-blind," let's take a quick look at a few of the minority medical school graduate successes.

Dr. Benjamin Solomon Carson, Sr., a graduate of the University of Michigan School of Medicine, became director of pediatric surgery at Johns Hopkins University at 33. "In the early days," he says, "every time I would go on the wards, they would mistake me for an orderly because I had my scrubs on." Carson is also professor of pediatrics, oncology, neurosurgery, and plastic surgery at Johns Hopkins.

Dr. Keith Black is director of neurosurgery at the Maxine Dunitz Neurosurgical Institute at Cedars-Sinai Medical Center and a professor in the department of neurological surgery at the University of California, Irvine Medical Center. Dr. Black recalls telling the chief of neurosurgery of the University of Michigan medical program that he wanted to be a surgeon. The reply was, "Who are your parents? You have to be really smart to be a neurosurgeon."

Dr. William J. Coffey, Jr., was the first African American resident admitted to the University of California's College of Medicine in San Francisco, where he helped create the "tissue culture" that set the precedent for techniques used today by scientists and doctors to grow living cells. He also established the dermatology program at Martin Luther King Jr. Hospital in Los Angeles.

California

Despite these and many other successes, many states have eliminated race-sensitive affirmative action, sharply decreasing the number of under-represented students enrolling in medical schools. In previous years there were four states— California, Texas, Florida, and Washington — that accounted for 16 percent of all medical school graduates on an annual basis. With the implementation of race-blind admissions this is no longer the case. The California system is a good example. The University of California (UC) has five medical school programs at the campuses of Davis, Irvine, Los Angeles, San Diego and San Francisco.

From 1994 to 2001, the number of underrepresented students admit-ted to the medical schools declined by 36 percent, from a total of 261 to 166. The enrollment also declined by 54 percent during this period, from a total of 107 to 49 for all students of color enrolled in medical schools at UC. In 1999, there were a total of 44 underrepresented students enrolled in all UC medical schools.

In 1996, only 5.3 percent of the admitted students were African Amer-icans, 1.2 percent Native American, and 10.1 percent Latino. The most out-landish numbers came from San Diego and Irvine, where in 1997, both schools admitted a total of eight underrepresented students, only one of whom was African American; no Native Americans were admitted for either school. Yet that same year both institutions received more than 400 applications from underrepresented students of color.

In 1999, however these numbers began to rebound from the 1997 lows. African American admissions in 1999 increased by 53 percent and Latino by 40 percent. For some of these institutions, like UC Irvine, the numbers could only go up. In 1997, UC Irvine received 170 African American appli-cations and admitted none, and in 2001, the university admitted only two.

While the acceptance rates in 1999 went up, the enrollments for underrepresented students went down. For African Americans in the same time for admissions there was a 12 percent drop, Latinos a 5 percent drop and Native Americans a .84 percent drop. However, for non–Hispanic whites enrollment increased by 3 percent. Yet in 2001, these numbers were still low, with five Native Americans admitted, 75 African Americans and 121 Latinos. During the same year only three Native Americans enrolled, 29 African Americans, and 56 Latinos. Also, UC Irvine did not admit any Native Americans and only four African American students that year even though many more applied.

The grim reality is that the state of California since 1997 has become successful in dramatically reducing the number of prospective doctors from underrepresented groups who are able to obtain access to quality education at public universities. Dean John Alksne, in 1997, was dean of the medical school at UC San Diego. He openly stated that the decline in minority admissions was nothing less than embarrassing. Out of 196 African American applicants, the university did not admit any.

In its screening process the school had identified 13 candidates it was interested in advancing to the next step and sent out secondary applications. All 13 applicants withdrew. When questioned on the withdrawals, Alksne stated that he believed Proposition 209 and SP-1 had a huge impact on those candidates. In addition, the slow pace of the university's process also had a hand, assuming that most applicants found places at other institutions.

Alksne made this statement during a public hearing of the Senate Select Committee on College and University Admissions and Outreach. Sen. Barbara Lee, a member of the committee, asked him to talk about the "real problems."[14] Alksne responded that the school would increase the application process time to coincide with Harvard and other institutions and that the school would also do more outreach with alumni, medical

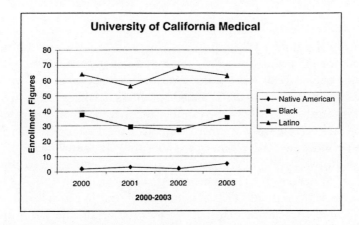

UNIVERSITY OF CALIFORNIA MEDICAL SCHOOL ENROLLMENTS				
	2000	*2001*	*2002*	*2003*
Native American	2	3	2	5
Black	37	29	27	35
Latino	64	56	68	63
Source: University of California, Office of the President				

organizations and those in the community to increase the pool of diverse applicants. Today, there are still very few African Americans admitted to UC San Diego's School of Medicine.

From 2000 to 2003 there have been no Native American students enrolled at the University of California, Irvine (UCI), UCLA, the Martin Luther King, Jr., Drew Medical Center, and University of California, Riverside (UCR). In the same time frame only five African American students have enrolled at UCR. In 2002, there were no underrepresented students of color enrolled at UCR. From 2000 to 2002 a total of three Native American students enrolled. In the fall of 2000 at UC Davis, a total of seven underrepresented students of color enrolled. UCR has had the lowest enrollment of underrepresented students of color. In 2000, a total of six underrepresented students of color enrolled. In 2001, that number dropped to four and for 2002 no underrepresented students of color enrolled. In 2003, at the campuses of Davis, Irvine, San Diego, and Riverside, no Native American students enrolled. In the same year, only two African Americans enrolled at the campuses of Davis, Irvine, San Diego and Riverside.

Texas

The outcomes were similar for Texas medical schools. The state has eight medical schools. While African American and Latino admittances increased in 1994 and 1995, they remained constant in 1996, with the admission of 65 African Americans, 183 Latinos, and 13 Native Americans. However, post–Hopwood actions made dramatic changes to the diversity of the student body. In 1997 the number of African Americans admitted dropped to 40 (14 enrolled); there were also 142 Latinos admitted (109 enrolled), and nine Native Americans admitted (four enrolled).

Pre-Hopwood numbers for enrollment in 1996 showed medical schools at 61 percent white, 5 percent African American, and 14 percent Latino. The University of Texas System Vice Chancellor for Health Affairs has indicated that the system will be looking at alternative means to increase diversity. Institutions are looking at different methods such as first-generation graduate student status, economic background, and extracurricular activities. The chart displays the 1997 declines for all underrepresented students of color seeking access to medical school. In 2002, the enrollment numbers had not fully recovered to the 1996 levels and only African Americans rebounded in 2003.

Texas, for instance, recently passed a law limiting the use of standardized tests in graduate admissions. Critics of standardized tests say that African American and Latino students tend to score lower on the tests

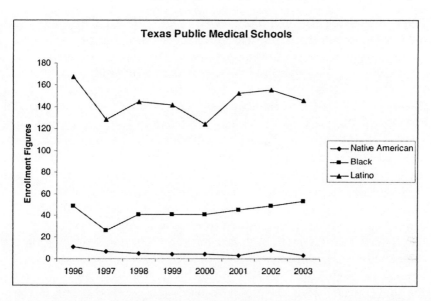

TEXAS MEDICAL SCHOOL ENROLLMENTS								
	1996	*1997*	*1998*	*1999*	*2000*	*2001*	*2002*	*2003*
Native American	11	7	5	4	4	3	8	3
Black	49	26	41	41	41	45	49	53
Latino	167	128	144	141	124	152	155	145

Source: Texas Higher Education Coordinating Board

than do white and Asian students. Albert Kauffman, regional counsel for the Mexican-American Legal Defense and Educational Fund, says that a disproportionate number of African American and Latino students come from low-income families and can't afford test-preparation classes while rich kids can buy a leg up through coaching.

"Actually we already have a working admissions system that is pretty much in compliance with the law," says William C. Powers, Dean of the University of Texas School of Law. However, this has caused some administrators to modify their admissions process in response to the new law. For instance, Flilomeno G. Maldonado, assistant dean of admissions at Texas A&M University's medical school, said that his office would probably need to conduct more personal interviews now that MCAT scores cannot be used to filter applicants. The medical school received 1,800 applications for the

2000–01 entering class and interviewed roughly 500 students. About 200 students were admitted, and 64 enrolled. "We don't know exactly how we're going to handle this," Maldonado said, "because we are so thorough, even reviewing the application for one student is an arduous task."

The Hopwood decision has had a devastating impact on African American enrollment at the University of Texas Center at Houston. In 1995 the medical school had a high enrollment of 13 African Americans. In 1996, that dropped to nine and in 1997, it plunged to only one student, and in the year 2000 the number rose modestly to three. In 1998, four medical schools (University of Texas at San Antonio, Texas A&M, Texas Tech and the University of North Texas at Fort Worth) together enrolled only six African American students. This enrollment accounted for 11 percent of all first-time enrolling African American freshmen that year.

This is not unique. In 2000, five medical schools in Texas had almost the same pattern (Tamus College of Medicine, Texas Osteopathic Medicine, Texas Tech University Health Center, University of Texas at Houston, and University of Texas at San Antonio) collectively enrolling thirteen African American students. This enrollment accounted for 25 percent of all first-time enrolling African American medical students that year.

For Latino students there is a dichotomy when it comes to enrollments. There were two medical schools responsible for over 50 percent of Latino enrollments in 1998 — the University of Texas at Galveston (enrolled 56) and the University of Texas at San Antonio (enrolled 36). In 2000, that was still the case as the University of Texas at Galveston enrolled 35 Latinos and the University of Texas at San Antonio enrolled 30 Latinos. There were also two medical schools that combined enrolled only nine Latino students. The Tamus College of Medicine enrolled only one and the Texas College of Osteopathic Medicine enrolled 8, which made up 6 percent of all first-time enrolling students. There were four medical schools that did not enroll any Native American students in 2000 even though several applied, the University of Texas Southwestern Medical, University of Texas at Houston, Tamus College of Medicine, and Texas Tech School of Medicine. In a 2002 report on medical education the Texas Higher Education Coordinating Board concluded that while efforts have been made to increase diversity, medical schools in the state have not made any real progress and the Hopwood decision has assisted in the continued decline of underrepresented students of color. "The availability of physicians in rural and urban underserved areas and the underrepresentation of Hispanics and African Americans are critical issues for Texas."[15] Yet, little progress has been made in enrolling African American and Latino students during the last 10 years.

Washington

In Washington, access to medical school for students of color has been declining since 1998. The University of Washington in Seattle is the only public medical school in the state. In 1997, the university enrolled five African Americans, seven Native Americans and six Latinos. In 1998, only two African Americans enrolled (seven admitted), six Native Americans enrolled (six admitted), and eight Latinos (11 admitted). In 1999, four African Americans, four Native Americans and six Latinos enrolled. In 2000, the university enrolled five African Americans, zero Native Americans, and five Latinos. In 2001, two African Americans enrolled (113 applied), three Native Americans (41 applied), and 12 Latinos (104 applied). In 2003, numbers declined to the lowest levels in a decade.

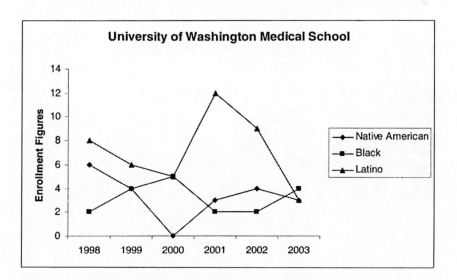

UNIVERSITY OF WASHINGTON MEDICAL SCHOOL ENROLLMENT						
	1998	*1999*	*2000*	*2001*	*2002*	*2003*
Native American	6	4	0	3	4	3
Black	2	4	5	2	2	4
Latino	8	6	5	12	9	3
Source: University of Washington Office of Diversity Research						

Florida

At the University of Florida, minority admissions have fluctuated but have sustained some growth since 1999. In 1999, 14 African Americans (10 enrolled), 12 Latinos (nine enrolled), and one Native American (zero enrolled) were admitted to the medical school. In 2000, 11 African Americans (nine enrolled), 24 Latinos (16 enrolled), and one Native American (one enrolled) were admitted. In 2001, 16 African Americans (12 enrolled), 17 Latinos (12 enrolled), and two Native Americans (two enrolled) were admitted. In 2003, 16 African Americans (11 enrolled), 35 Latinos (18 enrolled), and two Native Americans (one enrolled) were admitted. The prohibition on consideration of race at this time has not severely impacted access for underrepresented students in medical school.

However, that is not the case nationwide. According to the Association of American Medical Colleges the number of underrepresented students enrolled in medical school declined from 1992 to 2001. Nationwide

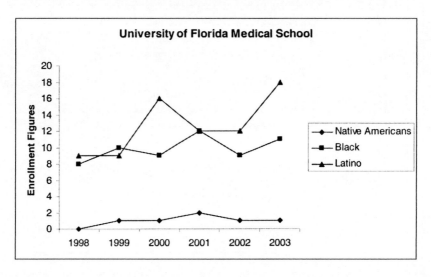

UNIVERSITY OF FLORIDA MEDICAL SCHOOL ENROLLMENT						
	1998	*1999*	*2000*	*2001*	*2002*	*2003*
Native Americans	0	1	1	2	1	1
Black	8	10	9	12	9	11
Latino	9	9	16	12	12	18
Source: State University System of Florida						

for African Americans from 1992–2001, the decline was -2.5 percent, Latinos -5.1 percent and Native Americans 0.6 percent. The largest increase in enrollment for the same period was for foreign students, whose numbers have doubled, and in 2001, had a 99 percent increase. Admission of underrepresented students to medical schools nationwide saw an increase from 1992 to 1996. As the chart below shows from 1996 on there have been declines and the growth has stagnated. For African Americans the admission numbers have not bounced back from a high of 1,386 in 1994. The same is true for Native Americans, who experienced a high admission of 155 in 1995 and have not surpassed that number.

The legal and medical communities believe that professional schools must take race and ethnicity into account in the admission process in an effort to obtain the most effective and diverse workforce representative of the population they will serve. This has been echoed by the some of the leading professional organizations. The Association of American Medical

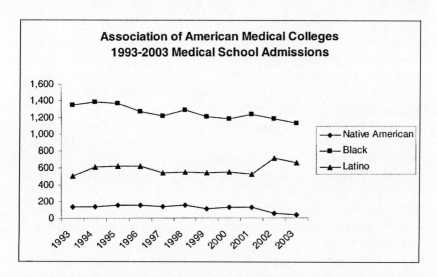

ASSOCIATION OF AMERICAN MEDICAL COLLEGE ADMISSION										
	1993	1994	1995	1996	1997	1998	1999	2000	2001	2002	2003
Native American	138	134	155	155	134	151	112	126	129	56	38
Black	1,349	1,386	1,366	1,268	1,213	1,282	1,208	1,177	1,230	1,178	1,123
Latino	504	614	621	618	541	549	536	548	522	708	652
Source: Association of American Medical Colleges										

Colleges (2003) asserts that the medical profession must be able to consider race and ethnicity in selecting students in order to graduate a capable, effective physician workforce prepared to meet the needs of a diverse society. Without race-conscious admissions policies, medical schools would be unable to increase the number of minority physicians necessary to serve America and its ever-growing minority population, expand areas of academic research, and raise the general cultural competence of all physicians.[16] According to a study on minority health published in the 1997 *Health Affairs Journal*, three medical physicians advocate that medical schools be allowed to use race as a criteria for admission to address projections of reaching racial parity of medical doctors to the population. They base their research on patient need and changing demographics. In their study they found that African American and Latinos sought care from physicians of their own race based on personal preference and language. In their study they sought to discover if minority physician supply will meet the needs of the United States. They say no. "We project the future racial and ethnic composition of the U.S. physician workforce under different assumptions. Our projections show that reaching racial and ethnic population parity with a managed care-based requirement of 218 physicians per 100,000 population would require the number of first-year residents to roughly double for Hispanic and black physicians, triple for Native American physicians, and be reduced by about two-fifths for white physicians and two-thirds for physicians of Asian or Pacific Island origin."[17]

Underrepresented minority populations have greater disparities in access to health care than those from the dominant group. In addition, minorities tend to receive less or differential care than white Americans. These disparities will grow as the population increases. This brings the issue of access to the forefront of the discussion. The results lead to increased human suffering, which is preventable. A U.S. Department of Health & Human Services study (2001) examining cancer, diabetes, infant mortality and heart disease found that minority groups had a rate three times higher of these aliments than whites. Latinos are diagnosed with diabetes at twice the rate of whites. For example, HHS noted that the death rate due to cardiovascular disease is 67 percent higher for African American women then for white women[18]

Komaromy (1996) stressed that this is especially true for minorities who live in inner-city and rural communities, "where an estimated 50 million people live and an additional 13,000 physicians are needed to serve their needs."[19] The attack on affirmative action has reduced the number of students of color obtaining medical degrees. This has created a significant decrease in the number of practicing doctors. In poverty areas with high concentrations of Latinos and African Americans there were nearly four times fewer physicians as comparable to non-poverty suburban areas.

A study conducted by the National Cancer Institute in conjunction with medical colleagues from Memorial Sloan Kettering Cancer Center in New York found that racial disparities existed between African American and white patients. Using data from more than 10,000 lung-cancer patients 65 and older, researchers found that African American patients were 12.7 percent less likely than white patients to obtain life-saving surgery. "The scientists who conducted the study estimated that the lack of surgery resulted in about 44 unnecessarily early deaths for every 1,000 black lung cancer patients. When Black patients did receive this surgery, their survival rate was similar to white patients."[20]

As demographics continue to increase across the country, so, too, will the demand for minority physicians. According to Health Affairs, "certain racial and ethnic minority groups are underrepresented among U.S. physicians. In 1990, African Americans, Hispanics, and Native Americans accounted for 21 percent of the U.S. population but only 8.6 percent of physicians." Policies aimed at increasing the number of minority physicians need to be implemented.

Minority physicians are unique in that they provide primary care for a large share of the nation's underserved communities, which are predominantly of color. Organizations like the Council on Graduate Medical Education and the American Medical Association all connected with the study assert that it is in "the public interest to increase the numbers of underrepresented minority physicians and therefore justifiable to use race as a factor in selecting medical students."[21]

Underserved Communities

Underrepresented students of color are twice as likely to return to their communities and set up practice. Research supports the idea that physicians of color are more likely than non-minority doctors to practice in underserved areas. In Moy & Bartmen (1995), minority patients are four times more likely to receive care from non-white doctors than were white patients. African American and Latino doctors have practices in areas where the percentage of minorities is twice as high as areas where other doctors practice. For example, a national survey (Saha, 1999) revealed that while African American physicians are only 5 percent of the total doctor workforce, they provide care to more than 20 percent of African American patients in the country.[22] This is not to imply that only physicians of the same race can deliver effective care to minority groups. It simply suggests that underserved communities tend to have more underrepresented physicians than white physicians.

Dr. James Curtis, a professor at the Columbia University College of Physicians, conducted a study on affirmative action's impact to medical school admissions of African Americans. Curtis' study examined African American medical school graduates from 1973–77. He found African American doctors set up more practices in their communities and were more committed than white physicians. Minority doctors work to meet the unmet needs of underrepresented minority groups. The result of his data reveal that 36 percent of African American doctors who graduated in 1977 were still practicing medicine in the inner city. Twenty-eight percent of African American graduates work in neighborhoods that are predominantly of color in comparison to 6 percent of whites.[23] Congress recognized the need for physicians in underserved communities and created the Disadvantaged Minority Health Improvement Act of 1990. The act is designed to provide funds and scholarship programs to increase the number of underrepresented students into the medical field. The need for diversity in the medical field will assist in improving access to health care for underserved communities. In addition to research, there are many examples of minority physicians reaching out to underserved communities.

For example, Dr. Sandra Hullett, who comes from the working-class side of Birmingham, Alabama, where most of the residents work in a nearby steel mill, earned her undergraduate degree in biology from Alabama A&M University, her medical degree from the Medical College of Pennsylvania, and her master's in public health from the University of Alabama. While in college Hullett realized that doctors rooted in and concerned with the community were needed in rural towns and small areas across the country. "When I had to choose an area to work in," she says, "I wanted to be where there was a need [for me], where there was an academic institution nearby, a 20-bed hospital for me to keep up my skills, and a four-lane highway so I had the illusion of going somewhere." Her choice was to work as a physician in a small rural community near Birmingham. Many other minority doctors have made the same choice. Unfortunately, the attacks on affirmative action have dramatically slowed this trend, and it has only gotten worse as the number of students of color in training to become doctors has declined.

Affirmative action is a policy designed to equalize access to high-profile professions like that in the legal and medical fields from which underrepresented students of color have been excluded for generations. Reprieve from racial discrimination through laws is not enough to eradicate the plight of second-class status from underrepresented minority groups in the country. Yet this is an automatic burden that many students of color have faced over generations.

Race-Conscious Admissions

Medical school admission is an intense process. Historically, medical schools have subjected applicants to a rigorous process including committee interviews, personal statements, letters of recommendation and community work. In addition to qualified academic criteria, institutions look for leadership skills, hardship, communication skills and community service experience, just to note a few. Critics of affirmative action assert that race-conscious admission policies compromise the institutions' integrity in allowing admission offices to admit incompetent underrepresented students into the medical field. The use of race in admissions does not lead to a less qualified or incompetent physician workforce. Many underrepresented students of color graduate from medical school. Cohen (1997) reported that by 1997, 87 percent of minority medical students who matriculated in 1990 had graduated from medical school; and by 1996, 88 percent of African American and 95 percent of Latino medical students had passed the national medical school examination.

Medical Research

Increasing the number of underrepresented students of color will assist in improving the nation's medical research. As underrepresented minority groups are disproportionately facing serious medical risks, it is vital that medical research expand into the areas that are affecting minority groups. Cohen (2002) asserts that underrepresented students of color tend to focus more of their research on health issues that impact racial populations. Through the Minority Health and Health Disparities Research and Education Act of 2000, Congress has provided funding for the training of individuals in biomedical research. According to the National Institutes of Health (2002), racial and ethnic minorities are projected to grow to 40 percent of the population in 2030. Now more than ever a stronger commitment to research and seeking solutions in preventing health disparities is vital to the country. The National Institutes of Health asserts that, "Our ability to sustain and even increase the momentum of recent scientific progress and our international leadership in medical research depends on recruitment, training, support and retention of diverse biomedical investigators."[24]

    In the United States for the last three and a half decades, affirmative action programs have played a critical role in allowing the government to put forth policies to remedy racial and gender inequality. While overt discrimination has been reduced, everyday subtle discrimination and informal practices of prejudice have not. The playing field is not level just because some of the players have had access, but no resources, to compete full-time. In our history, racial and gender discrimination were reinforced by laws, which created the need for government policies of intervention. Affirmative action was designed to remedy our racist past. Assessing the effects of affirmative action used to remedy discrimination will enhance this controversy because it is difficult to measure discrimination. The emotion behind the issue of race will always make it controversial, but to begin to create equal access for all we must maintain policies designed to redress the inequities of the past in order for real equality to exist in the future.

I think a great public university, and great public institutions, should reflect the public. And when they don't reflect the public, they should do something about that, and that's called affirmative action. It's not quotas — it's not giving anything to unqualified people.

— Secretary of State Colin Powell

3. Historical Perspective

The United States is one of the wealthiest and most diverse countries in the world. However, the nation is plagued with issues of inequity among its citizens. America was founded on the premise that with hard work, all of us have the opportunity to build our future.

It is the American dream, the rags-to-riches story, that any child can be president and everyone can find his fortune. However, making that dream a reality is not the same for all citizens. American society perpetuates the myth that life is fair and full of opportunity for all. If true equality of opportunity existed for everyone, people of color, women and those with disabilities would be equally represented in the nation's educational institutions.

Throughout our history many Americans have been denied basic rights to participate in our society. Native Americans, African Americans, Latinos and Asians were not openly invited to take part in our so-called democratic society. For most of this nation's history, people of color were denied educational opportunities afforded whites.

While Americans have always considered education an important value to a democracy, fear and ignorance convinced a majority that education was unnecessary and unattainable for people of color. As others have faced inequities and discrimination such as disability, gender, sexual orientation, age, and religion, this chapter focuses on affirmative action in the United States as it pertains to education as a means of providing access and opportunity for underrepresented students of color.

Our nation continues to grapple with overt and systemic institutional racism, and it is this reality that makes the history of affirmative action vital to sustaining the policy. Historically, affirmative action was a concept put in place prior to the civil rights movement. Yet at the time it was not called affirmative action. It was emancipation, and it began at the end of the Civil War.

Reconstruction

With the Emancipation Proclamation, President Lincoln ended slavery. After the Civil War and the freeing of slaves the president established the Freedman's Bureau. It was charged with assisting slaves with the transition to freedom, specifically to address their rights. The bureau developed plans and measures to help current and former slaves join the work force. This transition became known as the Reconstruction Period. Under Reconstruction the federal government intervened in the Southern states to expand opportunities for African Americans. The Constitution was amended through the Thirteenth, Fourteenth, and Fifteenth amendments, which abolished slavery and established the right of freed slaves to vote and obtain citizenship without reference to race.

The nineteenth century saw the end of slavery and the ratification of treaties between the U.S. government and peoples in the conquered territories, i.e., Native Americans and Mexican Americans. Reconstruction was a time of hope for many African Americans as they thought Reconstruction would give them the right to participate in white society, the right to own land, vote, and attend public schools. The federal government, abolitionists, and freed slaves from the North took on the task of providing education for former slaves, who were forcibly kept illiterate.

In 1866, the first Civil Rights Act passed, and it entitled all persons to equal employment, accommodations, and access to land ownership regardless of race or previous condition of servitude. However, when the abolitionists began to lose political power or died, a new, more conservative South was reborn. Reconstruction faded, and the gains made by African Americans were virtually lost. The promise of equality and opportunity evaporated and was replaced by racism and an unwillingness of the federal government to enforce the constitutional amendments designed to empower African Americans.

Separate but Equal

Segregation replaced Reconstruction and legally separated people of color from whites with a system of laws informally called Jim Crow laws. With the African American population growing, whites realized that they had to regain some sort of control. In 1883, the Supreme Court struck down the Civil Rights Act, claiming it was unconstitutional. While amendments to the Constitution made it illegal to discriminate on the basis of race, there was no restriction for private organizations or individuals. In an 8 to 1 vote the majority concluded that the Fourteenth Amendment to the constitution gave Congress no authority over private businesses.

Justice John Marshall Harlan asserted that the constitutional amendments passed during Reconstruction to give African Americans equal rights were just "baubles" unless Congress and the government enforced the rights. The Morrill Act, passed by Congress in 1890, permitted "separate but equal." For universities this presented clear financial discrimination. Historical Black Colleges and Universities in the South didn't have enough money, facilities or staff to do the job. Yet, for the white colleges, the resources, facilities and staffing were top notch.

In June of 1892, Homer Plessy, of white and African American descent, boarded a train in New Orleans believing he was entitled to all white privileges. He purchased a first-class ticket on East Louisiana Railway and entered the passenger car for whites only. The conductor asked Plessy to vacate the seat and move to the appropriate coach. When Plessy refused he was ejected from the train and arrested. Plessy filed suit in the Supreme Court against Judge H. Ferguson.

The Supreme Court ruled in Louisiana's favor and upheld its statute. Under *Plessy v. Ferguson*, the Supreme Court ruled that "separate but equal" was constitutional. Under that decision governments were permitted to separate individuals based on race in public transportation, housing, schools, and public facilities. The 1896 Supreme Court ruling solidified Jim Crow as the law of the land, and through this system segregated education continued.

In 1899, the Supreme Court ruled in *Cumming v. Richmond County Board of Education* that the educational policies of public schools were the responsibility of the states, unequal expenditures on separate schools were not unconstitutional and the federal government was not allowed to interfere unless it found a case of blatant disregard of rights. By the 20th century all Southern states had implemented Jim Crow laws.

According to civil rights organizations during the last four years of the 19th century there were 2,500 lynchings, and during 1900 there were over 1,000, a majority in the Deep South.

Tilly, an African American, explained the problems she experienced growing up in the South. "It was a different world for African Americans. You never disagreed with a white person. You addressed them as ma'am or sir and you never gave them any eye contact. If a white woman was walking down the same street as an African American man, he knew to get off the sidewalk and walk in the street or cross it. If anything happened to a white person and they did not have a suspect, that night an African American man would disappear and show up dead."[1]

Tilly indicated that many folks disappeared in Jackson, Mississippi, when she was growing up and that they were all of color. Several folks fled in the night to avoid death. "This is exactly how my family came to California. My brother was in a car accident that involved a white woman, and we knew if she died what that meant for him. In the middle of the night we packed our car and drove out of Mississippi. It was in that night that I left the house in which I was born and grew up in along with all of our belongings. While I had some happiness as a child, it is overshadowed with the dominance of fear, for I knew first-hand what it was like to grow up scared all the time."[2]

Civil Rights Movement

With racial discrimination legalized, groups began to form to protest the problem. One such group is the National Association for the Advancement of Colored People. Established as a non-profit organization, the NAACP is one of the oldest civil rights organizations in the country. The goal of the NAACP, comprised of a multiracial group of progressive thinkers, is to ensure educational, political and economic equity for minority groups. Specifically, its mission is to eliminate racial prejudice and discrimination.

Civil rights pioneer A. Philip Randolph tried to organize a march on Washington during Franklin Roosevelt's administration. To avert the march, President Roosevelt issued an executive order. It required all departments of the government involved in vocational and training programs for defense production to include full participation of citizens regardless of "race, creed, color, or national origin." It also stressed that "the democratic way of life within the nation can be defended successfully only with the help and support of all groups within its borders."[3]

This was yet another measure designed to take affirmative steps to reduce discrimination in employment and provide full participation in the defense program. In 1943 this policy was expanded to include all federal contractors. As a result of government intervention, African American, Latino, and Jewish workers began to gain access to the defense industry. However, once wartime criteria were relaxed, opportunities for people of color in the defense industry decreased.

The separate but equal doctrine also kept neighborhoods segregated under what was called redlining. Redlining of districts prohibited people of color from buying homes in white neighborhoods. This was a common and open practice until 1948. In that year the Supreme Court, in *Shelly v.*

Kramer, found laws preventing minorities from purchasing in white neighborhoods were illegal. The biggest blow to Jim Crow laws came in public education, where the Supreme Court ruled in the landmark 1954 *Brown v. Board of Education* case that "separate but equal" was unconstitutional. This case will be discussed in greater detail in Chapter Four. With this victory to desegregate public education the civil rights movement had begun.

Even though the landmark desegregation case was filed on behalf of students and parents in Topeka, Kansas, the first school integrated with federal troops was in Little Rock, Arkansas. Nine students, called the "Little Rock Nine," integrated Central High School on September 24, 1957, with the help of federal troops. Three years later college students organized lunch counter sit-ins, and the Student Non-Violent Coordinating Committee was founded.

"One hundred years of delay have passed since President Lincoln freed the slaves, yet their heirs, their grandsons, are not fully free. They are not yet free from the bonds of injustice. And this nation, for all its hopes and all its boasts, will not be fully free until all of its citizens are free."[4] President John F. Kennedy made this statement on television prior to sending civil rights legislation to Congress.

Nineteen sixty-three was the height of the civil rights movement. That August, 250,000 Americans from all ethnicities participated in the historic march on Washington, in which Dr. Martin Luther King delivered his "I Have a Dream" speech. Five days after the assassination of President Kennedy, Lyndon B. Johnson signed the Civil Rights Act of 1964. While some civil rights leaders did not see Johnson as a real civil rights supporter, it has been said he signed the act to honor the memory of Kennedy's policy.

The Civil Rights Act of 1964 also promoted equity and prohibited discrimination in housing, employment, and education. Under Title VI, discrimination on the basis of sex, religion, race, color or national origin is prohibited in public education and institutions of higher learning that receive federal funds. Title IV permits the U.S. Attorney General to investigate school districts and university systems that engage in racial segregation. Under Executive Order 11246, President Johnson established the Federal Contract Compliance Program, which allowed the collection of data to track and examine the racial makeup of the labor force to identify practices of discrimination.

For those who gave their lives during the civil rights movement, the greatest reward was the signing of policy, which acknowledged the problem of racism and set up prohibitions on discrimination. Passage of the Civil Rights Act of 1964 was a victory for equity, but some within the university community did not publicly support civil rights and saw regulatory procedures mandating funding as government interference.

Defining Affirmative Action

Why is affirmative action such a controversial issue for America? The controversy centers on the term. Most individuals do not understand the term affirmative action. Affirmative action is a policy designed to fully integrate society through education and employment opportunities for women and minorities. It was President Lyndon Johnson's words in 1965 that established the rationale for affirmative action. "You do not take a person who, for years, has been hobbled by chains and liberate him, bring him up to the starting line of a race and then say, 'You are free to compete with all others,' and still just believe that you have been completely fair."[5] The Equal Employment Opportunity Commission defines affirmative action as "one part of an effort to remedy past and present discrimination" and uses it to "insure that jobs are genuinely and equally accessible to *qualified* persons without regard to sex, racial or ethnic characteristics."[6] Affirmative action is designed to take proactive steps to reduce or address the impacts of discrimination with the ultimate goal of eliminating differences between genders, race and ethnicities, underrepresented groups and dominant groups.

During the Johnson era, affirmative action was understood to offer the opportunity to compete and was not a guarantee of access. According to the U.S. Commission on Civil Rights, it is a policy designed to eradicate discrimination and to put measures in place to eliminate its recurrence. Affirmative action operates in different ways and at different levels, within the realms of public vs. private sectors, in different governmental levels and is voluntary or involuntary. Based upon policy initiatives and court rulings, affirmative action has become a moving target, adding to the confusion and misunderstanding, which fan the flames of controversy.

Five Types of Affirmative Action

There are five race- and gender-conscious practices under the umbrella of affirmative action: quotas, self studies, preferences, outreach and counseling, and anti-discrimination.

Quotas

A quota is the use of fixed percentages in the selection of minorities and women. This is where a majority of the debate on affirmative action exists, but the issue is mute. The Supreme Court has consistently held that racial quotas by government, institutions and businesses are illegal. What affirmative action is not is an absolute requirement that an employer hire or a university admit a certain percentage of individuals from a specified group, without regard to the qualifications. In the 1978 Bakke decision, the Supreme Court declared quotas illegal. Race, however, could still be considered as one admission criterion, while educational qualifications should not be compromised.

Self Studies

Under affirmative action, self-studies are conducted to show how a business engages in employment selection and how decisions are made. Self-studies are the result of Executive Order 11246: "Any business public or private, doing substantial business with the federal government, is required to engage in a self study."[7] Self-studies are conducted to examine the actual hiring or contract selection by businesses and the actual admission selection by colleges.

Preferences

Preferences used in affirmative action take on many forms, but for this research we will look at school admission. In some states race can be considered as a factor in evaluating an applicant. This approach is identical to considering geographical location, athletic achievement and any other factors that promote diversity. This is why colleges and universities assert that race is one of several different factors they consider in evaluating and selecting all "qualified" candidates for the entering class.

The use of preferences is at the heart of the affirmative action debate. To proponents of affirmative action, preferences are necessary to remedy discrimination. For these individuals, affirmative action isn't about test scores and comparing standards. The choices for admission are between A and B students. Under academic freedom, colleges and universities have the right to seek student diversity. Since workplace success often depends on going to college, it is about guaranteeing access to eligible underrepresented students. To critics, preferences are reverse discrimination.

Supreme Court Justices Clarence Thomas and Antonin Scalia see them as stigmatizing for minority students.

Outreach and Counseling

Outreach and counseling are programs run by colleges and universities to recruit underrepresented students. These are programs designed to encourage underrepresented students of color to attend college as well as encourage women to pursue careers in male-dominated fields such as engineering.

Anti-discrimination

Federal civil rights laws have brought about tremendous changes for students facing discrimination. Since the adoption of the 1964 Civil Rights Act, racial barriers to educational opportunity have been coming down. According to the Department of Education Office for Civil Rights, the dropout rate for African American students declined from 20 percent in 1976 to 13 percent in 1996. High school graduation rates for students of color increased. In 1976 it was 19.5 percent. In 2000 the completion rates for students of color had increased to 30.3 percent. Total minority enrollment at colleges and universities increased 61 percent between fall 1986 and fall 1996.

Since 1990, the number of Latino students enrolled in higher education increased by 47 percent; Native Americans 30 percent and African Americans 20 percent. In order to compete on the economic playground a college degree is mandatory. According to a study conducted by the American Educational Research Association's panel on racial dynamics in colleges and universities, before 1996 and California's Proposition 209 underrepresented students of color had large gains in undergraduate admissions from 1982 to 1996.

Is There Still a Need for Affirmative Action?

While this country has made great strides in addressing discrimination, it still persists. Here are some facts.

• The United States has a history of over 300 years of slavery and racial oppression.
• Historically Black colleges and universities were created to provide

educational opportunities for students of color who were excluded from all-white universities.

• From 1964 to 1971, the Equal Employment Opportunity Commission had no enforcement powers and no authority to bring suits against employers who engaged in practices and patterns of discrimination.

• In 1965, 4.9 percent of African Americans were college students. In 1970 that number had climbed to only 7.8 percent, but with the help of affirmative action.

• According to the U.S. Census in 1969, the median African American family income in the United States as a percentage of the median white family income was 61 percent, and in 2001, 62 percent.

• *United States v. Paradise* ruled in 1970 that the State of Alabama Department of Public Safety discriminated against African Americans. In its 37-year history there had not been an African American trooper. Even after several lawsuits the department refused to promote any African Americans beyond entry level and did not implement an equitable hiring system. In 1987 a federal court imposed a numerical quota system on the department, mandating it to increase and promote African Americans into the upper ranks of the organization. This was upheld by the Supreme Court.

• The Contract Compliance Program in 1975 still had done no affirmative action enforcement, letting several government contractors continue to engage in practices of discrimination that are prohibited by law.

• In 1988, Detroit public schools spent $3,600 per child in largely minority communities while largely white suburbs spent $6,000 per child.

• In Richmond, Va., the courts in 1989 invalidated the minority-contracting program. As a result, the share of contracting dollars going to minority-owned firms in Richmond went from 38.6 percent to 2.2 percent.

• The Urban Institute study on college graduates with similar qualifications in the job market in Chicago, San Diego and Washington, D.C., concluded that Latinos and African Americans were systemically denied equal access in the recruitment process.

• The U.S. Department of Labor's 1995 report, "The Glass Ceiling," showed that while white men are only 43 percent of the Fortune 2000 work force, they hold 95 percent of the senior management jobs. The report concluded that barriers to advancement still exist for minorities and women in corporate America.

• According to the U.S. Census and the Department of Labor, there are three times more African Americans with incomes below the poverty level than there are whites.

• A study on senior management at the University of California by the Greenlining Institute found that in 2003, whites are six times more likely than minorities to serve as university presidents, chancellors or other top administrators.

• Research indicates that economic and social disadvantages are still linked to skin color, creating a huge barrier for opportunity in America.

• A white high school graduate is twice as likely to graduate from college as a Latino, Native American or African American high school graduate.

• In 1998, UC's prohibition on the use of race (the first year of the implementation of SP-1), resulted in a 40 to 50 percent drop in under-represented students of color entering the top tier universities of Berkeley and UCLA.

• More AP courses are offered in white-dominated affluent schools than are offered in poorer schools with a majority of students of color enrolled. This makes their ability to compete for admission much more challenging.

• According to a 1998 study conducted by the Fair Housing Council in Washington, D.C. minorities are discriminated against 40 to 50 percent of the time they attempt to purchase homes or rent apartments.

Former President Clinton asserts the continued need for affirmative action. "Despite great progress, discrimination and exclusion on the basis of race and gender are still facts of American life. Affirmative action is needed to remedy discrimination and to create a more inclusive society that truly provides equal opportunity."[8] Those who dismiss discrimination as ancient history must explain the data, which shows its persistence.

The Historical Misconceptions of Affirmative Action

The misconceptions created by the critics are just as much a part of the history of affirmative action as are the facts. Let's examine them one by one.

Misconception No. 1: "We've Done Enough Already" Theory

The critics are quick to state that laws against discrimination are sufficient and that people have opportunity to succeed. This is the "we've done enough already" theory, perpetuated by those who view history from the perspective that African Americans are no longer slaves and that women can vote, so we have reached the promised land — the American dream can be attained by all who seek it. To these critics, affirmative action was a temporary policy meant to redress those groups living under Jim Crow laws.

Critics believe that the policy prohibits the ability of qualified individuals to enter college and obtain jobs. However, while the statement sounds logical, it is inaccurate. Affirmative action does not allow unqualified applicants to obtain any benefits let alone those above a qualified applicant, and the most competitive job on average is filled through a network of colleagues and friends, at the exclusion of most people of color. Close to 75 percent of corporate executives obtained their jobs through friends and small networks.[9] This is the process that affirmative action was designed to eliminate.

There is an inherent belief by critics that those who benefit from affirmative action are less qualified than whites. Many individuals miss the most important term in the definition of affirmative action, and that term is "qualified." Affirmative action includes opportunities for qualified applicants to participate. The myth about this policy is that it is a government handout for individuals who do not meet entry-level qualifications. Affirmative action seeks to ensure that access to education and employment are available to qualified individuals. The courts and state governments have never advocated or placed in statute that unqualified individuals be employed or gain access to education based entirely on their race.

This country's history of discrimination disproves this belief. According to a study by the Russell Sage Foundation, African Americans with qualifications of education and experience equal to whites who search for employment much more aggressively than whites are 36 to 44 percent less likely to get a job in white suburbs. People of color who are more qualified than their white counterparts more often than not are passed over for promotions or are viewed as less competitive in the labor market because of the color of their skin. According to the U.S. Department of Labor, qualified professionals of color in terms of education and experience, on average earn 20 to 25 percent less than their white counterparts.[10] White males with high school diplomas tend to earn just as much as racial minorities with college degrees.

Researchers (Dovidio and Gaertner 1996) have found that white job applicants are favored over African American applicants. In a study in which white participants evaluated applicants in college admissions, researchers found that discrimination was low for white applicants with lesser qualifications and high for African American applicants who were highly qualified.[11] The studies show that race impacts judgment. According to Dovidio & Kawakami (2000), this is an example of aversive racism, a theory that refers to the unintentional expression of "anti-black" feelings by people who sincerely endorse, on a conscious level, egalitarian values and principles. Rather than reflecting bigotry or hatred, the "anti-black" feelings reflect fear and discomfort, and the discrimination is displayed through unconscious acts of avoidance.[12]

Misconception No. 2: The Preferential Treatment Myth

Critics believe that affirmative action is synonymous with preferential treatment. This is simply false, and the issue of privilege supports that fact. According to former California Gov. Pete Wilson, "Those who benefit from affirmative action today are granted preferential treatment simply because they were born into a protected group." For Wilson today, affirmative action is unfair to whites. Yet who really is the protected group? Opponents have never explained the result of white privilege. For most white individuals, racism is only viewed as individual acts of cruelty. They are not taught the "invisible" systems that bestow dominance on whites as a group.

According to McIntosh (1988), white privilege is defined as an invisible package of unearned assets that can be cashed in almost every day, but which whites are meant to remain oblivious about. Those in the dominant group are educated to believe that society is morally neutral. For Wilson and like-minded, there is a disconnect to the reality of white history. Racial preference has had a long white history.

According to Wise (2003), "Affirmative action for whites was embodied in the abolition of European indentured servitude, which left black slaves as the only free labor in the colonies that would become the U.S. It was the essence of the 1790 Naturalization Act, which allowed virtually any European immigrant to become a full citizen, even while African Americans, Asians and American Indians could not. It was the guiding principle of segregation, Asian exclusion laws, and the theft of half of Mexico for the fulfillment of Manifest Destiny."[13]

White privilege makes it easy to miss the privileges of belonging to a dominant group. For example, President George W. Bush attacked the University of Michigan's policy of awarding 20 points to underrepresented applicants. But he failed to mention the points awarded to whites, like the 16 points based on geography, given to students who reside in the upper peninsula of Michigan, which is almost all white. He did not mention the 20 points given to recruited athletes, the 20 points the provost awards to any student who has overcome an obstacle, the 10 points awarded to students from selective high schools (primarily attended by whites) and the 8 points given for students who complete AP and honors courses.

While all of these preferences are allowed, they are disproportionately awarded to whites, and any preference for underrepresented students of color become the basis for attack and anger. According to Paul Butler, law professor at George Washington University, "The favoritism of certain groups in the United States is so strong that it can only be remedied by actively encouraging the promotion of other groups." Butler goes on to assert that this is such an overlooked phenomenon that in order for any other groups to participate they have to be "actively considered." This will be discussed further in Chapter Five.

Misconception No. 3: Individual v. Group Perspective

There is a belief that what individuals become and the success they acieve are solely indicative of their own ability and ambition. After 35-plus years of civil rights, there is an illusion that all of us interact in an equal and fair society, that the individual is only hindered by his ambition or skill. This is a common inaccurate perception. Ferdman (1997) asserts this dynamic as the "individualistic perspective." The individualistic perspective makes the claim that it is unfair to take into consideration racial group membership as that should not influence outcome or opportunities for individuals in society. Critics of affirmative action subscribe to this philosophy because they view selection procedures as fair when individuals are viewed as simply human and when race is not considered. "Individual skills and achievements are viewed as legitimate criteria by which to judge individual competence because they are thought to be objective and orthogonal to ascribed characteristics such as race."[14]

The group perspective supported by proponents of affirmative action asserts that with the reality of inequities in resources and access to opportunities, there exists a power disparity. This makes it unfair not to take into account the racial background because of the degree of difference in access between majority and minority groups. This is a consideration vital in order for underrepresented groups to compete as individuals and to obtain more equitable opportunities. According to Duke University professor William Chafe: "The absence of an equal start in turn gets to the nub of the differences in the current debate. Advocates of affirmative action argue that membership in a particular group is what denies a person an equal start. Opponents insist that each person be treated as an individual."

That would be appropriate if it worked that way, but the history of the United States is the history of groups and not just individuals.

Affirmative action programs are designed to redress discrimination against groups and the individuals who belong to them. Affirmative action "is about the importance of understanding the inextricable connection between group identity and individual identity; the realization that a law without government's commitment to make its guarantees real is a hollow vessel."[15]

The individual perspective makes it impossible to view systemic institutional racism, for one is always looking at the issue as isolated individual assessments. According to the National Opinion Research Center, 43 percent of all Americans view hard work as the sole component to wealth.[16] The group perspective allows for the criteria of long-term systemic racism that is placed upon individuals in certain groups. The individual perspective asserts that folks must pull themselves up by their boot straps, and the group perspective will assert how do you begin if you have no boots and no straps from which to work.

Misconception No. 4: Dr. Martin Luther King Speech

Another myth of affirmative action is a belief that Dr. Martin Luther King himself did not support affirmative action. In his historic "I Have a Dream" speech, he spoke of the "content of their character and not the color of their skin." It is a statement many opponents cite but do not understand. In 1964, King wrote:

> Whenever this issue of compensatory or preferential treatment for the Negro is raised some of our friends recoil in horror. The Negro should be granted equality, they agree; but he should ask for nothing more. On the surface, this appears reasonable, but it is not realistic. For it is obvious that if a man is entering the starting line in a race three hundred years after another man, the first would have to perform some impossible feat in order to catch up with his fellow runner.[17]

The entire quote makes the statement that 300-plus years of racial segregation can only be redressed through affirmative action. Identifying only one phrase without looking at the quote in its entirety is a common mistake critics make. It was King who asserted that civil rights include both economic opportunity and race-conscious measures that go beyond anti-discrimination.

Linda Chavez, with the Center for Equal Opportunity, states: "Highly competitive public colleges and universities admit blacks and Latinos with significantly lower grades and test scores than whites. We don't expect these students to measure up, so we are giving them a pass."[18] The statement by Chavez perpetuates the inferiority myth of affirmative action. In some cases underrepresented students of color as well as whites are admitted with low test scores, as discussed in Chapter One. If they are eligible, they are qualified.

The students of color who are admitted with lower scores than whites are still qualified to be considered for college because they are eligible for admission. As discussed in Chapter One, eligibility and admission can have different outcomes for all applicants, but if they are eligible they are qualified for consideration. For example, at Harvard most students of color admitted have a lower mean SAT score than whites. However, African American graduation rates are almost identical to that of whites: at 92 percent compared to 96 percent.[19]

The Center for Individual Rights (CIR), founded by Michael McDonald and Michael Greve, had been searching for five years for a test case that would get the center to the 5th U.S. Circuit Court of Appeals, considered one of the most conservative benches in the nation. Greve sought out plaintiffs at the University of Texas Law School because he felt it was vulnerable to the courts. The center's strategy paid off in 1996. In *Hopwood v. State of Texas*, the court concluded the law school could no longer use race as a factor in deciding which applicants to admit.

Civil rights leaders attribute the 15 percent decline in underrepresented minority enrollment in Texas medical and law schools to the Hopwood decision. CIR wants the complete removal of race or gender as a consideration for any school admissions.

The ultimate goal for CIR is to overturn the Bakke decision. In an interview with The Washington Post, Greve stated: "We don't have a problem with any admissions system, provided it doesn't use race as a factor, period. These schools can use a lottery or run applicants around a track if they like, but they can't use race."[20]

Samuel Issacharoff, who defended the University of Texas in the Hopwood case, told a local newspaper that CIR has this "messianic sense that every person on the other side of this issue was lying and evil. Meanwhile, they totally missed the issue of what were the purposes and justifications of an affirmative action program at a university which stood at the head of a statewide education system that still doesn't afford equal opportunity to all citizens."

CIR, which represented the plaintiffs in the University of Michigan cases, has a $1.2 million yearly budget funded from conservative foundations. When the center was researching Michigan, it hired a publicist, and the staff reviewed biographies of several potential plaintiffs sent to them by Michigan legislators who support CIR's cause. After conducting several interviews, CIR chose Jennifer Gratz and Barbara Grutter. The center openly admitted it sought out individuals who would appeal to the American public. These individuals had stellar grades, good backgrounds and were fairly attractive. CIR's simplistic view of the issue has come under scrutiny for turning back the clock on access, distorting the issue and using disingenuous tactics. These cases will be discussed in greater detail in Chapter Four.

Misconception No. 5: The Reverse Discrimination Myth

Another misconception of affirmative action is one of reverse discrimination. Opponents have been successful in distorting the use of affirmative action as a policy that is discriminatory toward whites. To claim reverse discrimination ignores the fact that courts have taken steps to balance affirmative action remedies. Discrimination is illegal. If affirmative action were reverse discrimination for white males, then with evidence they should be in court to process their claim.

The parameters of affirmative action policy have been set by the Rehquist and Burger courts and have required that there be a strong basis for invoking race to remedy past discrimination (*Johnson v. Transportation Agency*. Santa Clara County, CA, 480 U.S., 107 S. Ct. 1442, 1987). The court has required affirmative action programs to be narrowly tailored to the purpose of remedying discrimination and have limited affirmative action to ensure the interests of whites are not put at a disadvantage. In remedying discrimination what the court means is a plan must be flexible, employing goals rather than quotas; it must be limited to fully qualified applicants; it must provide for some continuing opportunities for whites and for men; it must not require the reduction of existing positions held by incumbent whites and men; and it must be temporary, designed to last no longer than necessary to remedy the discrimination that justified the plan.

Lawful affirmative action does not promote merit or goals in a discriminatory way. The federal government allows for goals and timetables to be established and allowed in court-ordered sanctions to eliminate discrimination. A goal or a timetable will form the basis of an affirmative action policy when it is ordered under law to address specific discrimination. For example, the U.S. Department of Justice's Civil Rights Division monitors 400 school districts that are under desegregation orders for the practice of racial segregation.

The division has established specific goals that schools must meet, including student assignment, transportation, faculty and staff hiring and placement, availability of equitable facilities, distribution of district resources, and quality of education. In 1968, in *Green v. County School Board of New Kent County* (Virginia), the Supreme Court ruled that desegregation of schools in the South is mandatory and required affirmative action to achieve integrated schools. Goals and timetables were established in this case. The Equal Employment Opportunity Commission says that of the 91,000 employment discrimination cases before it less than 2 percent are reverse discrimination cases and only 1.7 percent of the totals are made by white males on the basis of race. Whites are 50 to 60 percent more likely than African Americans and 93 percent more likely than Latinos to have professional jobs, while they are twice as likely not to hold service level positions.[21]

If affirmative action is reverse discrimination, why do Ivy League schools, in an attempt to accommodate more underrepresented students of color, have a mere 5,500 African American students out of a total student population of over 95,000?[22] If underrepresented groups of color are taking advantage of racial preference, where are the huge benefits?

Critics insist that reverse discrimination allows unqualified minority students to enter universities. The numbers make that a hard sell. For example, 1996, the year Barbara Grutter (U-Michigan plaintiff) was denied admission to law school was the same year that California's voters chose to prohibit consideration of race in admitting students to colleges and universities. As a result, in 1997, the University of California admitted 59 African Americans to all three law schools out of 1,294 applications, 14 Native Americans out of 162 applications, and 170 Mexican Americans out of 1,790 applications. From 1994–2001 the number of African Americans admitted to UC law schools declined by 55 percent, Latinos 33 percent and Native Americans 65 percent. These numbers do not indicate that white students are suffering irreparable harm. Yet none of these students who were denied admission filed a lawsuit claiming discrimination.

Misconception No. 6: The Myth of Stigmatization

Critics claim that affirmative action admits minority students who cannot compete at the same level as whites, marking those students inferior. Labeling affirmative action as some sort of crutch that implies students are incapable of making it on their own is an inaccurate theory. There are many students who deserved the opportunity to get their education because they were qualified, not because they were students of color.

Judith Soto, for instance, the daughter of farmworkers, said, "I got into Berkeley through affirmative action, and I'm not ashamed to say it because no one else is doing my homework."[23] Monica, a Boston University student asserts, "I got in on affirmative action, and I am proud to bring more diversity to this campus. I am not ashamed. I work in my classes along-side my other classmates and compete at the same level."[24] Cedric, a student at the University of Georgia, explains, "I am a product of affirmative action, and I am proud of it. The problem is that white students have an advantage coming from privilege. I came to this institution with offers from three other universities, a 3.8 GPA and good test scores. White students who don't get it look down on us. I am just trying to go to school."[25]

Charles J. Ogletree, professor at Harvard Law and a graduate of Stanford University, observed: "When I arrived on campus, I found there was no affirmative action in course selection or grading. I was expected to compete with my peers on an equal basis. I learned that success was not automatic. I got my bachelor's degree in three years and graduated with distinction."[26] These student experiences are reinforced by the Bowen and Bok (1998) study. They found that 75 percent of African American students entering selective colleges graduated, as compared to a 59 percent rate for white college students. Bowen and Bok's findings suggest that "since the retention rates for underrepresented students in elite schools is high, it makes sense to invest even more for minority students to attend those schools."[27]

The damage of stigmatization from affirmative action as a presumption of preferences is rather interesting. According to Wise (1996): "If blacks are damaged by affirmative action, shouldn't the same damage, and in greater abundance, extend to whites, who have continuously received privileges and opportunities due to racial discrimination on their behalf? Is no one concerned about the self-esteem of white children who get into Harvard because of alumni preferences? Do children who inherit millions of dollars — money they clearly didn't earn — wallow in self-doubt, or do they take advantage of their opportunities with hardly a second thought?[28] If the belief that affirmative action is a blow to self-esteem, should those who benefited from the policy as recipients of opportunity feel shame or embarrassment?

Should Colin Powell, a successful leader in the armed forces and Secretary of State to former and current presidents, as a recipient of affirmative action, feel shame or inferiority because of his success? How about Clarence Thomas? He went to Yale Law School, was an appointee in the Reagan administration and is a Supreme Court justice, filling the seat held by Thurgood Marshall. Thomas is a lifelong recipient of affirmative action, knowing that without the policy he would not be where he is today. Does he feel inferior or embarrassed?

Misconception No. 7: The Myth of Eligibility

The focal point of the critics' argument is that school admissions should be based solely on quantifiable means, like that of test scores and grades. These critics overlook eligibility and the reality that minority children receive unequal opportunities in elementary and secondary education compared to whites. Most students of color attend segregated schools. According to a recent study by the Civil Rights Project of Harvard University, the 2000–01 academic year shows whites are the most segregated group in the nation's public schools; they attend schools in which 80 percent of the student body is white. But as minority student enrollment is increasing to 40 percent of U.S. public schools. These schools educate close to one-third of the nation's students of color. These schools are predominantly faced with poverty, dilapidated facilities, scarce resources, and uncredentialed teachers. The rationale of the study indicates that we are in a trend of resegregating public schools and that minority students will be severely impacted by this trend.

In his book *Savage Inequalities*, Kozol (1991) researched the inequities in American schools. He found that education and funding were linked to race. The result was that white children were provided with twice as much funding as children in predominantly minority schools. Kozol found in New York that the average expenditure per pupil in largely minority public schools was $7,299; in white suburbs on Long Island, the funding levels were $15,000. At East St. Louis High School in Missouri, where the school is predominantly African American, the students in home economics class are trained for fast-food jobs. Chicago spent about $5,500 for each student in its secondary schools. This compared to an investment of some $9,000 in each high school student in the highest-spending suburbs to the north. The better teachers are attracted to the wealthier districts or the magnet schools, and other neighborhoods must settle for the rest. The principal of Goudy Elementary School in Chicago said simply, "I take anything that walks in." The National Center for Education Statistics asserts the average public education expenditure in districts serving students in the poorest communities is $4,375 versus $7,000 in districts serving students in the nation's suburban/affluent communities. This will be discussed in greater detail in Chapter Five.

Misconception No. 8: Affluent Minorities
Don't Need Affirmative Action

Another myth of affirmative action is that it benefits some people who do not need it, like members of affluent minority groups. The issue of class does not discount discrimination. This assumption is making a claim that there are some individuals who are more deserving of equity than others. This does not make sense. If a policy exists to address inequities, it should apply to all, not just those who are considered more deserving. Affirmative action is not a need-based economic (poverty) program. Affirmative action as defined earlier is established on the basis of redressing discrimination against historically underrepresented disadvantaged groups. Affluent minorities with professional careers still experience discrimination in the labor market, education and housing regardless of their class. Lastly, this assumption asserts that affirmative action is not assisting those in need, which is false. Affirmative action helps many individuals and groups in every social class. As a policy designed to provide opportunities it has opened the door to access for groups that had been largely excluded.

Misconception No. 9: The Playing Field is Level Myth

For proponents, the playing field is not level if the ground is tilted and equal opportunity to succeed does not mean equal resources to compete. Affirmative action cannot be reduced to simple categories of "fair, unfair" or "right versus wrong," for it is much more complex an issue. Critics want no use of race at all. The use of race should be judged differently. If a university does not want an all-white freshman class, shouldn't it use race as one of several criteria in selecting a student body? The answer is yes.

The push for no use of race at all has created a race-neutral movement, which pushes percentage plans as the new alternative. Percentage plans will be discussed in greater detail in Chapter Six. If the United States had not enacted Jim Crow laws and the use of race was a consideration when colleges and universities were established, we might not have racial diversity as a need we face today.

Audit studies have become a popular means of documenting the so-called level playing field. In audit studies researchers test the field by sending in individuals from different racial backgrounds with similar or identical education and experience to employers. The outcome of treatment on each individual can provide results on the status of discrimination in the labor market. Audit studies conducted by several researchers (Neumark, 1995; Wissoker, 1994; Bendick, Jackson, and Reinoso, 1994; and Kenney, 1994) indicate that in almost every study white males were given job offers twice as often as minorities and women. The difference favoring whites and males on a numerical percentage range from 6 to 20 percentage points. These studies all concluded that discrimination is still an issue in the labor market. The playing field among different groups is not level. If affirmative action were not a governmental policy it is highly possible that discrimination in the labor market could be worse.

Former White House staffers George Stephanopoulos and Christopher Edley, Jr., conducted research derived from federal agencies. Their report examined affirmative action programs, primarily contracting. From 1982 to 1991 there was a 125 percent increase in contracts awarded to minority owned firms and a 200 percent increase in firms owned by women. The most important part of their report was the findings that by 1993, affirmative action in contracting had almost reached parity with representation of minority-owned businesses.

Equality or equal access is a phrase that dominates civil rights, court decisions and the affirmative action movement. Yet, it is also a phrase the courts and we as individuals struggle with. From the time of Reconstruction to the twenty-first century the debate on how to achieve equity is still as controversial as it was in the nineteenth century. Today, there is still massive confusion over the meaning of equal access and a lack of consistency by the courts in enforcing it. Our forefathers stressed that all citizens should be free to achieve their highest potential. However, at the time this only applied to whites. In 1974, Justice Thurgood Marshall stated, "Equal opportunity to reach their potential as citizens is tied directly to everyone's having an equal start in life." This concept is not widely understood or used. We still need to work for effective enforcement of civil rights laws.

For the protection and preservation of democracy, the government must provide leadership in alleviating odious discrimination. Affirmative action is the principal remedy available in correcting great disparities among people of color in the United States. Affirmative action must be a part of our society, otherwise, the dream of an equal society will never be realized. We must create equitable opportunities for all Americans if we are to transcend issues of racism, discrimination and privilege. If we fail we will be caught in the endless cycle of white against brown and black, women against men, and economic inequities of rich versus poor.

Of all the civil rights for which the world has struggled and fought for 5,000 years, the right to learn is undoubtedly the most fundamental.

— W.E.B. Du Bois

4. The Courts and Affirmative Action

The issue of race and college admissions has a long and documented history within the United States courts. Prior to the landmark Supreme Court decision in *Brown v. Board of Education* (1954), the court had struggled with the equal protection clause of the Fourteenth Amendment and provided varying rulings over the centuries regarding race and access to public education. Under affirmative action, strict scrutiny requires the courts to assess the need and impact of race-conscious policies. Yet over the years, the overall question that many states struggle with is, is the need to achieve diversity in educational systems a compelling state interest that is consistent with equal protection principles of the Fourteenth Amendment? In the process of answering that question this chapter will examine the background and role the federal government and the courts have played over the years regarding education and race. In order to understand how pivotal the courts are we must examine how the issue of racial discrimination has been played out in the configuration of legal cases and policies that for centuries have been utilized to denigrate people of color. This background will be critical in building an understanding of how affirmative action made its way back to the U.S. Supreme Court in 2003.

While this chapter addresses the question of whether diversity serves as a compelling state interest that supports the Fourteenth Amendment, the limitation of this chapter is its inability to include all of the court cases related to affirmative action. Therefore, this chapter is limited to only the court cases that provide vital insight on decisions and patterns of outcomes related to affirmative action policies as they pertain to public education and college admissions.

Affirmative Action and Educational Institutions

First, let's identify the current federal laws that apply to affirmative action. Below is an outline of the major statutes that apply to affirmative action and education. Most of the statutes provide the basis for affirmative action used in admissions and employment, which are aimed at prohibiting discrimination, and encourage goals to remedy past effects of discrimination and targeted recruitment to increase access for underrepresented groups. The use of affirmative action is governed by the following laws:

Fourteenth Amendment of the U.S. Constitution: the "equal protection clause" prohibits discrimination based upon sex or race and applies solely to public institutions. Under the amendment, affirmative action programs must be designed and implemented to remedy specific evidence of past discrimination.

Title VI of the Civil Rights Act of 1964, 42 U.S.C.: The Civil Rights Act prohibits race discrimination in all programs receiving federal funds. At educational institutions this law applies to employees and admissions. The most recent cases brought under Title VI are the U-Michigan cases of *Gratz v. Bollinger*, 539 U.S. S.Ct. 123 (2003), and *Grutter v. Bollinger*, 539 U.S. S.Ct. 123 (2003).

Title VII of the Civil Rights Act of 1964, 42 U.S.C.: This prohibits employment discrimination based upon color, religion, race, national origin, and sex by employers and public and private educational institutions with 15 or more employees.

Title IX of the 1972 Education Amendments, 20 U.S.C.: This prohibits sex discrimination in all educational institutions that receive federal funding. Title IX applies to college admission and employment.

To understand how the United States moved to the need for anti-discrimination laws we must begin by looking at the issue of slavery. Human beings were once considered property. This established whites as the superior race. It has been this establishment of an inferior race that became the foundation for the need for equity, and affirmative action as a means by which we strive for equity.

It started with slavery. The original Constitution condoned the institution of slavery; the federal government passed laws that sustained and supported it; with racial oppression, state and federal courts devised and perpetuated policy that dehumanized African Americans at every level — even to those who were free. In 1857, a pivotal case, *Dred Scott v. Sandford*, established an apartheid of enslaved African Americans. In this case the court articulated that there was no real distinction between free African

Americans and slaves. This case set the precedent on how the Constitution could be used to dehumanize people of color.

Dred Scott v. Sandford (1857)

In 1856, Dred Scott brought suit against his slave owner, John Sandford, for assault against him and his family. Scott, who sought his freedom in court and won his case, which was later overturned by the Supreme Court, was at one point a free man as well as a slave. When he sued his slave owner he filed his case as a citizen of Missouri. Even though his owner admitted to accosting Scott, his wife and two children, the court ruled in the owner's favor as it declared Scott had no rights because he was not a citizen. The jury and the court ruled that the word "citizen" under the Constitution did not apply to an individual of "negro race." A "negro," therefore, could not become a citizen based upon residence in a free state. The Declaration of Independence did not include slaves as part of the human race; thus, slaves were not allowed rights and privileges guaranteed by the Constitution. Specifically, the court stated, "When the framers of the Constitution were conferring special rights and privileges upon the citizens of a state in every other part of the Union, it is impossible to believe that these rights and privileges were intended to be extended to the Negro race."[1]

The establishment of slaves as property was affirmed in the Constitution. Therefore, any citizen holding property of this kind while traveling in northern territories of the United States was legal. Sandford as a slave owner had every legal right to "restrain" Scott and his family, as they were his property. The Scott case confirmed that slaves as well as free men had no rights and were considered inferior to the white race, and the court upheld this as legal. After the abolition of slavery the Fourteenth Amendment was ratified, but there was no sign of equity for African Americans.

Freedmen's Bureau

The proponents of the Fourteenth Amendment were those who supported the establishment of the Freedman's Bureau. The amendment was constructed to provide a broad consideration of race designed to assist in state-sponsored policies aimed at improving the conditions of underrepresented minorities. The framers of the Fourteenth Amendment were the same representatives that supported the Freedman's Bureau and worked to enact race-conscious reconstruction programs.

The courts have been inconsistent over the decades in the true intent of the Fourteenth Amendment. History shows that the Fourteenth Amendment was intended primarily to assist Africans coming out of slavery as "free men." There were specific reconstruction measures that were intentionally "race-conscious" that were passed by Congress at the same time as the Fourteenth Amendment, leaving little doubt that the Fourteenth Amendment was designed to support affirmative action.

The Freedmen's Bureau Bill of 1864

Congressman Thomas Eliot proposed legislation that would create the Bureau of Freedmen's Affairs to provide assistance to "blacks." The goal of the bureau was to oversee the implementation of laws for freedmen or "persons of African descent." The legislation applied solely to former slaves in the Southern, or "rebel," states. Opposition to the bill was based upon two criteria: First, that this issue was a matter for the states and not for the far-reaching arm of the federal government, and second, that it benefited only persons of African descent. For example, the taxes paid under the bill by whites would go to aid "blacks." Eliot responded that this legislation was needed to truly assist and fully support persons of African descent in becoming self-sufficient members of society. While the bill used taxes to aid former slaves, in the long run it would be less-costly than to keep them on public assistance indefinitely. The Freedmen's Bureau Bill was a mandatory requirement to ensure rights and opportunities for freedmen.[2]

While the House and Senate ultimately passed the legislation, it was held up in conference committees as members argued over where to place the new department. A final decision was never made on where the bureau should be housed, and the bill died.

The 1865 Freedmen's Bureau Act is "40 acres and a Mule"

Following the failed first act another piece of legislation was established that held most of the provisions of the 1864 legislation, giving the bureau latitude to produce assistance solely to persons of African descent. The 1865 proposal created a Bureau of Refugees, Freedmen and Abandoned Lands, which would be placed in the War Department. The House of Representatives and Congress adopted the measure, it was signed by President Lincoln, and it became law in March 1865. The 1865 act promised

40 acres and a mule to former slaves. The act called for 40 acres of abandoned land for any freedman or refugee. The act also required the Secretary of War to authorize clothing, fuel and furnishings to "destitute refugees and freedmen."

The 1866 Freedmen's Bureau Act

Introduced by Sen. Lyman Trumball, this new act (S. 60) was established as a companion to the Civil Rights Act of 1866. The act was designed to continue the operations of the bureau and extend its jurisdiction nationwide. The act authorized Congress to provide funds to purchase school buildings and required the president to reserve 3 million acres of land to be sold to refugees and freedmen in parcels that did not exceed the 40 acres rule of the previous act. Through the Civil Rights Act the legislation prohibited discrimination against refugees and freedmen. Opponents of the legislation presented the same arguments expressed today regarding affirmative action. Congressman Nathanial Green Taylor stated the act was "a distinction on account of color between two races. This, sir, is what I call class legislation for a particular class of the blacks to the exclusion of all whites. Such partial legislation, Mr. Speaker, cannot be lasting; it seems to me to be in opposition to the plain spirit pervading nearly every section of the Constitution that congressional legislation should in its operation affect all alike."[3] During this time in the nation's history there were many Congressmen who saw the white race as superior to African Americans and any legislation that was designed to support the needs of freedmen was an unjust threat to the longevity of the white race. Giving 3 million acres of land to freed men was seen by such members as discrimination because there was no land provisions for poor whites.

Proponents of the bill noted that 4 million former slaves, with no education and an inability to own anything and accomplish nothing without permission from the white man, could not be thrown to the wayside. To do so would allow the democracy of our country to perish.

In the end, S. 60 did not become law; President Johnson vetoed the bill. In his veto message the president raised concerns similar to those expressed by opponents. Johnson justified his veto by asserting that the responsibility was left to the individual states and that the founding fathers did not design the country as a government to support "indigent" persons. He saw it as class legislation and discriminatory to people who were not black. The next month Johnson also vetoed the Civil Rights Act of 1866, stating it provided blacks with special treatment.

H.R. 613 (1866)

However, this backfired for Johnson, and Congress passed the Civil Rights Act by overriding his veto. On the momentum of the Civil Rights Act, Congress established a new bill, H.R. 613, to replace S. 60, and it expanded the scope of the previous bill to address Johnson's concern of class legislation. The new bill allowed white refugees to be afforded all of the same supports offered freedmen. The 3 million acre land provision was eliminated from the bill. Unfortunately, Johnson vetoed the bill, citing the same reasons for his objection to S. 60 in his veto message. Once again, the House overturned the veto, and the Senate voted the bill into law.

The Freedmen's Bureau 1866–1870

In 1868, Eliot introduced legislation to continue the work of the bureau, noting its good educational work in assisting refugees and freedmen in transitioning into society. While opposition was still based on the same previous arguments, Congress overturned the president's veto, providing a statute that indefinitely continued the educational functions of the bureau. Since 1866 the bureau had been self-supporting as a result of funds from the rental of abandoned property from the Civil War. However, the 1868 act terminated all other bureau functions as of January 1869. As education became the main focus of the bureau, it was successful in providing funds, land and sometimes construction to establish more than 13 colleges and universities for the education of freedmen "black" students. One of the institutions was Howard University, established in 1867. In the spring of 1870 the bureau ran out of funds, and subsequently all of its educational activities also ended and soon most of the freedmen schools established by the Bureau were closed. The bureau was abolished in 1872.

Fourteenth Amendment

Race has been embedded in the Fourteenth Amendment and has been litigated in the courts since its inception. The equal protection clause is the fundamental basis for most cases involving civil rights and equity. The Fourteenth Amendment asserts that no state shall make or enforce any law which shall abridge the privileges or immunities of citizens of the United States nor deny to any person within its jurisdiction the equal protection of the laws. The objective of the Fourteenth Amendment was designed to provide equity for newly freed slaves, an objective that has yet to be completed today. The original purpose of the Fourteenth Amendment was to provide redress against discrimination for African Americans as a group.

The establishment of the Fourteenth Amendment was to ensure the constitutionality of race-conscious legislation enacted by the 39th Congress. The 39th and 40th Congresses, which were comprised of the framers of the Fourteenth Amendment, viewed and recognized race as a legitimate and constitutionally acceptable factor in Reconstruction legislation. Therefore, they enacted measures that conferred benefits that used race as a factor of eligibility. Congress and federal statutes dating as far back as 1866 promoted and supported race-conscious legislation. For example, public school funding for the District of Columbia (Ch. 217, 14 Stat. 216, 39th Cong., 1st. Session) provided funding for the education of "colored" children. Public lands for public schools (Ch. 308, 14 Stat. 343, 39th Congress) donated lots in Washington for schools for children of color.

The Fourteenth Amendment was established at about the same time as the Freedmen's Bureau acts. The author of the Fourteenth Amendment was Congressman John Armor Bingham; the sponsors of the Amendment were Congressman Thaddeus Stevens and Senator Benjamin Franklin Wade; they all supported and voted for the Freedmen's Act. The purpose of the Fourteenth Amendment, like that of the bureau, was to establish a humane life for freedmen and eliminate the poverty and despair of former slaves. The actions of President Johnson led to the establishment of the Fourteenth Amendment. When Johnson vetoed the 1866 bureau bill, he called into question whether the Constitution allowed such legislation, specifically whether Congress could spend funds to provide for such services. At that time Congress was working on a draft to the Constitution that would clearly provide it with the authority. According to Bingham, the Fourteenth Amendment would give Congress the authority to "make all laws which shall be necessary and proper to secure to the citizens of each *State* all privileges and immunities of citizens in the several States, and to all persons in the several States equal protection in the rights of life, liberty, and property."[4] The actions by Congress in 1866 have been viewed as making it clear that race-conscious assistance programs under the Fourteenth Amendment and the Freedmen's Bureau were not in violation of the principle of equal protection. Bingham made it clear that the amendment before the House was designed to arm Congress with the power to enforce the Bill of Rights as it was written. While these programs were originally designed solely for individuals of African descent, these programs were offered to refugees and all destitute individuals during the years of the Freedmen's Bureau. The bureau fed all who were hungry no matter what their ethnic background.

When the Fourteenth Amendment was established it applied solely to the states. The Supreme Court in the 20th century extended the equal protection clause to the federal government through the Fifth Amendment. The movement by Congress from 1866 to 1869 and the Civil Rights Act of 1866 make it clear that race-conscious programs were not only constitutional, but fell in line with the principle of the Fourteenth Amendment and its guarantee of equal protection. The adoption and work of the Freedmen's Bureau made it clear that race-conscious policies were not only permitted, but had constitutional merit under the Fourteenth Amendment.

Ward v. Flood (1872)

Many people of color interpreted the Fourteenth Amendment as opportunities they themselves had missed out on. For example, the strive for access to desegregated schools is an ongoing issue in the United States, but one that started as early as the 1800s.

In July 1872, Harriet Ward attempted to register her daughter, Mary Frances, at Broadway School, but she was refused entry. Principal Noah Flood informed Ward that the San Francisco Board of Education required all "black" children to enroll in separate "all-black" schools and directed her to one of two institutions in the city for "colored children." Ward took her case to court, and it became California's first school segregation court case. In an effort to end segregation of colored children in California, the case was submitted to the State Supreme Court on September 22, 1872. Her attorney, Mr. Dwinelle, argued that education was a right protected by the Fourteenth Amendment. While Justice C.J. Wallace agreed that education was protected under the equal protection clause, the court believed that Mary was not denied an education as she was directed to a school that could provide her with enrollment. The court upheld the rule of separate but equal in California law and thus triggered more than a century of litigation regarding school segregation.[5]

From the early to mid–20th century, most children of color were forced into impoverished schools. Separate schools made it impossible for any real advancement for children of color. The case was the same for higher education. Under the guise of the Fourteenth Amendment, legal battles were waged to undo the injustices.

The Civil Rights Act of 1875 provided citizenship to all African Americans and proposed elimination of discrimination based on race. In 1883, the court threw out the Civil Rights Act of 1875 that outlawed racial segregation. After 200-plus years of slavery, the court declared that remedies for racial discrimination were beyond the power of Congress. While separate but equal was widely practiced, this decision solidified it in history and opened the door to the "separate but equal doctrine" embodied the 1896 *Plessy v. Ferguson* case. This was the steppingstone to legalized white supremacy in all facets of social life, especially education. This changed the perception and implementation of the Fourteenth Amendment. The equal protection clause was once again used to deny people of color the rights of full citizenship. Ultimately, people of color lacked the authority to establish a better life and seek representation since they could not vote to change the very government that imposed the discriminatory system upon them and denied them resources to create change. By the start of the 20th century every Southern state had enacted separate schools for children of color and whites. Many African Americans began migrating to the North in search of better opportunities, but found their children forced into segregated schools there as well. *Ward v. Flood* is one such example of segregation.

Missouri ex rel. Gaines v. Canada (1938)

In 1935, Lloyd Gaines graduated from Lincoln University with a bachelor of arts degree. Lincoln University, at that time, was the college designated for the education of "colored" people in Missouri. Lincoln had no law school so Gaines applied for admission to law school at the University of Missouri. The University of Missouri was designated for whites only, and the university denied his application for admission based on his race. The university claimed it had the right to do so because state statute prohibited whites and blacks from attending the same schools. The state constitution provided that separate free public schools shall be established for the education of "colored" children. The state also provided that any minority resident may attend the university of any adjacent state with his tuition paid until the full development of Lincoln University was complete. Based upon this statute, the university asserted that it was not the intention of the legislature that African Americans and whites attend the same university. With this law in place the university claimed it acted in accordance with state policy by denying Gaines' application for admission to the School of Law based upon his race. Gaines sued for admission.

Mr. Gaines' attorneys argued, in Missouri ex rel. *Gaines v. Canada*, Registar of the University of Missouri (1938), that the issue was not what other states may offer as an opportunity but what opportunities Missouri itself offered to white students and denied to students of color. According to the court brief:

"By the operation of the laws of Missouri, privilege has been created for white law students which are denied to 'negroes' by reason of their race. The white resident is afforded legal education within the state; the Negro resident having the same qualifications is refused it there and must go outside the state to obtain it. That is a denial of the equality of legal right to the enjoyment of the privilege which the state has set up, and the provision for the payment of tuition fees in another state does not remove the discrimination."[6]

While the state argued that separate facilities could be afforded to Gaines, at that time those facilities did not exist. Gaines refused to travel outside the state to attend another law school because he would be put at a disadvantage; he wanted to practice law in Missouri. Gaines contended that there were advantages to staying within the state. By obtaining access and experience with the local courts and having the prestige of attending the University of Missouri, Gaines argued that his contacts within the community could become prospective clients. The court found that it was impossible to conclude that what otherwise would be an unconstitutional discrimination, with respect to the legal right to the enjoyment of opportunities within the state, could be justified by requiring the denied person to resort to opportunities elsewhere. That option may mitigate the inconvenience of the discrimination but cannot serve to validate it.[7] The courts ruled in favor of Gaines and ordered that the university admit him, arguing that he could not be denied admission based upon his race.

Sipuel v. Board of Regents of the University of Oklahoma (1948)

Sipuel v. Board of Regents of the University of Oklahoma (1948) concerned Ada Sipuel, an African American woman who was denied admission to law school. In 1946, Sipuel sought admission to the School of Law of the University of Oklahoma, which at the time, was the only institution for legal education supported and maintained by the state. Her application was denied by the university based on her race. As a result of *Missouri ex rel. Gaines v. Canada* (1938), Thurgood Marshall argued on her behalf that African American people are qualified to receive professional legal education offered by a state and cannot be denied that education because of their race. The state must provide such education for her in conformity with the equal protection clause of the Fourteenth Amendment and provide it as soon as it does for applicants of any other group. The Supreme Court of Oklahoma affirmed that Sipuel was entitled to a secure legal education afforded by a state institution. The court asserted that the right to a legal education had been denied Sipuel while it was afforded to many white applicants by the state. Therefore, the court concluded that the state must provide a legal education for Sipuel in compliance with the equal protection clause of the Fourteenth Amendment.

Sweatt v. Painter (1950)

Sweatt v. Painter (1950) concerned Herman Marion Sweatt, an African American student who sought admission to the University of Texas Law School for the fall 1946 term. The university denied his application because of his race. Sweatt brought suit against school officials to compel his admission. At the time he filed his case, there was no law school in Texas that admitted students of color. Like most states, the university was restricted to white students in accordance with state law. The state court recognized that denying the petitioner access to the law school was depriving him of his Fourteenth Amendment right to equal protection under the law. The state court at the time continued the case for six months to allow time for school officials to establish a state law school for African Americans. Once university officials announced they would open a law school, the court denied Sweatt's petition for admission, contending that separate and equal facilities were available to the petitioner. He appealed and while his appeal was pending, a law school was made available for blacks, but Sweatt refused to register. Sweatt's attorneys contended that the University of Texas Law School was considered one of the nation's top ranking law schools. The law school was staffed by a faculty of 16 full-time and three part-time professors, its student body numbered 850 and the library contained over 65,000 volumes along with a law review, moot court facilities, and scholarship funds. The law school for students of color had no independent faculty or library. The teaching staff was comprised of four instructors from the University of Texas Law School who maintained their offices at the university. The library would contain 10,000 volumes that had yet to arrive and there was no full-time librarian. Finally, the school lacked accreditation.

The attorneys for the petitioner concluded in their appeal that these facilities were not equal to those provided for white students at the university. Sweatt's attorneys asserted that excluding him from that school is no different from excluding white students from the new law school. "This contention overlooks realities. It is unlikely that a member of a group so decisively in the majority, attending a school with rich traditions and prestige, which only a history of consistently maintained excellence could command, would claim that the opportunities afforded him for legal education were unequal to those held open to petitioner. That such a claim, if made, would be dishonored by the state is no answer. Equal protection of the laws is not achieved through indiscriminate imposition of inequalities."[8]

In the Supreme Court's decision, the court concluded that the law school designated for people of color was not an institution equal to that of the University of Texas. The court asserted that with such inequities in resources and facilities along with a substantial number of people excluded from the University of Texas law school, the education offered would not be equal. Under the ruling, the petitioner could claim his full constitutional right in seeking a legal education equivalent to that offered by the State of Texas to white students. The court held that the equal protection clause of the Fourteenth Amendment required that the petitioner be admitted to the University of Texas Law School.

Unlike the previous cases addressing college admissions, the courts did not deal with the issue of segregation in education directly because separate facilities were not available to the petitioners in the cases of Missouri and Sipuel at the time at which they applied for admission to law school. Although the Texas case was similar to *Sweatt v. Painter*, Texas attempted to circumvent the rulings of Missouri and Sipuel in claiming that African American students had full access to an education because the state had provided a separate institution that provided graduate education opportunities for non-white students. The state was not successful because the court ruled that the separate institution was not equivalent to the facilities offered for white students.

McLaurin v. Oklahoma State of Regents (1950)

In *McLaurin v. Oklahoma State Regents for Higher Education* (1950), the issue of segregation in separate facilities established a different precedent. An African American man possessing a master's degree was admitted to the Graduate School of the University of Oklahoma as a candidate for a doctorate in education. Mr. G.W. McLaurin was permitted to use the same facilities as white students. However, because state law required that institutions of higher education operate on a segregated basis, he was assigned to a separate table in the library, a separate row in the classroom as well as a separate table in the cafeteria, all of which were designated for Negro students only. He filed suit against the university, claiming that the conditions under which he was required to attend school deprived him of his personal and present right to the equal protection of the laws on the basis of race, which the Fourteenth Amendment prohibits.

Oklahoma regents argued that they were acting in accordance with state law. State-owned or -operated colleges or institutions of higher education established for and/or used by whites which offered programs of study not found elsewhere for the "colored race" could provide them on a segregated basis. Segregated basis was defined as "classroom instruction given in separate classrooms, or at separate times."[9] Regents asserted that they were in compliance under segregation laws and concluded that they were not in violation of McLaurin's personal and present rights under the Fourteenth Amendment. Oklahoma State Regents indicated that McLaurin used the same classroom, library and cafeteria as students of other ethnicities with no indication that the seats he was assigned put him at a particular disadvantage. "He may wait in line in the cafeteria and stand there and talk with his fellow students, but while he eats he must remain apart."[10]

McLaurin's attorneys insisted that the State, in administering facilities that it established for professional and graduate study, intentionally excluded McLaurin from interaction with other students. In court documents McLaurin's attorneys stated: "The result of these facilities is that appellant is handicapped in his pursuit of effective graduate instruction. Such restrictions impair and inhibit his ability to study, to engage in discussion and exchange views with other students, and in general to learn his profession."[11] Overall, state obligatory limitations produce impossible inequities that any student would suffer under and they should not be sustained. The final decision on this case was handed down by the Supreme Court, which concluded that the conditions in which McLaurin was required to receive his education were a violation of his personal and present right to equal protection of the laws. The court held that the Fourteenth Amendment prohibited differences in treatment based upon race. Since McLaurin was admitted to a state-supported institution, he therefore must receive the same treatment as students of other races do.

Federal laws founded during slavery that promoted discrimination contributed to segregated schools and institutions. While these cases preceded Brown, they set a legal precedent of great importance regarding the policy dilemma that continued to curtail the efforts of underrepresented students in securing increased access to higher education. In *Brown v. Board of Education* (1954), the issue of segregation was definitely addressed by the courts.

Brown v. Board of Education (1954)

In 1952, four cases, from Kansas, South Carolina, Virginia, and Delaware were consolidated and presented to the U.S. Supreme Court. In each case the primary objective was to undo the "separate but equal" doctrine and provide desegregation for public education. All the plaintiffs were children of color seeking the aid of the court for the right to attend all-white schools in their communities. Like so many plaintiffs before them, they based their argument upon the Fourteenth Amendment. At the local level, except in the Delaware case, all the plaintiffs had been denied relief under the separate but equal doctrine. In the Delaware case, the Supreme Court of Delaware adhered to that doctrine, but it required that the students be admitted to the white schools because the resources and facilities far exceeded the negro schools.

The plaintiffs appealed to the U.S. Supreme Court, where the case was argued on December 8, 1953. The question before the court was whether segregation of children in public schools, based solely on race when all other factors may be equal, still denied children of color equal educational opportunities. Once the case was presented, the team of attorneys, parents and students stood back and prayed they would be successful where so many had failed before. What the court noted was that education of negroes was almost nonexistent, and at one point, was forbidden by law. Then the court examined the status of public education at that time when education of white children had taken place, in large part, by private groups. Free public schools supported by taxes were absent in the South and scarce in the North, with degrading conditions.

According to court documents, the conditions of public education did not approximate those existing today. The curriculum was usually rudimentary; ungraded schools were common in rural areas; the school term was but three months a year in many states; and compulsory school attendance was virtually unknown. As a consequence there is very little with regard to the Fourteenth Amendment as it relates to the impact on public education.[12] By the time *Brown v. Board of Education* arrived at the Supreme Court, the courts had labored with "separate but equal" over half a century. Previously the courts looked at cases with findings that negro and white schools have been equalized or were being equalized with respect to facilities, access, curriculum and other tangible factors. What made Brown different is that half a century later, the court was asked not to look at the tangible factors between negro and white schools, but to look at the impact of segregation itself on education.

In his opinion, Chief Justice Earl Warren concluded that education is perhaps the most important function of state and local governments. Compulsory school attendance laws and the great expenditures for education demonstrate our recognition of the importance of education to our democratic society. In these days, it is doubtful that any child may reasonably be expected to succeed in life if he is denied the opportunity of an education. Such an opportunity, where the state had undertaken to provide it, is a right which must be made available to all on equal terms. On May 17, 1954, the court ruled that separate does not mean equal.[xiii] The face of education was changed forever when the court found that state policies to segregate students on the basis of race were unconstitutional. In the field of education the doctrine of "separate but equal" was determined to have no place in a democratic society. The court required all school systems to take affirmative steps to remove past discriminatory practices.

In the pivotal case following the Brown decision, the court ruled in Florida ex rel. *Hawkins v. Board of Control*, 350 U.S. 413 (1956) that Brown also held for higher education. People of color could not celebrate a decision of equity too soon as they quickly discovered few victories existed for public education because full access was not the case for all. Until the passage of the 1964 Civil Rights Act, the executive branch of government had no real power to enforce the *Brown v. Board of Education* mandate in school desegregation, which left the compliance to the courts. Dr. William T. Trent, a professor of policy studies at the University of Illinois, believed it was Title VI that set the pace toward desegregating higher education. According to Trent, despite the rulings in the Brown court case, progress in desegregating higher education in those states was not forthcoming. Title VI of the 1964 Civil Rights Act provided for federal regulation of higher education by prohibiting the distribution of federal funds to colleges and universities that discriminate on the basis of race, color or national origin.[14]

North Carolina State Board of Education et al. *v. Swann et al.* (1971)

After the Brown decision, the need for desegregation was pivotal in public education, and the federal government devised busing as one means to create equity. In the spring of 1969, the district court of North Carolina directed the school board to devise a method of desegregating the district. The school board had the option of altering attendance areas or consolidating schools or bus transportation to racially balance the system. The school board submitted several proposals, which were all rejected by the district court. The North Carolina State Board of Education, a local school board, and four North Carolina officials challenged the judgment of a three-judge court in U.S. District Court granting an injunction against its enforcement. In an attempt to intervene during the course of this litigation, the North Carolina Legislature passed legislation known as the "anti-busing bill." The bill forbade any assignment of any student based on race or for the purpose of desegregating public schools. The school board that planned to transport close to 4,000 black children into white suburban schools faced a suit by defendants in state court to impede the federal court order.

The court concluded that the "anti-busing" statute exploited a form designed to control school assignment plans by demanding that they be color-blind. That requirement prohibited the implementation of *Brown v. Board of Education.* Since the race of students must be considered to assess if a constitutional violation had occurred, race must also be used to devise a remedy. To prevent all placements made on the basis of race would deprive school authorities of the one tool necessary and essential for fulfillment of their constitutional obligation to eliminate existing dual school systems. Bus transportation had long been an integral part of all public education systems; a true remedy was impossible without reliance upon it.[15] The "anti-busing bill" was found unconstitutional, and the district court mandate was upheld.

Pasadena City Board of Education v. Spangler (1976)

In 1968, the Pasadena Unified School District Board of Education was charged with unconstitutional segregation of its high schools. Numerous students, joined by their parents, brought a suit in U.S. District Court seeking relief from unconstitutional segregation of the Pasadena Unified School District. Under Title IX of the Civil Rights Act of 1964, the U.S. District Court intervened. The court ruled that the defendants procedures violated the Fourteenth Amendment by failing to adopt a desegregation plan. The school board was then ordered to submit a desegregation plan to begin with the 1970 academic school year that would result in no school "with a majority of any minority students." The court retained jurisdiction to ensure the plan would be carried out, and even though the case was appealed to the U.S. Supreme Court, the United States was the victor and Pasadena maintained a desegregation plan. On many occasions, the courts had to step in to ensure compliance with the Civil Rights Act.

Wygant et al. v. Jackson Board of Education (1986)

Teachers within the Jackson, Michigan, district filed suit against the Jackson Board of Education for discrimination. The suit claimed that the board's policy of laying off white teachers violated the Fourteenth Amendment and Title VII of the Civil Rights Act of 1964. The school board claimed that the policy was designed to remedy past discrimination and therefore was constitutional. The district court agreed and found the policy was good in providing teachers of color as role models for students of color. The U.S. Supreme Court found the policy unconstitutional and found the layoff policy was not narrowly tailored enough to promote a compelling state interest, and consequently the policy was eliminated. The court concluded that societal discrimination as the sole basis is not sufficient enough to justify a racial classification layoff policy. There must be evidence of a compelling nature of prior discrimination by the school board that would allow racial classification in teacher retainment; the court suggested less intrusive means of accomplishing diversity, including hiring goals as an appropriate alternative.

Five decades ago, *Brown v. Board of Education* was the promise of a more racially inclusive society. Yet, today resegregation of American public schools exists. Racial isolation of students of color has increased to levels larger that those experienced three to four decades ago. Today, the largest city school systems in the United States are predominantly non-white. According to a study released by the Civil Rights Project at Harvard University, white students are the most segregated; on average as they attend school where 80 percent of the student body is white.[16]

Racial isolation in American schools is a result of the deeply embedded discriminatory racial hierarchical system that permeates our society and continues to reduce opportunities for children of color. When the court ruled in *Brown v. Board of Education* that "separate but equal" was decisively unequal, it was the appropriate ruling. Yet, today one-sixth of all African American students in the nation and one-fourth of African American students in the Northeast and Midwest are educated in schools characterized by concentrations of enormous poverty and with inadequate resources. Many students of color, especially African Americans, regardless of their family income, have strikingly diminished opportunities for educational, social, and economic advancement.[17]

Overview of Strict Scrutiny Rule

"Strict scrutiny" was devised by the U.S. Supreme Court to interpret the execution of the Fourteenth Amendment. Justice Thurgood Marshall asserted that strict scrutiny was needed in order to have a better understanding and ability to interpret the Constitution. Strict scrutiny and the Fourteenth Amendment were designed to protect freed slaves from unlawful legislation enacted by the states. However, by the time the court got to *Plessy v. Ferguson* (discussed in Chapter Three), the equal protection clause had been interpreted as separate but equal laws for African Americans and whites. This interpretation was the majority view of the Court up to the mid–1950s, placing at risk the constitutional rights of people of color against racism.

Next, the court used the equal protection clause to address the issue of classifications. In the 1920 F.S. *Royster Guano Co. v. Commonwealth of Virginia* case, the court wanted to make sure certain classifications would not be used against businesses to deny them equal protection of the law. The court held that equal protection did not prohibit states from "resorting to classifications for the purpose of legislation." In addition, it ruled that classifications "must be reasonable, not arbitrary, and must rest upon some ground of difference having a fair and substantial relation to the object of the legislation, so that all persons similarly circumstanced shall be treated alike."[18] Thus, the court decision established a standard that verified that a law is unreasonable if a classification is not "rationally related" to a government interest.

In *Hirabayahi v. U.S.* and *Korematsu v. U.S.*, strict scrutiny was applied to racial classifications. In these two cases, the court held that distinctions between citizens solely because of their ancestry are by their nature odious to a people whose institutions are founded upon the doctrines of equality.[19] In the Korematsu case (1944) the court held all restrictions thar curtail the civil rights of a single racial group are immediately suspected. That is not to say that all such restrictions are unconstitutional. It is to say that courts must subject them to the most rigid scrutiny.[20] Based upon case law in Hirabayahi and Korematsu, once strict scrutiny is invoked, the responsibility falls upon government to prove a compelling state interest for racial classifications. This was the standard until the Bakke decision. In Bakke, the court moved away from its previous stance on racial classifications and held that racial inclusion is not solely protected under racial classifications. Under strict scrutiny any use of race or ethnicity in admissions must be narrowly tailored to serve a compelling governmental interest. According to the College Board (2001), a compelling education interest in diversity encompasses the following:

"Educational benefits of racial and ethnic and nonracial and nonethnic diversity,

Is particularized to the structure, pedagogy, and mission of the specific school, department or program that uses race or ethnicity in admission or financial aid decisions, and

Is supported by strong evidence that educational diversity is not a pretext for racial and ethnic balancing and that student body diversity in fact enhances educational outcomes."[21]

Dr. J. Owens Smith, a researcher and professor of political science and Afro-Ethnic studies at California State University, Fullerton, asserted that the Bakke case was the first time that the court reviewed a government policy designed to protect minority groups against the tyranny of the majoritarian political process. This case touched the nerve system of the American society. It led to the most emotionally charged debates since the Civil War. The critics' arguments were so compelling that they were successful in convincing the majority of the court to accept the notion that the proscription against discrimination contained in Section 601 of Title VI of the 1964 Civil Rights Act was intended to protect individuals against discrimination and not groups.[22] Let's examine the most pivotal case regarding college admissions and the courts, the Bakke decision.

University of California Regents v. Bakke (1978)

University of California Regents v. Bakke (1978) was the most controversial and the single most important case ruling on affirmative action and college admissions of the 20th century. Before the 2003 University of Michigan court ruling, Bakke stood as the pivotal case regarding the use of race that most colleges and universities follow as a guide today.

In 1973 and 1974, Allan Bakke was denied admission to the Medical School at the University of California, Davis. Unfortunately, Bakke had been turned down by all 12 of the medical schools to which he applied, even the University of Minnesota, his alma mater.

With the shortage of underrepresented doctors, UC Davis, like most institutions, had an affirmative action program for disadvantaged students. It has been said that if Bakke had not discovered that the medical school had a program that provided specified slots for underrepresented students, he might not have sought to charge racial discrimination. At the time, the university had two admissions programs for the entering class of 100 students: the regular program and the special admissions program, utilized to consider applications of disadvantaged students. Bakke filed suit against the university, seeking a mandatory injunction for admission, claiming that the institution had excluded him on the basis of his race, which was in violation of the equal protection clause of the Fourteenth Amendment and Section 601, Title VI of the 1964 Civil Rights Act. This section of the Civil Rights Act, pertinent to the case and most cases regarding affirmative action, states that "No person in the United States shall, on the grounds of race, color, or national origin, be excluded from participation in, be denied the benefits of, or be subjected to discrimination under any program or activity receiving federal financial assistance."[23]

Bakke's suit also claimed that all students admitted under the special program were underrepresented minorities, to whom the university applied separate, preferential standards of admission. In 1973, over 2,000 applications were submitted for admission to the medical school, and in 1974, that number was over 3,000. There were only 100 slots available for acceptance into UC Davis Medical School each year, of which 16 were filled under the special admissions program for "disadvantaged" students. Bakke argued that the "racial quota prevented him from competing for 16 of the 100 slots at the Davis Medical School and, as a result, barred him by reason of race alone from attending the school."[24]

The court contended that quotas existed "if a fixed number of seats were set aside or an unyielding number is set to achieve a goal" (Bakke, 438 U.S. at 288, 98 S. Ct. at 2747). The University argued that the 16 slots presented a goal, not a quota. They stated: "In light of California's sizable minority population and the current underrepresentation of minorities in the medical profession, the allocation of 16 out of 100 places to the special admission program can hardly be criticized as unreasonably generous. Moreover, only *fully qualified applicants* were admitted under the program and thus if there had not been a sufficient number of qualified disadvantaged minority applicants the medical school would not have accepted minority applicants simply to fill a quota."[25]

The university asserted that if special consideration was not afforded to disadvantaged applicants, most of them would not gain admission because their test scores and grades more often than not were lower than those of white students. Two years prior to the establishment of the university's special program, only two African Americans and one Mexican American were selected for admission. Upon implementation of the program 33 Mexican Americans, 26 African Americans, and one Native American were admitted.

The Supreme Court ruled in favor of Bakke, finding the university's special admission program unconstitutional, but still allowing the university to consider the use of race in its admissions process. Justice Lewis F. Powell contended that the use of race was a plus when administered appropriately. He asserted that while race could be a plus in consideration of admissions, race and ethnicity should not be used to insulate the individual from comparison with all other applicants for available seats. Powell believed that it was the goal of the institution to assure applicants were treated as individuals in the admissions process. The court ruling stated: "Regardless of its historical origin, the equal protection clause by its literal terms applies to any person, and its lofty purpose, to secure equality of treatment to all, is incompatible with the premise that some races may be afforded a higher degree of protection against unequal treatment than others. The rights created by the first section of the Fourteenth Amendment are, by its terms, guaranteed to the individual. The rights established are personal rights. It is, therefore, no answer to these petitioners to say that the courts may also be induced to deny white persons rights of ownership and occupancy on grounds of race or color. Equal protection of the laws is not achieved through indiscriminate imposition of inequalities. We conclude that the program, as administered by the university, violates the constitutional rights of nonminority applicants because it affords preference on the basis of race to persons who, by the university's own standards, are not as qualified for the study of medicine as nonminority applicants."[26]

The Bakke ruling ran counter to the court's ruling in *Regents v. Roth* in 1973. In that case, the court held that the constitution does not create rights, but protects them through due process. Under the "Fourteenth Amendment procedural protection of property is a safeguard of the security of interests that a person has already acquired in specific benefits."[27] Basically, before an individual can make a "property" claim to a government benefit, there must be a law in place that provides that benefit. The University of California, Davis, had no law that *mandated* that students had a right to attend medical school based on merit. This would mean that all qualified students have a mandatory right to attend medical school no matter the institutional availability, university's ability to accommodate them or the institution's academic freedom to make the decision on how to compose a student body. Not everyone who applies gets in, and there is no statute that mandates that scenario.

Justice Byron R. White agreed with this perspective; he felt it was the court's responsibility to determine if Bakke had an individual right or "private" cause of action under the Civil Rights Act. Without this cause the courts would not have the jurisdiction to consider his claim. White stated that Title VI of the Civil Rights Act does not give individuals a private cause of action. There is no expressed "provision for private actions to enforce Title VI, and it would be quite incredible if Congress, after so carefully attending to the matter of private action in other Titles and the Act, intended silently to create a private cause of action to enforce Title VI."[28] When the court allowed Bakke to make a private cause of action claim, it should have also allowed the other 2,000 applicants with higher credentials then Bakke the same claim. The private claim was not the ability to apply under the special admissions program, but the benefit was a medical education that all the applicants were seeking to obtain. "In ruling that affirmative action classification discriminates against individual whites, the court used the proscription against racial discrimination in Title VI as a legal tool to preclude governmental actors from adopting affirmative action measures unless it includes whites."[29] The flaw with that approach is that the program did not prohibit whites from regular admission; out of the 100 open seats, 84 were available to whites.

The court's ruling in Bakke dismissed the inherited societal discrimination that groups face. The ruling did not address the group reality of discrimination, but predicted its decision on an individual basis. For some, that meant that the court neglected to review the United States' history and track record on discrimination against groups. UC Davis was making light of that reality in its justification of the 16 slots. The court neglected to define "societal discrimination" in its ruling, and it has yet to be defined.

Justice Marshall's opinion criticized the court for not acknowledging the history of discrimination, which gave validity to UC Davis' medical school in providing a special program for disadvantaged students. He stated: "It is more than a little ironic that, after several hundred years of class-based discrimination against Negroes, the Court is unwilling to hold that a class-based remedy for that discrimination is permissible. This ignores the fact that for several hundred years Negroes have been discriminated against, not as individuals, but rather solely because of the color of their skins."[30] Marshall meant that our devastating history requires us to take steps of special consideration to bring underrepresented groups into the mainstream of American life with the same opportunities afforded whites. Our consistent failure to do so will ensure that the United States will always be divided by race.

The Bakke case is what white applicants use as their foundation to attack affirmative action based on race. The Bakke case has been characterized as the sample case of how affirmative action negatively affects white applicants. The true facts of the case make that a challenging assumption. Bakke was denied admission not once, but twice, to UC Davis Medical School. Bakke asserted that the reason for this rejection was the special admissions program at the medical school and formed the basis for his case on racial discrimination. The special admissions program was not designed to afford admission based upon race, but on the basis that all applicants had to meet the university eligibility requirements, and consideration would also be given to economic and educational disadvantage. In the court record, Dr. George H. Lowrey, chairman of the special admissions program, stated that the program was an effort to give preference to applicants from disadvantaged backgrounds; minority group status was one factor in determining disadvantage.[31] In 1973, 73 of the 297 special applicants were white, and in 1974, 172 of the 628 special applicants were white. While no white student was ever admitted through the special admission program, Bakke did not apply for admission as a disadvantaged student nor claim to be disadvantaged.

It was surprising that Bakke attributed his denial of admission solely to race. "Not only is there no sound basis for inferring that the 16-seat set-aside caused Bakke's rejection, there is also no basis for believing that Bakke was excluded from the special program based on his race as opposed to his lack of disadvantage."[32] Disadvantaged whites and students of color applied to the special admissions program at UC Davis. Those who were not considered disadvantaged were moved to the regular admissions process. Had Bakke made a claim as a disadvantaged student and applied to the special admissions program, he may have had a stronger legal standing to claim racial discrimination.

UC Davis Medical School concurred that with or without a special admissions program it would not have admitted Bakke. Dr. Lowrey testified in court that Bakke would not have been admitted in 1973 or 1974 even if there was no special admissions program. While the California Supreme Court and the U.S. Supreme Court agreed that the special admissions program was unconstitutional, the university stood its ground that the special program would have had no impact on its decision or Bakke's ability to gain admission.

In Bakke's original suit, he sought an injunction from the court that mandated the university admit him. The university asserted: "Petitioner was not denied admission to the Davis Medical School as a result of the operation of the special admissions program at said school. Petitioner would not have been admitted to said school even if there had been no such special admissions program."[33] In both years that Bakke applied, there were more than 15 applicants who had higher ratings, which gave them priority over Bakke. After the first state court trial, while the special admissions program was ruled unconstitutional, the judges did not order Bakke's admission to the medical school. The court findings concurred with the university that in both years, even with the special program, the plaintiff would not have been admitted. Bakke's injunction mandating admission was not awarded until the U.S. Supreme Court ruling.

Though much has been written about the Bakke case, there is very little that ponders another alternative as to why Bakke may have not been admitted. For example, in 1974 when Bakke applied he was one of 3,109 regular applicants. Bakke was one of 520 students under regular admission invited for an interview. Neither the case record nor the university specifically divulges what qualities Bakke lacked to be selected for admission. However, Judge Powell's opinion asserted that the chair of admissions, who interviewed Bakke, did not find him to be a sound candidate. He described Bakke's approach to the study of medical problems disturbing as he based his solutions primarily on his personal views and opinions. In addition, he asserted that Bakke's ability and approach to examining problems of the medical profession were limited in scope. It could be that Bakke's poor rating in his interview led to his inability to maintain a strong standing in the admissions process. Acknowledgment of all these other factors in their entirety makes it quite interesting yet puzzling as to how Judge Powell came to the conclusion that the special admissions program with 16 seats was the main reason for Bakke's rejection to the medical school. Maybe the answer lies with UC Davis. The university acknowledged to the court its inability to carry its burden of proof, that absent the special admissions program, Bakke still would not have been offered a letter of admission. The university clearly stated that with or without the special admission program, Bakke would not have been admitted. It however, never fully proved that statement in court. This raises several questions: How much did the special admissions program weigh into the university's admission decision and, How did his interview affect his candidacy? These are questions to which we may never know the real answers. However, there are some key points that lead the author to believe it was more than his interview that led to his rejection. Most individuals are not aware that Bakke submitted his application to the university after the deadline and after most of the students had been selected. Also, Bakke was 32 when he applied to UC Davis. While age should not matter, it was rather late to decide to start an eight-year medical education. Today, Bakke practices medicine part-time as an anesthesiologist in Minnesota.

In summary, Bakke's admission to the UC Davis Medical School was an astonishing accomplishment because the results were based on litigation not related to the merits of his legal claim. The ruling in the Bakke decision, while still allowing colleges and universities to consider race as a plus factor in admission, did not address the continued controversy of affirmative action. It perpetuated what so many folks find unfair about affirmative action. For many white applicants, the Bakke decision gave them credibility to blame affirmative action and ignore the qualifications

of the other candidates for college admissions. This belief by the dominant group that affirmative action is eliminating access to selective institutions is what Liu calls the "causation fallacy."

Causation Fallacy

The causation fallacy "is the common, yet mistaken, notion that when
white applicants like Allan Bakke fail to gain admission ahead of minority applicants with equal or lesser qualifications, the likely cause is affirmative action. The causation fallacy reflects white anxiety over the desire to
gain admission and it accounts for much of the moral outrage that affirmative action inspires among unsuccessful white applicants."[34] Affirmative
action becomes the scapegoat, and the fallacy of causal relationship develops without all the correct information. This creates a conclusion developed by error in logic, and critics often base their beliefs on this without
factual support. It is eligibility versus admission as discussed in Chapter
One, because not everyone who applies is guaranteed admission. Qualified
students of color as well as white applicants are denied admission to selective institutions. Affirmative action does not solely benefit students of
color; disadvantaged whites also benefit. Just as in selective admissions,
affirmative action is not the sole reason and, in some cases, not the reason
white applicants may be denied admission. After the Bakke decision, other
breakthrough cases made their way to the Supreme Court. One such case
dealt directly with the "de jure segregation" of colleges in the Deep South
and set a precedent toward ending desegregation. In *United States v. Kirk
Fordice*, Mississippi's university system was labeled as segregated.

United States v. Fordice (1992)

In 1848, Mississippi established a public university system provided
solely for whites. Over the years, the state developed additional publicly
supported educational institutions, but they were single-race facilities.
Those decades turned into a century and despite the *Brown v. Board of Education* decision ending separate but equal, Mississippi continued to operate segregated educational institutions. In 1962, the first African American
student was admitted to the University of Mississippi under court order
(see *Meredith v. Fair*, 306 F 2d. 374 (5th Cir.), cert. denied, 371 U.S. 828
(1962)). Even though other colleges within the system had begun admitting their first African American students, the system remained almost

entirely white for several years. In 1969, the U.S. government became involved when the Department of Health, Education and Welfare (HEW) initiated steps to enforce the 1964 Civil Rights Act, requiring the state to develop and implement a desegregation plan. That plan was not developed until June 1973, and it called for improving educational opportunities and access for all the citizens of Mississippi. The plan established goals for enrollment, hiring, remedial programs, and special recruitment to diversify the system. HEW rejected the plan because it felt it did not go far enough in eliminating the "de jure segregated" nature of the Mississippi system. The Mississippi Board of Trustees nonetheless adopted the plan without HEW's approval and deemed it compliant with Title VI of the 1964 Civil Rights Act.

In 1975, a group of private citizens of color filed a lawsuit against the state for maintaining a racially segregated college system in violation of the equal protection clause of the Fourteenth Amendment as well as the Fifth, Ninth, and Thirteenth Amendments, and Title VI of the Civil Rights Act of 1964. The United States intervened, charging that state officials failed to meet their obligations of the Fourteenth Amendment and the equal protection clause to desegregate the state's college system. After the lawsuit was filed, the parties involved worked to achieve a resolution through "voluntary dismantlement." This went on for 12 years and, in 1987, the parties resigned themselves to the fact that they could not agree if the state had met its obligation to dismantle its segregated system. The education system was split, with the University of Mississippi, Southern Mississippi, Mississippi State, and Delta State predominantly white, while 71 percent of the state's African American students attended Alcorn State, Mississippi Valley, and Jackson State. For these campuses, the racial demographic was 92 percent African American (see *Ayers v. Allain*, 893 F. 2d. 732, CA5, (1990)).

In Mississippi, college and university admission standards relied heavily on standardized tests. Test scores were used as the minimum and, in some cases, the sole criteria for admission into public institutions, even though students of color scored lower than their white counterparts on these tests. Under the dual college system, the state had duplication of programs at historically black colleges and predominantly white institutions. This duplication was evidence of a separate but equal system that was left in place from the vestiges of discrimination. Instead of institutions desegregating and admitting students of color, they continued to operate separately. This separate but equal process is what led many states to establish historically black institutions because they could not assure qualified applicants of color access to all-white institutions.

Federal involvement in efforts to desegregate Mississippi's colleges and educational institutions go as far back as 1962, when the first African American student was admitted to an all-white institution. As a result, in 1969, 19 states in the South were ordered by HEW to develop desegregation plans. Since this was a federal order, state agencies and judges did not have a Supreme Court ruling that would supercede previous state court rulings. According to Gary Orfield of Harvard, the U.S. Office for Civil Rights was much too easy on states, focusing on whether they met certain minimal goals instead of seeking full opportunity for black students. OCR's clearing of states was not valid under the constitutional theory of the Supreme Court decision.[35]

The state contended that it had taken affirmative steps to desegregate and that the process would take time. The plaintiffs and the U.S. government saw it differently. Simply changing the law to no longer discriminate against students of color was not an affirmative step to change the system. The Supreme Court agreed and ruled that Mississippi public institutions were still operating as segregated campuses. The Supreme Court asserted that states must do more than simply eliminate laws of discrimination, that they must make a concerted effort to desegregate and develop other remedies to make institutions more accessible to students of color. The ruling made the state obligated to end desegregation otherwise it lose federal funds. The majority decision, was written by Justice White, who stated: "In a system based on choice, student attendance is determined not simply by admissions policies, but also by many other factors. Thus, even after a state dismantles its segregative admissions policy, there may still be state action that is traceable to the state's prior *de jure segregation* and that continues to foster segregation."[36] Justice Scalia was the only one who did not join in the decision. He wrote that he believed the court's decision on duplication could be potentially damaging to the longevity of Historically Black Colleges and could put them at risk of elimination. Justice Thomas asserted that the court's decisions should not be seen as an attack against Historically Black Colleges. These institutions sustained African Americans during the days of Jim Crow laws; they cannot be destroyed in an effort to correct the segregationist days they were created to respond to.

Universal Declaration of Human Rights

After 1994, what becomes a glaring omission in the discussion of civil rights issues and affirmative action case law is the court's inability to make decisions that are consistent with universal human rights laws. The ruling in University of California *Regents v. Bakke* of 1978 and *Adarand v. Pena* in 1995 run counter to human rights principles outlined in the Universal Declaration of Human Rights. The International Covenant on Civil Rights in 1992 and the International Convention on the Elimination of All forms of Racial Discrimination in 1994 adopted universal human rights principles. These principles prohibit oppression of all racial groups and require governments to devise special measures to protect underrepresented groups and ensure their equal access to human rights and freedom.

As human rights laws supercede all domestic laws, the U.S. Supreme Court rulings since 1994 that view race-conscious policies as a violation of the equal protection clause run counter to international human rights laws. The system of human rights provides a theoretical blueprint for how societies should be structured by specifying which important human interests should be specifically protected by national governments.[37] Human rights laws are not binding in the United States until they are adopted as treaties. These treaties then must be ratified by the U.S. Senate to be valid. When the Senate ratifies the treaty, it becomes the law of the land. The Supreme Court can and should recognize treaties as the law of the land. This makes the court's subsequent decisions void. For example, the court's ruling in *Adarand v. Pena* is at odds with Article 1(4) of the International Convention on the Elimination of All Forms of Racial Discrimination. The article states: Special measures taken for the sole purpose of securing adequate advancement of certain racial or ethnic groups or individuals requiring such protection as may be necessary in order to ensure such groups or individuals equal enjoyment or exercise of human rights and fundamental freedoms shall not be deemed racial discrimination.[38]

Dr. J. Owens Smith, a professor at California State University, Fullerton, has studied the issue of civil rights for many years. In a personal interview he asserts that Titles VI and VII of the Civil Rights Act are human rights laws and have been misinterpreted by the courts. Smith (1998) contends that the Supreme Court has attempted to make the equal protection clause fit into Titles VI and VII in concluding that equal protection is a personal right. Smith's research asserts that human rights laws are superior to domestic laws. This distinction between the two makes the Supreme Court's rulings involving the use of race-based decision-making a violation of the civil rights act. Thus, it is a complete contradiction with the international law of human rights. Smith asserts that the Fourteenth Amendment extends to all individuals. The text of the Fourteenth Amendment is explicit in declaring that no state has the right to deny anyone equal protection of the laws. The Fourteenth Amendment guarantees rights to the individual, and those guaranteed rights are personal property rights. Property is a right and not an object or thing. "It is a right in or a right to things. The Constitution does not create these rights, but safeguards them through procedural due process. The only way that affirmative action can infringe on an individual's right is to require governmental actors to take away a benefit from a non-affirmative action applicant and give it to an affirmative action applicant for the sole purpose of fulfilling its affirmative action obligations."[39]

Smith believes that the only way Bakke could have been deprived of his equal protection rights to attend UC Davis Medical School would have been to become accepted and then dropped and replaced with one of the disadvantaged minority students admitted through the school's minority program. After he was admitted he would have had a property interest in this benefit. Smith further asserts (1998) that the boundary of the equal protection clause agreement is solely limited to safeguarding the property interest. Section 601 of Title VI does not create a property interest and without a property interest there can be no discrimination.

Smith contends that the failure to provide a clear definition of racial discrimination within Titles VI and VII of the Civil Right Act has contributed to the reverse discrimination theory for which proponents of race neutrality laws have argued for years. According to Smith, the U.S. government has an obligation to its people to amend the 1964 Civil Rights Act to include the international definition of racial discrimination. The inclusion of this definition would make the Civil Rights Act and the terms used in that act consistent with the international law of human rights. The definition for racial discrimination is found in Article 1 of the Constitution, which defines the term as any distinction or exclusion based upon race, color, national or ethnic origin with the purpose of nullifying on an equal basis access to human rights and freedoms in any field of public life.

Putting this language into statute would remove any gray areas regarding equity and reverse discrimination, allowing the country to keep its laws designed to create equity through affirmative action in place. Smith was successful in placing the definition of racial discrimination into statute. During the 2003–04 California legislative session, Assembly Bill 703 authored by Dymally, was signed into law by Gov. Gray Davis. The bill defined race discrimination in the California Constitution as the same meaning as the term racial discrimination found in Article I of the International Convention.

Smith contends that if Congress does not take affirmative steps to amend the Civil Rights Act we will soon see an end to policies designed to eliminate racial discrimination and a systematic exclusion of underrepresented groups from mainstream society. Proponents of race-blind decision making have prevailed in launching a war and a campaign of language designed to mobilize public opinion against civil rights. It is this mobilization that will ultimately prevent the United States from fulfilling its international obligation to eradicate racial discrimination. The need to eradicate racial discrimination has been an incentive needed to maintain diversity and equity in higher education.

Adarand Constructors, Inc. v. Pena (1995)

In 1995, in *Adarand Constructors, Inc. v. Pena*, the U.S. Supreme Court held that affirmative action was illegal because it violated the equal protection clause. Federal contracts usually contain a clause that allows a financial incentive for contractors who subcontract and hire small businesses owned by "economically disadvantaged" individuals, minorities and women. A federal highway contractor awarded a contract to a business identified as disadvantaged. Adarand Constructors submitted a bid that was lower than the bid from the business awarded the contract. When Adarand was not awarded the contract, it sued, claiming race-based practices used in awarding the contract violated the equal protection component of the Fifth Amendment. The Supreme Court invoked strict scrutiny rule when it held that racial and ethnic classifications of any sort are inherently suspect and call for the most exacting judicial scrutiny.[40] As a result of Adarand, the court held that all racial classifications imposed by governmental actors must be reviewed by the court under strict scrutiny.

This ruling gives credence to those Americans who feel that affirmative action is an unfair policy and fueled the efforts of the Center for Individual Rights Movement to take the courts to task to eliminate affirmative action for good. The flaw with this ruling is that it neglects to examine the unintended consequences. The harmful effect of applying the strict scrutiny rule to affirmative action is that it is strict in theory, but fatal to attempts to maintain equity for people of color. It places the onerous burden on governmental actors to demonstrate a compelling state interest in order to adopt positive laws to protect racial minority groups' human rights against the tyranny of racism and oppression. Prior to the Adarand case, the strict scrutiny rule was used to force governmental actors to show a compelling state interest for adopting a policy that operated to exclude racial minority groups from sharing in resources.[41]

The Supreme Court ruling in *Adarand v. Pena* was a setback to race-conscious policies. The ruling allowed any plaintiff the constitutional right to prevent any governmental entity from establishing or adopting measures designed to provide equity or opportunities for people of color to a level of that enjoyed by the dominant group. As a result of the case, the Fifth Circuit used the Adarand decision to eliminate affirmative action in Texas in the Hopwood ruling.

Hopwood v. Texas (1996)

In *Hopwood v. Texas* (1996), once again, the issue at hand was whether it was constitutional for a public college or graduate school to use race or national origin as a factor in its admissions process. Cheryl Hopwood brought suit against the University of Texas after being denied admissions, alleging violations of the Fourteenth Amendment and Title VI of the Civil Rights Act of 1964. The main issue before the court was whether the affirmative action program employed by the university was constitutional. Hopwood contended that it was not because she was discriminated against by the University of Texas Law School when it administered a quota system and provided preferential treatment to less qualified Mexican and Black American applicants in admitting them to the university.

Texas has a long history of discrimination. In 1978, the Federal Office of Civil Rights conducted an investigation of Texas' public higher education system. OCR concluded that Texas had failed to eliminate vestiges of a former segregated system of public higher education between whites and students of color. In 1983, the United States District Court for the District of Columbia entered a Title VI enforcement suit against Texas after it found that Texas had not committed itself to a desegregation plan. This resulted in the court ordering the U.S. Department of Education to begin enforcement proceedings against the state unless it submitted a plan in full conformity with Title VI. The state did comply in submitting a desegregation plan 45 days from the deadline contained in the court order. Prior to the court order, the Office of Civil Rights provided Texas with suggested measures for increasing African American and Latino student enrollment in graduate programs at traditionally white institutions. One of the suggestions was that graduate admission officers re-evaluate each underrepresented candidate's entire record in admitting African American and Latino students who demonstrate the potential for success, but "who do not necessarily meet all the traditional admission requirements."[42]

In 1992, the University of Texas Law School admissions committee was comprised of 15 individuals from faculty, staff, and students. The university also had a minority subcommittee whose members all belonged to the full committee. The minority subcommittee was made up of three individuals whose sole responsibility was to review files of the underrepresented candidates and make recommendations. When students applied, their applications were placed in individual folders in which additional material was added as it became available to the university. Each folder was color-coded based on two criteria: residency and race or ethnicity. Their application deadline was Feb. 1 for fall admissions. However, to ensure that the university would increase the chances of admitting the top underrepresented candidates, the chair of the minority subcommittee would conduct what the members called "presumptive" applicant reviews. What this meant is that once the university had a computer printout of the student's test scores and qualifications and the candidate seemed likely to contain the appropriate admission qualifications at first review (such as a high Texas Index score which was a combination of GPA and LSAT scores), the candidates would receive an offer of tentative acceptance. The offer was tentative, based on completion of any current course requirements in which the candidate was enrolled. The university's process of separate review for underrepresented candidates verses those of nonminority candidates was the crux of the lawsuit. However, presumptive admissions were also conducted for nonminority resident candidates. In addition, the University also implemented a separate admissions process for nonresident applicants. What became the issue of concern was not the presumptive admissions process, but that of the qualifying requirements for each category of students.

The plaintiff's suit claimed that the university set a higher level of requirements for white candidates than it did for students of color. The university set required scores lower for resident and nonresident African American and Latinos than those set for nonminority resident and nonresident applicants. The University of Texas Law School is highly rated nationally. The institution receives over 4,000 applications each year for 500 available seats. According to the university, the law school received 4,494 applications for the fall 1992 incoming class. It offered admission to 936 applicants to fill a class of slightly over 500 students. The overall median GPA for entering students was 3.52, and the overall median LSAT was 162. The median figures for white applicants was a GPA of 3.56 and an LSAT of 162; for African Americans, a GPA of 3.30 and an LSAT of 158; and for Latinos, a GPA of 3.24 and an LSAT of 157.[43]

The university contended that part of its admissions process was established by the Office of Civil Rights through the Texas desegregation plan. The plan required the state to admit 10 percent Mexican-American and 5 percent black students in its entering class. In adhering to the need for equity and diversity, the University asserted that these percentages were not quotas but goals consistent with the numbers of black and Mexican-American college graduates. The university also asserted that the implementation of the OCR plan was contingent upon the quality of the pool of applicants. This meant that the University was not just admitting underrepresented students based on color, but that these students were qualified and showed promise for achieving a law degree. For these reasons the university contended that the admission process was constitutional.

Hopwood had a Texas Index (TI) score of 199. Her TI was reflective of a 3.8 GPA and a 139 LSAT score combined, which placed her in the "presumptive" resident admission range. According to the university, when Hopwood applied it was more concerned about her commitment to the program and the previous undergraduate institutions she attended. Hopwood received an associate's degree in accounting from Montgomery County Community College in 1984 and a bachelor's degree in accounting from California State University, Sacramento, in 1988. She was a certified public accountant from California who worked 30 hours a week while attending school. In addition to being active in community organizations such as the Big Brothers and Sisters in California she also had a disabled child who required additional care.

Because of the needs of her child, Hopwood submitted a letter to the university requesting to attend school on a limited basis the first year in order to attend to her child. The university had additional concerns regarding the lack of information Hopwood provided in her application. Her application contained neither letters of recommendation nor a personal statement. Further, her responses to questions included within the application were brief, failing to elaborate on her background. Based on her application the university did not consider her a strong candidate. Because of this, Hopwood was not offered admission in the first cut of students. She was wait-listed for admission by the University. The institution asserted that it believed Hopwood's ability to work a significant number of hours while maintaining a high GPA was indicative of earning her GPA while on a "fairly slow track" at a noncompetitive institution. In contrast, Dean Michael Sharlot found that Hopwood's achievement of a high GPA while working was a "definite plus." This plus, however, was insufficient to overcome Hopwood's below-median performance on the LSAT and attendance at a series of "very weak schools."[44]

The university's letter to Hopwood indicated that it could not admit her to the 1992 class at this time. However, it instructed Hopwood to return an attached form to the law school within three weeks if she wished to be placed on the waiting list. In addition, the letter asked all applicants not to place their names on the waiting list unless they could accept an offer of admission as late as August. Hopwood testified before the court that she contacted the admissions office and personnel within the office could provide no insight on the possibility of admittance from the waiting list. At the time, because of her child-care needs, she chose not to place herself on the waiting list for fear that she would not be in a position to accept admittance a week before school would start. Based upon this information, the court declared that under Hopwood's circumstances, she was denied admission to the university based on its letter.

Under the court's standard of review, it contended that the university's affirmative action plan based on race was applicable to strict judicial scrutiny. The university asserted that the court's decision to apply a strict judicial scrutiny to the affirmative action program administered by the university was inappropriate because the plan was adopted pursuant to a federal mandate. The Texas plan for desegregation submitted to OCR equates to a federal mandate in keeping compliance with Title VI, which is within the power of Congress, as argued by the university. The university held that it was protected under the Supreme Court's ruling on affirmative action plans. In 1990 the Supreme Court held that affirmative action plans adopted under federal mandate are not subject to strict scrutiny, but that these plans must only show whether they serve an important governmental objective and whether "they are substantially related to the achievement of the objectives" (Supreme Court's holding in *Metro Broadcasting v. FCC*, 497 U.S. 54, 110 S. Ct. 2997, 111 L. Ed. 2d 445, 1990).

The court disagreed with the university and asserted that the equal protection analysis of strict scrutiny applies to all race-conscious affirmative action plans, including those adopted by consent agreements such as those conducted between Texas and OCR. The court pointed to a 1992 ruling in *Podberesky v. Kirwain*, 956 F. 2d 52, 55, in which an affirmative action scholarship under OCR guidelines was upheld by the lower court's application of strict judicial scrutiny. The application of strict scrutiny, according to the court, involves a determination of whether the law school process served "a compelling governmental interest" and whether the process is narrowly tailored to the achievement of that goal. The "compelling governmental interest" test exists to smoke out illegitimate uses of race by ensuring that the goal is important enough for the implementation of race-conscious policies. The narrowly tailored analysis ensures that the means chosen fits this compelling goal so closely that there is little or no possibility that the motive for the classification was illegitimate racial prejudice or stereotypes.[45]

The university, in its defense, contended that a compelling governmental interest existed which justified the need for the affirmative action program implemented by the law school. The reasons for justification were put forth in the school's policy on affirmative action. In order to achieve the school of law's goal of providing real opportunities for a legal education to African American and Latino students as two of the largest minority groups in the state, the institution implemented the following goals for diversity:

To achieve the diversity of background and experience in its student population essential to prepare students for the real world functioning within the law of our diverse nation;

To assist in redressing the decades of educational discrimination to which African Americans and Mexican Americans have been subjected in the public school systems of the state of Texas;

To achieve compliance with the 1983 consent decree entered with the Office of Civil Rights of the Department of Education imposing specific requirements for increased efforts to recruit African American and Mexican American students;

To achieve compliance with the American Bar Association and the American Association of Law School standards of commitment to pluralist diversity in the law school's student population.[46]

The university contended that race-related remedies could be used in attempts to address past and present effects of discrimination. Hopwood asserted that any past discriminations against African Americans occurred so long ago that it had no present effects on the law school. In addition, the law school had not discriminated against Latinos. The separate review process for admission to the law school was unfair to nonminority candidates.

The court contended that Texas' "consent decree" with the Office of Civil Rights in an effort to remedy past discrimination in the higher education system was not a valid justification by itself for the current structure of the admissions program. In the end, the court sided with Hopwood, asserting that the law school's affirmative action program, which gave underrepresented applicants a plus, was unlawful. But the court said the lack of an evaluative comparison among all individual applicants to determine who were the most qualified was not lawful. On March 18, 1996, the Court ruled that constitutional infirmity of the 1992 law school admissions procedure, therefore, is not that it gives preferential treatment on the basis of race, but that it fails to afford each individual applicant a comparison with the entire pool of applicants, not just those of the applicant's own race. Because the law school's 1992 admissions process was not narrowly tailored, the court found the procedure violated the equal protection clause of the Fourteenth Amendment.[47] In the Hopwood decision, the court ruled that diversity was not a compelling state interest, and the university failed to make its burden of proof on the need for affirmative action programs.

The court ruled in favor of Hopwood, stating that she should be allowed to reapply for admission to the law school for the 1995–96 school year without having to pay administrative fees and that her application would be reviewed by the admissions committee along with all other applications. The court ruled 2–1 that Justice Powell's opinion on diversity in the Bakke decision was not law, as it did not garner the majority of the court and no other justice joined him in that part of the opinion regarding diversity. The panel stated: "Justice Powell's argument in Bakke garnered only his own vote and has never represented the view of the majority of the court in Bakke or any other case. Moreover, subsequent Supreme Court decisions regarding education state that nonremedial state interests will never justify racial classifications."[48]

This ruling changed the college admissions process in Texas in that educational institutions within the state could no longer use race or ethnicity as a basis for offering preferential admissions to students. As a result of the Hopwood decision, the University of Texas at Austin and Rice University both announced they would no longer consider race in admission decisions. The Hopwood decision handed down by the Fifth Circuit covered Texas, Mississippi, and Louisiana. William H. Cunningham, chancellor of the Texas system, asserted that the system would seek an appeal but in the meantime would comply with the law. While some praised the decision, they were outnumbered as many students at the University of Texas were outraged. College officials throughout the Fifth Circuit reexamined their admission policies in the wake of the decision in preparation for changes. Some of those race-neutral factors consist of personal talents, extracurricular activities, and socio-economic background.

The U.S. Supreme Court rejected Texas' appeal to hear the case, and the Fifth Circuit decision was left in place. The court rejected the case because the Texas Law School had abandoned its use of race in 1994, so to the court it was no longer relevant. Laurence Tribe, a professor of law at Harvard University, said he believed, "The Fifth Circuit's decision had absolutely no implications for colleges outside of Texas, Louisiana, and Mississippi." Tribe discouraged institutions from removing affirmative action too quickly.

Attorney General Dan Morales began advising colleges and universities on the court decision. He issued guidelines to assist institutions in increasing enrollment of underrepresented students of color without the use of race. Morales' stated that institutions "should avoid racial preferences but consider other 'race-neutral' factors in compiling a diverse student body." Many within the education community condemned the Fifth Circuit decision and predicted it would drastically reduce access for underrepresented students.

University of Georgia (UGA)

The Board of Regents of the University System of Georgia did not have a lot of support in general for affirmative action. Attorney General Michael Bowers encouraged public colleges in Georgia to alter their admission policies to reflect issues presented in the Hopwood case. Bowers sent a letter to Chancellor Stephen Portch expressing his concerns, along with a copy of the Hopwood decision. Bowers cited *Adarand Constructors v. Pena, Shaw v. Reno* and *City of Richmond v. J.A. Croson* and said the court was making it clear that racial classifications of any kind are only permissible in egregious cases and that the equal protection clause requires each person to be treated as an individual, not viewed as a member of a group. He then recommended that the university system review its admissions policies and revise them into compliance with Hopwood.

Bowers' letter created a firestorm within the education community. The U.S. Department of Education's Office for Civil Rights sent a letter to Bowers expressing its concern over his directive regarding the institutions in Georgia. Regional Director Archie B. Meyer, author of the letter, wanted to make sure that Bowers understood the Department of Education's position on issues of this nature as well as to make it clear that the Hopwood decision was a Fifth Circuit court decision and did not apply to Georgia. Specifically, Meyer stated: "The decisions of the U.S. Supreme Court in *Regents of the University of California v. Bakke*, 438 U.S. 265 (1978) and *United States v. Fordice*, 112 S. Ct. 2727 (1992) are the governing precedents for the department and all 50 states. The Office for Civil Rights is guided by these decisions in interpreting and enforcing Title VI of the Civil Rights Act of 1964 and its implementing regulation, which prohibits discrimination on the basis of race, color, or national origin in programs that receive federal funding."[49] The letter wanted to make it clear to Bowers that it is still legal to take race into account in higher education programs.

The attorney general indicated that his letter should be viewed as a letter to a client and that it does not carry any legal weight. In an interview, he stated: "It is legal advice to a client. I can't force them to do anything. But they can't go to any other lawyer. If the colleges get sued, I'm going to defend them and I'm not going to defend something that's illegal."[50] Responding gently for political reasons, Chancellor Portch informed the Attorney General that he would ask the 34 campuses in the system for reports on their use of race.

Wooden v. Board of Regents of the University System of Georgia (1997)

In 1997, 11 students filed suit against the University System of Georgia, claiming that as a result of affirmative action, racial segregation was dominant in the university system's 19 campuses. The students (seven white, four African American) demanded that the system eliminate "racial identifiability" at the predominantly white colleges and the Historically Black Colleges and Universities. This case was unique because the plaintiffs attacked both desegregation and affirmative action. They wanted the university system to stop considering race in all facets of the institution, hiring, contracting and admissions. The plaintiffs claim was that in Georgia, the three HBCUs were predominantly black, which allowed all other 19 campuses to remain predominantly white and thus, dependent upon racial preferences.

The lawsuit stated, "The use of race in admitting students at these institutions has been employed for the purpose and has had the effect of deflecting attention from the need for realistic desegregation; persuading influential black legislators and citizens to not seek a truly desegregated higher education system."[51] The 1992 U.S. Supreme Court decision in *United States v. Fordice* established standards for desegregation in colleges, and those standards did not conclude that HBCUs must close their doors because their student body was more than 70 percent African American.

Robert Davis, a law professor from the University of Mississippi, found the plaintiffs' claim unable to hold water when closely examined. "There have to be additional policies that the state is responsible for to support a complaint that vestiges remain. Racial percentages of students, in and of themselves, are not enough."[52]

The university found the lawsuit far-fetched and asserted that it had admitted students in a lawful manner with the use of affirmative action and that the efforts of affirmative action helped to increase diversity within the system.

The plaintiffs' case also sought to merge historically black Savannah

State University with Armstrong Atlantic State, a predominantly white institution, which physically is almost impossible as the schools are 8 miles apart. Portch stated that the campuses continue to move away from the days of segregation, noting that some public predominantly white universities have student populations that come close to reflecting the state population, which is 27 percent black.[53] In January of 1999, Judge B. Avant Edenfield dismissed the system's diversity defense and ruled that the University of Georgia used an unconstitutional admission policy for five years, 1990–95, which gave preference to African Americans. At the time of the ruling the university had stopped using race in admissions, so the decision had no impact. The ruling only dealt with previous admissions policies, but the university system asserted that the decision should be thrown out as the policy was no longer in place. Edenfield felt compelled to rule on the previous policy to ensure that it would not be reinstated. However, in March of 1999, Edenfield dismissed a portion of the lawsuit brought by four of the plaintiffs because they could not establish direct injury based upon the system's alleged misconduct.

Texas v. Lesage (1999)

Francois Lesage, a white African immigrant applicant, sued the University of Texas Ph.D. program after he was denied admission to the doctoral program in education. Under Title VI the plaintiff challenged the school's race-conscious policy of admission. The court ruled in favor of the university based upon evidence that the plaintiff would not have been admitted even with a race-neutral policy. The case went all the way to the U.S. Supreme Court, which upheld the original decision. The court asserted that an institution can avoid liability if it can show that the same decision would have been made absent affirmative action.

Green v. Board of Regents of the University System of Georgia (1999)

In 1997, Craig Green and Kirby Tracy sued the University of Georgia, claiming their rejection was the result of affirmative action admission policies. Their claim was that the University System of Georgia and Chancellor Portch discriminated against them based upon their race (white). This case went before the same court that previously ruled that UGA's admission policy was unconstitutional from 1990–95. That previous decision by the court included Tracy (the plaintiff). The court found that Tracy's rejection was in violation of his equal protection rights (Wooden, 32 F. Supp.2d at 1378–84). However, UGA changed that policy in 1996, and Tracy was not considered a lead plaintiff in the Green suit.

When Green applied to UGA as a freshman, the university screened applicants in three categories: (1) Academic Index (AI); (2) Total Student Index (TSI); and (3) the edge read (ER). At the AI level, students were screened solely on academic criteria (grade point average and SAT). In 1997, UGA admitted close to 88 percent of its freshmen based solely on academic criteria. Students who did not meet the criteria based on their AI level were moved to the next stage, the TSI, for which the university used bonus points in calculating a student's TSI score. The bonus points consisted of academic (high GPA, high SAT, high school curriculum), demographics (racial/ethnic background, Georgia residency, alumni and parental education level) and extracurricular activities (summer work, school work, hours spent in extracurricular activities). When students were evaluated under the TSI score, UGA offered admission to almost all students in this category. The plaintiffs claimed that the TSI score bonus points were unconstitutional because they considered race. TSI applicants are borderline applicants who are given bonus points based on criteria other than academic measures such as those listed above.

Green's GPA was a 3.3, and he had an ACT score of 27 (SAT equivalent of 1170), which placed him in the middle range of admission or denial. He was then sent to the TSI level, by which he obtained bonus points for his parents' education level and his Georgia residency, and male gender. Green then moved on to the ER (edge reader) category, where two readers reviewed his file. As a result of their review, Green lost points and was denied admission. Judge Edenfield, indicated that the race criteria may be unconstitutional, but he did rule on that basis. He ruled that the university's rejection of Green had nothing to do with preference. In reality, because Green did not have the necessary test scores, grades and other extracurricular factors, preference did not prevent him from gaining admission to UGA. In this matter, the equal protection clause stands for individuals who are denied individually equal treatment by the "challenged discriminatory conduct. A person who fails to satisfy lawful, nondiscriminatory requirements or qualifications for the benefit lacks standing to raise claims of discrimination in the denial of the benefit."[54] In a nutshell, Green needed to show that the current admissions process prevented him from competing on a level equal to all other applicants. Green was unable to do that because he would have needed to show that his application was exposed to a separate and distinctly different admission process and had it not been for affirmative action he would have been admitted. But that was not the case. Therefore, Green lacked standing and was unable to meet his burden of proof.

Green attended a community college and then sought transfer into UGA in 1998, but the university denied his transfer from the community college because he lacked the necessary credit hours and was not at junior status, a requirement to be considered for admission as a transfer. Green indicated he planned to reapply once he completed the necessary credits.

While Edenfield dismissed the case, he took the opportunity to chastise the university for policies he adamantly disagreed with. Edenfield stated: "The court would be remiss if it didn't briefly note what the record evidence now compels: UGA cannot constitutionally justify the affirmative use of race in its admissions decisions."[55] Edenfield believed that the University System of Georgia was engaging in discriminatory practices. He felt university officials were promoting racial stereotyping in its admissions process.

While the Board of Regents was happy with the dismissal, members felt Edenfield's statements were made with malevolent intent. The chancellor stated, "Our state's future economy depends on the University System of Georgia being accessible to all qualified Georgians, so we will continue to work with the University of Georgia and the Attorney General's office to explore all of the options that will enable UGA to have an inclusive student body."[56]

One Florida Plan and the NAACP

When Florida Gov. Jeb Bush eliminated affirmative action at colleges and universities under his One Florida Plan and replaced racial and gender preferences in admissions with a percentage plan for students ranked in the top 20 percent of their high school graduating class, he claimed that affirmative action was no longer needed since the university system had increased underrepresented student enrollment. Three months later the Board of Regents adopted the governor's proposal to end affirmative action in college admissions. As a result of that vote the National Association for the Advancement of Colored People took the Board of Regents to court claiming that it had no authority to make monumental changes. The NAACP claimed that only the individual institutions could make those decisions. The rush to put the One Florida Plan in place concerned some within the education community. They said the regents did not act reasonably and did not properly notify the public of the extent of the changes required by the plan.

The NAACP filed the case on behalf of Mattie Garvin, an African American high school student. The claim was that Garvin would be denied the benefit of affirmative action programs that govern admissions. Keith Goldschmidt, a spokesperson for the regents, asserted that the regents have "precedent for their One Florida decision. They have been developing admissions policies as long as there has been a board."[57]

In July 2000, Administrative Law Judge Charles Adams upheld the regents' elimination of affirmative action. The judge asserted that affirmative action was no longer needed to ascertain diversity in college admissions. He also noted that Florida did have the top 20 percent plan ready as an immediate replacement. According to Adams, "Consideration of race as a factor in admission should not be allowed if Florida were to avoid the problems experienced in California and Texas where race as a consideration in admissions policies was removed without the prior opportunity to adjust to the eventuality."[58] Bush moved forward with the Florida Talented 20 Program, and it remains in place today.

Castaneda v. Regents (2002)

The case started out as *Rios v. Regents* in February 1999. It involved the complaint of underrepresented students denied admission to the University of California, Berkeley. The plaintiffs claimed that implementation of the new undergraduate admissions process used at Berkeley, which prohibited the consideration of race, discriminated against students of color. The complaint stated that Berkeley relied solely on advanced placement college preparatory courses and standardized test scores. Students with more advanced placement (AP) courses were awarded bonus points to their GPAs, making it impossible for underrepresented students of color to fully compete since these courses were not offered in large numbers at their high schools in comparison to the suburban high schools attended by a majority of whites. So, you had a larger number of whites with 4.2 to 4.5 GPAs and underrepresented students of color with 4.0 GPAs creating an inequity in access based upon AP courses. The plaintiffs requested mandated changes to the Berkeley admissions process as relief.

The plaintiffs argued that the disparity in admission in 1998 (first year of the implementation of the new policy) when Berkeley experienced a 45 to 50 percent drop in admissions from the three underrepresented minority groups, which were substantially below the admission rate of white and Asian applicants.

In 1999, the plaintiffs and the defendant agreed to place the litigation on hold to allow for discovery to reveal the functions of the admissions process at Berkeley. Later the parties decided on a settlement, and the terms were agreed upon in November 2002.

The settlement provided for a portion of the plaintiffs' litigation costs. In an effort to disclose any potential disparities, the settlement also required that specified public records regarding Berkeley's undergraduate admission procedures and admissions decisions be made public. Lastly, the third section of the settlement required the retention of an admissions consultant to advise the university on a range of admissions issues. The main factor that led to the settlement is that in 2001, the U.S. Supreme Court decided that private parties do not have a cause of action for disparate treatment under Title VI of the Civil Rights Act.

Smith v. The University of Washington Law School (2002)

Katuria Smith, Angela Rock and Michael Pyle filed suit against the University of Washington Law School, claiming that the law school had violated their constitutional right to equal protection under the admissions program. The plaintiffs claimed that the law school used different standards for students of color and white applicants. Smith, Rock and Pyle, all white applicants, were denied admission individually three consecutive years: Smith was denied in 1994, Rock in 1995 and Pyle in 1996. All three plaintiffs contended that race was used as the majority factor and that the law school failed to narrowly tailor its use in the admissions process.

The lead plaintiff, Smith, scored in the 95th percentile on the LSAT. She was represented by the Center for Individual Rights which successfully sued the University of Texas in the Hopwood case. Michael Greve, CIR executive director, was convinced the plaintiff's denial was primarily the result of racial discrimination. While CIR could not find any proof that the law school lowered its standards to admit underrepresented students of color, Greve was infuriated that underrepresented students gained in numbers. He said that "under its former dean, Wallace Loh, the school in a few years had more than doubled its proportion of students from minority groups, to about 40 percent in 1994. The only way to do that is to lower admission standards."[59]

The law school contended that the admissions policy met the Bakke criteria and was narrowly tailored to adhere to the law school's objectives on educational diversity. The law school also asserted that race was not the reason for the denial of the plaintiffs. According to the school, none of them would have been admitted even if diversity was not used as a plus factor in the process.

The law school considered the use of race as a "plus" under its diversity factor in admissions from 1989 to 1998. The law school's diversity factor was not solely based on race. These factors consisted of race, ethnic origin, cultural background, career goals, disadvantaged background and environment, physical disability, special talents, and accomplishments or activities. The school asserted that the list is not exhaustive, "and the factors are not of equal weight; moreover, no single factor is dispositive. Furthermore, no factor will confer admission on an academically unqualified applicant."[60]

From 1994 to 1998, the presumptive admission group was 89 percent white and the remainder were underrepresented students of color. The law school annually received an average of 2,000 applicants for 165 seats. All applicants that applied to the law school with a valid GPA and LSAT score were assigned an index score by the law school admission council. The index score is a combination of the LSAT and GPA. The committee sets an index score by which students fall within the admit or deny category. In 1994, white applicants with a 195 or higher index score were placed in the "presumptive admit category" and referred to the admissions committee. All other applicants were read by the dean of the law school for consideration to admit, deny or refer to the admissions committee. All the dean's decisions were also reviewed by the admissions coordinator for the Law School. In 1995 and 1996, the dean of the law school read most of the presumptive admission files. The admissions coordinator also reviewed the dean's decisions on the files. The dean did not participate in the admissions committee, which was a separate group of six professors and three students. The admissions committee would assign additional points (from 0 to 15) to applicants for consideration in making an offer of admission.

When Smith applied in 1994, her index score was 192, which placed her in the "presumptive" deny category. Smith was one of 94 applicants with a 192 index score. According to the law school, in 1994 the applicant pool was extraordinarily qualified. In the year that Smith applied, the law school experienced a record number of applicants (a total of 2,552), the largest it had ever experienced, producing an increase of qualified underrepresented students.

In 1994, 546 students were offered admission and 187 enrolled. In that year there were 664 applicants with index scores higher than Smith's index score of 192. There were also 292 candidates with an index score higher than Smith's who were denied admission. Of those 292, 281 were white and 11 were underrepresented students. That year there were 1,792 applicants with an index score at or below 192. There were 1,633 remaining applicants with an index score of 192 or lower, and they were all denied admission. The dean testified before the court that students were not considered for admission unless they had at least two diversity factors, which included race, foreign language skills, geography, advanced degrees, disabilities, business or military, public service, and unusual life experiences. The dean asserted that she did not keep track of the race of the applicants selected for admission under this category.

The dean read 2,140 of the 2,276 applicant files with index scores below the admission level. The dean referred, admitted or rejected these applicants. Dean Sandra Madrid that year admitted 11 applicants with "non-standard" index scores, and four were white. A total of 158 applicants had an index score of 195, and according to policy, Madrid referred some of them to the admissions committee and reviewed the rest. Of the 158 applicants, 136 were white and 22 were underrepresented applicants. The dean reviewed the 22 underrepresented students with index scores of 195 and higher, and the remaining 136 were sent over to the admissions committee. Upon review by the dean, she made an offer of admission to 18 of the underrepresented candidates. The admissions committee admitted 40 of the other 136 candidates. The plaintiffs objected to the separation of the 136 white candidates, and Smith assailed the high admit count of the underrepresented students. They claimed that the separation was evidence of racial discrimination. According to court documents, "Dean Madrid testified and the Court finds that this separate treatment of the 22 minority candidates was for the purpose of making an early decision on minority applicants who were extremely well qualified based solely on their high index scores. Madrid testified that the law school did not want to delay decision on these minority candidates because they might otherwise choose to attend another school."[61] While the institution offered the 22 well-qualified underrepresented candidates admission, only two candidates accepted, and the remainder accepted offers at other institutions. While the court had concerns with the handling of the 22 applicants with the index score of 195, all the files were read in concurrence with all other candidates scoring in similar categories and therefore were not isolated from comparison with other underrepresented applicants.

All three plaintiffs submitted personal statements with their applications. The application indicates that the personal statement is very important to the law school in assessing the whole student. In addition, in the personal statement, students are asked to articulate in their own words how they will contribute to the diversity of the law school based upon the criteria of diversity as described. Smith did not provide any additional information regarding her race and background or how she would enhance the diversity of the law school.

All applicants denied admission can seek an appeal from the law school. In their cases, all three plaintiffs choose not to appeal the law school's decision. The law school asserted that it did not use racial quotas or goals in its admissions process. Nor did it establish different cutoffs for the index scores of white applicants compared to underrepresented students of color. The court agreed and found that the establishment of index scores was used for all applicants and did not "systemically" exclude whites from access to seats nor insulate underrepresented applicants from comparison with whites. Lastly, the 136 white applicants referred to the admissions committee were not a violation of Smith's equal rights. All 136 applicants had higher index scores than Smith along with the 2 underrepresented applicants admitted. They were all highly qualified and had higher index scores than Smith. Thus, applicants referred to the admissions committee for review were more qualified than the applicants not referred and not all of those referred were offered admission. Thus, there were 169 white applicants referred to the admissions committee for review who were denied admission. That same year 142 underrepresented students were also admitted with a plus diversity factor calculated in their admission. Smith contends that race was the sole basis for their admission, thereby, discriminating against the plaintiffs. The court disagreed because all 169 applicants had higher index scores than Smith. The court found that 142 spaces given to underrepresented students under a race-neutral policy would have been reallocated to the 169 white applicants denied admission, meaning that Smith would not have been admitted.

When plaintiff Angela Rock applied in 1995, her index score was 196, making her a "presumptive admit" applicant. She, along with 252 applicants, fell within this category. Rock was one of 26 referred to the admissions committee for consideration. The committee that year was assigning scores to candidates ranging between 5 and 15. Four applicants were offered admission three of them received a score from the committee ranging from 11 to 14. They were residents, and one nonresident received a score of 15. Rock was given a score of 10 and placed on the waiting list. The admissions committee did not offer admission in 1995 to any candidate receiving a 10, resulting in Rock being denied admission. During that year, there were 18 Washington resident applicants with the same index score of 196 as Rock who were admitted. However, Rock was a "presumptive admit" in which race was not a factor in the decision making for presumptive admits that year. Rock's application was referred to the admissions committee for reasons other than race. The law school felt that Rock was lacking significant life experiences, had weak letters of recommendation, a weak personal statement and issues regarding specific grades. All of these issues resulted in her ranking of 10. The school did not believe that her ranking would have changed if the admissions committee had given any weight to race. Therefore, race did not play a role in her rejection.

In 1995, Dean Madrid was in charge of reviewing all applicants that fell below the presumptive admission level with oversight from the admissions coordinator. The dean offered admission to 152 applicants, which included 30 African Americans, 30 whites, 34 Latinos, 14 Native Americans, and 33 Asian candidates. The dean also denied admission to 65 African Americans, 332 Asians, 1,128 whites and 95 Latinos.

In 1996, the third plaintiff, Pyle, a Washington resident, applied for admission. That year the law school began using a two-digit index score ranging from 00 to 99. Pyle had an index score of 89. The Law School identified the "presumptive admit" score as resident applicants with an index score of 91 or higher and nonresident applicants with scores of 92 or higher. There were 275 candidates who met the criteria: 27 Asians, 242 whites and five Latinos. Twenty-three candidates were referred to the admission committee, one was Asian and the remainder were white. The admissions committee provided scores for these candidates ranging from 6 to 14 points. The admissions committee made offers to 11 whites. Pyle's application was not referred to the admissions committee, and he was denied admission after initial screening.

The dean reviewed 1,644 applicants below the presumptive admit level and made offers to 112 applicants and referred 290 applicants to the admission committee. Of the 114 the dean admitted, 41 were white, 16 Latinos, 32 Asians, 10 Native Americans, and 15 African Americans. The dean denied admission to 1,242 of the 1,644 applicants. Of the 290 applicants referred to the admissions committee, offers were made to 121 students. This included 99 whites, one African American, seven Latinos, 13 Asians, and one Native American.

The plaintiffs in all three cases argued that race was used as more than a plus factor in admitting underrepresented students of color over whites. Even though there were different scales of measurement for the three years in question, the plaintiffs' expert combined all five years (1994–1998). The witness focused all the equations around the use of race and not allowing for the other diversity factors which were used. For example, the school could not explain to the court if race was the prevailing factor of preference in admission. So how did 802 whites, who had lower scores than some underrepresented students, gain admission? The reality was that each year in question and during the five-year period, whites were admitted with equal or lesser scores than underrepresented students. The court found that the expert could not fully explain the claim of discriminatory racial preference. In addition, the court also found that race did not play a significant role for the applicants referred to the admissions committee because there were more qualified candidates who were not referred to the admission committee. According to court documents, for example, admission rates for the presumptive admission groups was the same as the admission rates for white applicants for all years in question. The admission rate for whites was 94.64 percent, and 94.19 percent for all applicants. Therefore, the expert witness could not clearly express or articulate that any of the plaintiffs would have been admitted to the law school had a race-neutral criteria been in place. The court found that race and "nonracial" factors were implemented by the law school in admitting a diverse student body for all years in question.

The court found that educational diversity is a compelling state interest. A diverse law school assists in better preparing students to participate in a diverse and democratic society. The law school's admissions process for the years in question was appropriate in establishing a quality legal education and experience through the exchange of ideas among students from diverse backgrounds.

The law school's admission process did resemble a "Harvard-type" process consistent with Bakke. "A Harvard-type admissions program treats each applicant as an individual in the admissions process. The applicant who loses out on the last available seat to another candidate receiving a 'plus' on the basis of ethnic background will not have been foreclosed from all consideration for that seat simply because he was not the right color or had the wrong surname. It would mean only that his combined qualifications, which may have included similar nonobjective factors, did not outweigh those of the other applicant. His qualifications would have been weighed fairly and competitively, and he would have no basis to complain of unequal treatment under the Fourteenth Amendment."[62] The Law School's consideration of race met the "Harvard" criteria established under Bakke and is consistent with constitutional mandates. On June 5, 2002, the court ruled that the University of Washington Law School did not violate the Fourteenth Amendment and the admissions program from 1994–1996 was narrowly tailored to achieve diversity in an area of compelling state interest.

The Gratz and Grutter Decisions

The two most relevant cases regarding affirmative action and college admissions are the Gratz and Grutter cases. The author views these two cases as the "Bakke of the new millennium" since this was the first time since the Bakke decision that the U.S. Supreme Court tackled the issue of race and college admissions. Both cases involved the University of Michigan and its affirmative action programs.

The University of Michigan cases took six years to get to the U.S. Supreme Court, starting in 1997:

Oct. 14, 1997 Jennifer Gratz and Patrick Hamacher file lawsuit against President Bollinger, the University of Michigan and the Undergraduate College of Literature, Arts and Sciences. The case went before the Eastern Michigan U.S. District Court.

Dec. 3, 1997 Barbara Grutter files lawsuit against Bollinger and University of Michigan Law School Admissions. The case went before the Eastern Michigan U.S. District Court.

Aug. 10, 1999 Both cases were delayed for one year as the court of appeals reversed previous rulings in both cases and allowed intervention to take place by civil rights organizations and interested parties.

Oct. 16, 2000 Twenty Fortune 500 Companies file amicus briefs in the Gratz case in support of the University of Michigan.

Dec. 13, 2000 Judge Patrick J. Duggan rules that diversity is a compelling state interest and that the university's current undergraduate program meets the Bakke standards. However, the admission program from 1995–1998 was ruled unconstitutional. Appeals were filed in the sixth Circuit Court of Appeals.

March 27, 2001 Judge Bernard Friedman rules that the law school's policy weighs race too heavily and if the law permitted the use of race-conscious admission, Michigan's use of it would still remain unconstitutional. The judge issued an injunction prohibiting the school from using race. The court of appeals issued a stay which allowed the law school to continue its admissions process while the case was on appeal.

October 16, 2001 The Sixth Circuit Court of Appeals sets oral arguments for Dec. 6, 2001.

May 14, 2002 The Sixth Circuit Court of Appeals found the University of Michigan Law School's admission policy was constitutional and struck down Friedman's March 27, 2001, decision. The ruling was derived from Bakke, and the court found that the law school met the constitutional test of a compelling state interest in maintaining diversity.

August 9, 2002 The Center for Individual Rights filed a petition to the U.S. Supreme Court to review the law school case.

Oct. 2002 Plaintiffs in both cases file petitions to the Supreme Court before judgment.

October 29, 2002 The university files a petition in response to Gratz and Grutter to the U.S. Supreme Court.

December 2002 The U.S. Supreme Court agrees to hear the Gratz and Grutter cases.

February 2003 Over 100 amicus briefs are filed with the Supreme Court in support of the university.

April 2003 Oral arguments were heard by the Supreme Court.

June 23, 2003 The Supreme Court ruling upheld diversity as a compelling state interest in higher education in Gratz and Grutter. Race is upheld as a plus factor in college admissions. However, the court found the university's 150-point scale in its undergraduate program was not narrowly tailored and was unconstitutional.

July 18, 2003 Grutter files a petition with the Supreme Court to rehear her case.

August 25, 2003 The Supreme Court denies the petition to rehear the Grutter case.

August 2003 The university unveils its new undergraduate admissions policy, which includes more personalized individual review without a point system.

Gratz v. Bollinger *(1997)*

Petitioners Jennifer Gratz and Patrick Hamacher, two white students, applied for admission to the University of Michigan's College of Literature, Science, and the Arts in 1995 and 1997. While the university considered both students to be within qualified range, both were denied admission. Gratz and Hamacher filed a lawsuit based solely on the 20 points given by the university to underrepresented students of color. They claimed that the university's use of racial preferences in undergraduate admissions violated the equal protection clause of the Fourteenth Amendment and Title VI of the Civil Rights Act of 1964. As petitioners they sought compensatory and punitive damages for past violations.

The Office of Undergraduate Admission had considered African Americans, Latinos and Native Americans as underrepresented students, and the university said that every qualified applicant from these groups is admitted. The office used several guidelines for admission, such as high school grades, quality of the high school, standardized test scores, geography, alumni relationships, leadership, curriculum strength, and race. Those guidelines changed frequently during the period of the litigation. What the lawsuit focused on was the guidelines in place when the plaintiffs applied. These guidelines included a 150-point scale that the university employed for all qualified students. The guidelines provided 20 automatic points to underrepresented students of color, an automatic 20 points to recruited athletes, 4 points for alumni relationships, 16 points for geography, 20 points for low-income status, 10 points for attending a top high school, and 20 points to students that overcame a tremendous hardship.

Gratz had aspirations to become a doctor and as a resident of Michigan had always wanted to attend the University of Michigan, so much so that it was the only school she applied to. When she was denied admission she was devastated. She ended up attending the University of Michigan, Dearborn campus. Gratz graduated in 1999 and is currently a project manager for a software company in Oceanside, California. Patrick Hamacher, who applied to U-Michigan in 1996, graduated from Michigan State University in 2001 with a B.A. in public administration and is an accountant for a parks and recreation agency in Michigan. Both plaintiffs were recruited and represented by the Center for Individual Rights. CIR is a nonprofit organization that represents free of charge the legal interests of individuals whose civil rights it believes have been violated. As discussed in Chapter Three, CIR is widely known as an anti-affirmative action organization.

Grutter v. Bollinger *(1997)*

Barbara Grutter applied to the University of Michigan Law School in 1996. She was denied admission and filed suit alleging that she had been discriminated against based upon her race in violation of the Fourteenth Amendment and Title VI of the Civil Rights Act of 1964 because the law school uses race as a "predominant factor" giving applicants with similar credentials from majority racial groups less consideration. Grutter, a white female, felt that with a 3.8 grade point average and a 161 LSAT score, she was well qualified for admission. However, the law school follows an admissions policy tailored after the Bakke decision. The law school focuses on the students' academic ability coupled with a flexible assessment of their talents, broad background experience, undergraduate school of attendance, and potential for success. Admissions officers review and evaluate the whole student, looking at everything in the file, which includes the personal statement, letters of recommendation, an essay on how the student will contribute to the graduate program, undergraduate grade point average and LSAT score. The law school does not define diversity based in terms of race and does not restrict the types of diversity contributions eligible for "substantial weight." The law school does commit to diversity with special attention to underrepresented students of color by enrolling a critical mass of students of color.[63] It is this critical mass that was criticized as a quota system favoring underrepresented students over whites.

Once again, the Fourteenth Amendment and Title VI of the 1964 Civil Rights Act are at the forefront of a court case involving race and admissions. In the Gratz and Grutter cases, the questions before the court were under the equal protection clause: (1) Is the goal of a race-conscious policy important enough to constitute a "compelling government interest"? and (2) Is the policy "narrowly tailored" to advance as a "compelling government interest"?[64]

On June 23, 2003, the U.S. Supreme Court handed down its decisions in both the Gratz and Grutter cases. The court affirmed that race-conscious admission does meet the strict scrutiny test and that it is constitutional for a university to use race as a criteria. As the court articulated, colleges and universities do have a compelling interest in obtaining a diverse student body. The court upheld the law school admissions policy and struck down the university's undergraduate policy for not being narrowly tailored. In the Grutter case, the court concluded that there was a degree of deference and that an institution had academic freedom, within constitutional limits, to use race-conscious policies.

The Grutter opinion confirmed that student body diversity held educational benefits, is vital in reducing racial stereotypes and will help develop a racially tolerant society. The court stated student body "diversity helps to break racial stereotypes, and diminishing the force of such stereotypes is both a crucial part of an institution's mission, and one that it cannot accomplish with only token numbers of minority students. Just as growing up in a particular region or having particular professional experiences is likely to affect an individual's views, so too is one's own, unique experience of being a racial minority in a society, like our own, in which race unfortunately still matters.[65]

Narrow Tailoring

A critical evaluative component in the Gratz and Grutter decisions fell under the concept of narrow tailoring of strict scrutiny. This is where the court evaluated the connection between a compelling interest and race-conscious admissions employed to adhere to that interest. Narrow tailoring encompasses key elements such as: "A race and ethnicity-conscious admission or financial aid criteria that is narrowly tailored to further educational diversity is a policy that is necessary to promote the institution's educational interest in diversity; is more effective than any race and ethnicity neutral means of pursuing the same interest; in the case of admission, uses race and ethnicity as no more than 'plus' factors and does not use racial and ethnic quotas or racially and ethnically segregated admission processes; uses race and ethnicity flexibly; does not impose undue burdens on individuals who do not benefit from the racial and ethnic classification, and; is subject to periodic review by the institution to determine whether the continued use of race and ethnicity is necessary."[66]

The court used the narrow tailoring test guideline from Bakke. The test must fit the issues raised by the use of race to admit a diverse student body. In other words how was the admissions policy being implemented that gave validity to the use of race? In developing the narrow tailoring test, the court came up with five areas, and they applied all five to the University of Michigan's admission policies.

COMPETITIVE REVIEW. The first was competitive review, when the court implemented prohibition of quotas as outlined by Bakke. In examining if the school was implementing a full individualized review of all applicants, justices looked closely at the school's use of race. If race is used as a plus factor in an admissions policy, even if it offers a larger weight, it does not make it a quota. However, quotas are different from goals. A quota is a fixed number that is reserved for a group of applicants. A goal is a good faith effort to admit a range of particular qualified applicants, while ensuring that each candidate competes among other qualified applicants. According to the court, a goal that seeks underrepresented racial enrollments beyond a specified number but does not establish a "fixed" number or percentage of applicants admitted is an appropriate objective for universities.

INDIVIDUALIZED CONSIDERATION. Second, flexible individualized consideration must exist in a narrowly tailored test. The court examined both schools' admissions policies to investigate whether a race-conscious policy was narrowly tailored to allow for flexible and individualized consideration of all applicants. According to the court, when using race as a "plus" factor in admissions, a university's admissions program must remain flexible enough to ensure that each applicant is evaluated as an individual and not in a way that makes an applicant's race or ethnicity the defining feature of his or her application. The importance of this individualized consideration in the context of a race-conscious admissions program is paramount.[67] The court was clear that while race can be used, it cannot be the deciding factor; and while institutions have the ability to imply qualifications, they must consider nonracial factors to ensure that all factors that contribute to a diverse student body are meaningful in the final decision. In the Grutter case, the court endorsed the law school admissions policy because it weighed diversity factors outside of race that make a real difference for white students as well as students of color.

With regard to the Gratz case, the court felt that an assigned "automatic" number based on race was not a flexible individualized consideration. As the court articulated, a flexible admissions program does not contemplate that any single characteristic automatically ensures a specific and identifiable contribution to a university's diversity. Instead, each characteristic of a particular applicant is to be considered in assessing the applicant's entire application. It was the automatic assignment of a set of points based on race that the court found lacked the appropriate flexibility to meet the narrow tailoring test. Assignment of points can work; it becomes problematic if they are automatic and set at a high mark. The fact that every single qualified underrepresented student of color was admitted indicated that the 20 points provided a guarantee that should not have existed.

The university made the argument that 20 points was not the deciding factor and that the 150-point scale assisted with the large volume of applications they received for admission. The court's response was that "administrative convenience" as a mechanical approach over an individual one to address the volume of applications is not synonymous with constitutionality.

In the Gratz decision, Justices David H. Souter and Ruth Bader Ginsburg, in their dissenting opinion, raised the issue that there were substantive points assigned to nonminority applicants, including attendance at a predominantly minority high school, attendance at a top high school in the area, or socioeconomic disadvantage. All of the points for these categories far outweigh the 20 points applied to underrepresented students. Further, Souter argued that the fact that every qualified underrepresented student was admitted could merely be a reflection of how few had applied. Ginsburg's dissent was weighed from the current disparities. She argued that a racial caste system exists in this country, which still has vestiges of racial disparities in poverty, unemployment, health care and neighborhood schools that remain racially isolated. "Bias, both conscious and unconscious, reflecting traditional and unexamined habits of thought, keeps up barriers that must come down if equal opportunity and nondiscrimination are ever genuinely to become this country's law and practice."[68] Ginsburg's interpretation is that the Constitution is both color-conscious and color-blind. For that reason the Fourteenth Amendment, under equal protection of the laws, gives government the decision-making authority to appropriately differentiate between policies of exclusion and inclusion in implementing policies of equity.

Ginsburg, like Souter, found the undergraduate program in the Gratz case to be constitutional. In her interpretation of the admissions process, she observed that all students involved in the 150-point scale are qualified because they meet the eligibility requirements for admission, and that has not been disputed. Like other institutions, the University of Michigan is a selective institution, meaning it has many more applicants than it can accommodate. Since these students are qualified, the special consideration the institution affords underrepresented students of color is appropriate as these are the same groups that historically have been deterred and forced into inferior status. Today, and for centuries, the dominant group has far outnumbered applicants of underrepresented groups in applying to college, and consideration of race will not vastly diminish the opportunities for admission of white applicants. Both Souter and Ginsburg commended the university for its frankness in outlining the plus factor it provided to underrepresented groups and for its ability to clearly articulate how qualified students were judged. However, their arguments were not successful in convincing the majority of the court.

Justices Clarence Thomas and Antonin Scalia were the only two members who disagreed with the majority holding that diversity constitutes a compelling state interest. In Scalia's dissent, he asserted that diversity is a lesson of life, not of law; and diversity is not an educational benefit on which students will be tested or that will be reflected on their transcript. Diversity is a life lesson, the same life lesson "taught to people three feet shorter and twenty years younger than the full-grown adults at the University of Michigan Law School."[69] Thomas agreed only in part with the court. Part of his concurrence was that the use of race in admission will cease in 25 years and thus the expansion of the use of race will be unlawful. Thomas asserted that the "majority" has placed a 25 year limit on affirmative action, but this is an aspiration and suggestion by Justice Sandra Day O'Connor with the hope that in time, race-conscious admissions will no longer be needed. Thomas primarily dissented based on his belief that blacks can achieve without the meddling of the university.[70] You can be certain that Scalia and Thomas' opinions will be used in future litigation on this matter.

RACE-NEUTRAL ALTERNATIVES. Third is race-neutral alternatives as a requirement of narrow tailoring. However, it is critical that race-neutral alternatives are appropriate and work for the goals the institution has in selecting a diverse student body. For example, race-neutral alternatives like percentage plans and high school ranking are not workable for graduate programs and preclude individualized review, so this criterion may not work for all colleges and universities.

UNDUE BURDEN. Fourth, undue burden on nonminorities is a requirement of narrowly tailored programs. Those from the dominant group must
not be discriminated against in favor of underrepresented students of
color. To be narrowly tailored, race-conscious admissions programs must
not unduly burden individuals who are not members of the favored racial
and ethnic groups.[71] A fair and flexible admissions policy that employs
racial and nonracial guidelines will allow underrepresented students to be
competitive with white students, does not create an undue burden, and is
deemed constitutional. The law school met this criteria under all guidelines. The undergraduate school did not meet that criteria under the points
scale, yet it did in all other areas.

TIME LIMIT. Fifth, a time limit is a requirement of the narrow tailor
test. While a college or university may hold the interest of a diverse student body, its ability to use race to accomplish that goal is set by a time
limit. According to the court in the Grutter case, the requirement that all
race-conscious admissions programs have a termination point assures all
citizens that the deviation from the norm of equal treatment of all racial
and ethnic groups is a temporary matter, a measure taken in the service
of the goal of equality itself.[72]

The Supreme Court held that the use of race is one of several plus
factors that can be used in comprising a diverse student body. The University of Michigan Law School passed the constitutional narrowly tailored test. In addition, the court also found the Law School's goal of
admitting a critical mass of underrepresented students was constitutional
and did not amount to a quota system. Specifically, a critical mass is permitted so long as it does not advance diversity based on fixed numbers or
percentages. Critical mass is a goal institutions use to obtain a desired
number of qualified underrepresented candidates beyond specific numbers. However, in the Gratz case, the court held that affirmative action is
a compelling interest that legitimizes the use of race in admissions. The
court found that the manner and structure of the College of Literature,
Science, and the Arts did not meet the narrowly tailored standard with
regard to the distribution of an automatic fixed 20 points for underrepresented students of color out of 150 total possible points.

The court's decision has provided a clear opportunity for the use of
race-conscious policies, but it is unclear if those policies expand beyond
admissions. The other programs pertinent to access in higher education
are financial aid, recruitment, outreach, retention and scholarships. Questions with regard to other policies beyond admissions will remain. For
example, can an outreach program pursue and seem to attract solely under-

represented students of color? Are scholarships based upon race constitutional? For example, in the case of *Podberesky v. Kirwan* in 1994, the
court ruled a race-conscious scholarship failed to comply with the strict
scrutiny rule. The U.S. Department of Education also has a policy guide
on programs of this nature that many institutions use. However, if these
policies comply with the Court's narrow tailoring test and its criteria mentioned earlier, then its use could be deemed constitutional. It is unclear at
this point if that would ever be an issue since the use of race was ruled a
plus factor. While the court was silent on these specific issues, it would be
left open to future legal interpretation of how race-conscious programs
would be judged after Grutter and Gratz.

The court's majority support for the need to value diversity in education is seen as a compelling interest in support of diversity in other areas
beyond the scope of higher education. Specifically, in elementary and secondary public education, the court cited *Brown v. Board of Education* as
valid in pursuing the need for public education to prepare students for
work in a diverse democratic society. The desegregation mandate in Brown
makes a compelling argument and a solid case for integrated schools, but
K-12 education does not enjoy some of the same decision-making freedoms as higher education. Students in K-12 who are unable to gain access
to their school of choice based upon space or district assignment do have
the right to attend another school.

Before the Grutter and Gratz decision, many courts addressing educational diversity in elementary and secondary schools produced a mixed
bag of decisions, with some using the desegregation mandate of Brown and
the compelling interest argument of Bakke in reaching conclusions on
school district assignment policies by race. While some assignment policies have been struck down, others have remained intact. For example, in
June 2003, the Washington Supreme Court upheld the district policy on
school assignments within the Seattle School District Once again, this may
remain an issue of legal interpretation for the courts. While the Michigan
cases address legal questions regarding the use of race, like Bakke, we can
anticipate there will be additional gray areas open for legal interpretation
by the courts and state legislatures.

In the conclusion of both cases, history was made, once again, when
the court made it clear that colleges and universities have constitutional
boundaries within which they can implement race-conscious admission
policies. Like the Bakke decision, the court was clear that automatically or
fixed assigned numerical benefits and quotas on the basis of race are unconstitutional. An institution cannot use administrative convenience as its
defense to a fixed numerical scale. Policies that use race are constitutional

so long as they are flexible, comply with some race-neutral alternatives, do not create undue burdens, and have a time limit. Justice O'Connor, who gave the opinion of the court in Grutter, indicated in her decision that she believed that 25 years from now affirmative action should not be needed. She set a dangerous time limit on equality when she ruled: "There's a compelling state interest in having diverse student bodies at public universities. But race-conscious admissions policies must be limited in time. The court expects that 25 years from now, the use of racial preferences will no longer be necessary to further the interest approved today."

Twenty-Five Years for Affirmative Action

While 25 years was a suggestion, there are many who look at that statement by O'Connor as a fundamental time frame. Opponents of affirmative action have seen this as a structured timeline and goal to eliminate all elements of race-conscious decisions in college and university admissions. Now 50 years after the historic *Brown v. Board of Education* decisions, our country is still dealing with school segregation. Today, more than 25 percent of elementary and secondary school students in the country attend schools with nonwhite majority enrollment ranging between 80 and 100 percent.

A recent study released by the Lewis Mumford Center for Comparative Urban and Regional Research show a continued existence of racial divide. After examining segregation in a yearlong project called the Metro Boston Equity Initiative, the report found that after three decades of Boston challenging school desegregation battles, almost half of the white children in the city attend private segregated schools while most students of color have little, if no access, to suburban school resources and opportunities. The research found that most of the children of color, predominantly African American and Latino, attended Boston public schools concentrated in pockets of poverty and with reduced resources. In contrast, the suburban schools were predominantly white. White children have almost entirely left the city, and those who remain live in increasingly advantaged city neighborhoods; half of them attend private schools, according to the study. The vast majority of them live in the suburbs, and they grow up in neighborhoods and attend schools that are typically 90 percent white and remarkably affluent.[73]

One thing history has taught us is that the United States has a slow pace of change. For example, 100 years after the Emancipation Proclamation, Martin Luther King Jr. led the historic 1963 march to Washington in search of equality for African Americans. When half a century was not enough to desegregate the schools and a century of so-called freedom did not provide equity for slaves, can we now expect just 25 years to end the need for affirmative action?

According to Dr. Mark Fogel, president of the University of Vermont, by 2028, we need to be out of the affirmative action business. That time limit constitutes a call for urgent and extraordinary efforts. To win the race with that ticking clock, we have to bring American society to the point at which diversity can be attained through admissions processes that give no conscious attention to diversity itself. We need to ensure that all students and new Americans from around the globe have equal access to strong and effective preparation for postsecondary education.[74]

While diversity has been ruled to be a compelling state interest under the Fourteenth Amendment, this country still faces challenges. The United States still faces a crisis of racial inequality that has displaced numbers of underrepresented students of color at the elementary and secondary school level, and that displacement greatly reduces the pool of individuals eligible to compete for admission to elite universities. This result has provided an unfair advantage to whites as a group, who have benefited over the centuries from the racialized inequities of economic and social opportunity in the country. This timeline is counter to the court's own decision, for even the court stated in the Grutter case that "race unfortunately still matters." This continued systemic inequity, from birth, makes consideration of race not only relevant but vital to public universities in today's society. If 25 years is our new time frame, public education and the communities it serves need to come together with a sense of urgency to maintain equity and the integrity of the Fourteenth Amendment and Title VI of the 1964 Civil Rights Act if we are going to eradicate racial disparities in America. A true democracy involves effective participation by individuals of all racial backgrounds if the dream of one nation is to become a reality.

You must be the change you wish to see in the world.

— Mahatma Gandhi

5. Inequities in the System

If we are going to level the college admissions playing field, then it must be level for everyone. In conducting research for the California Senate Select Committee on Higher Education Admissions and Outreach, I discovered glaring discrepancies. Today, there are fairness problems within the whole system.

College Elitism

Basically, college elitism has to do with colleges that select their applicants based on the amount of prestige they will add to the university. This often boils down to what class of students are admitted. Often this does not always increase racial diversity. At America's Ivy League colleges, for instance, some groups of the American population have been severely underrepresented in the student population for over 30 years.

Jonathan Tilove of the Newhouse News Service in his special report on "Race in America" points out that the subject is touchy and until now undebated in spite of its three-decade history. Does it really matter? It does.

Sociologist E. Digby Baltzell, in his book The *American Business Aristocracy*, indicated that 50 percent of the secretaries of state from the beginning of the republic through the twentieth century have been graduates of Harvard. The Business Week 1000, an annual compilation of America's top 1,000 CEOs, routinely demonstrates that about 100 of these executives are Harvard graduates, approximately 80 are from the University of Pennsylvania's Wharton School of Business and Finance and 50 percent of the total are from 10 elite universities. Just half the country's business leaders come from less than 0.5 percent of the nation's colleges. Similarly, presidential cabinets, the U.S. Supreme Court justices and the judiciary as a whole are graduates of the choice universities.[1]

Colleges act like a private world unto themselves when they have certain admissions criteria unique solely to their institution. Some universities require additional exams for admission that no other universities require. For most students this is an additional gatekeeper to access. For example, the University of California requires the SAT II, a subject matter exam, in addition to the SAT I, and is the only public university in California that does so.

Advanced Placement Courses

Advanced Placement courses are essentially a good idea gone bad. The Advance Placement program (known as the Kenyon Plan) began in 1951 to give outstanding high school students a chance to advance their knowledge in 11 subjects including Latin, French, chemistry, physics, biology and math. In 1954, the Kenyon Plan officially became the Advanced Placement Program of the College Board and now offers 33 courses to over a million students each year. This gives students a chance to follow their interests beyond what conventional high school courses offer. The problem doesn't lie with the courses themselves but occurs because schools give an extra grade point for completion of these courses. For example, if a student gets an A in A.P. History, that A is worth 5 points instead of 4. Under the conventional grading system schools give 4 points for an A, 3 for a B, 2 for a C, 1 for a D, and none for an F.

The Big Imbalance

Before A.P. grading, a student who received all A's in high school came out with a 4.0 grade point average. But with the extra points allowed for A.P. courses, a student could end up with a 4.2 or above. Also, an A.P. student who got a few B's could end up with the same grade point average as a student who received all A's but didn't take any A.P. courses. What difference does this make? Probably not much if all students have an equal chance. But they don't, because not all high schools offer Advanced Placement courses or the same number as other schools.

Schools in affluent districts offer up to 33 A.P. classes in 14 subjects, but high schools in high poverty areas cannot reasonably compete with this. For instance, San Francisco's Balboa High School, in a low-income minority* neighborhood, offers very few A.P. courses, while Lowell High

---

*Minority and underrepresented students of color are used to identify Latino, African American, and Native American students.

School, a predominantly Asian, college-preparatory school, offers students the choice of 21 A.P. courses and eight honors courses that qualify for extra grade points at universities.

Even at Lowell, with all its A.P. courses, there is still a problem. The students can't always take the A.P. courses they want. In fact the school holds a lottery in high demand courses to see who can take the course and who can't. That means that even at Lowell some students lose out. Studies by the Tomás Rivera Policy Institute and the Public Policy Institute of California reveal a strong correlation between fewer A.P. course offerings and high minority enrollment schools.[2]

The Problem

This still wouldn't make much difference if the universities didn't consider grade points over 4.0 for admission but they do. That means that at some schools a student with all A's from a high school that doesn't offer many A.P. courses just can't compete for admission.

A good example of this is Faten Abushaer, a graduate of Balboa High, who always dreamed of going to the University of California at Berkeley. Despite the fact that she received mostly A's in high school and had taken A.P. calculus and physics, she was turned down. The reason was that students from more affluent high schools had taken more A.P. courses. Says Abushaer: "When a high school offers few A.P. courses, as Balboa does, it limits the student's ability to get into a quality college. This doesn't seem fair."

Of course it isn't fair. What it means is that students entering a high school like Balboa will be rejected at the elite colleges before they have taken one high school course. Wade Curry of the College Board in an *LA Times* article asserted: "The real problem in terms of access is that about one-fourth of the high schools don't have enough A.P. classes. Schools will offer two or three courses and not go beyond it."

According to the National Center for Public Policy and Higher Education, 42.6 percent of college freshmen have not taken any A.P. courses in high school. Some states require public high schools to offer A.P. courses. In South Carolina and Virginia, public schools must offer at least two A.P. courses. In Indiana, each school must offer an A.P. math and an A.P. science course. The cost is at an estimated $76 to 80 a student to take the A.P. exams— money that some families can't afford. As a result, some states are now picking up this cost.

The real purpose of A.P. courses is to increase the student's knowledge in a field and to give students the confidence they need to do well in college. Some students, however, have made a college admissions game out of it, taking A.P. courses just to beef up their transcripts. Bob Laird, the University of California's retired director of undergraduate admissions, says that if A.P. courses didn't carry additional grade points, strong students who are less sure of themselves than straight-A students are likely to shy away from taking A.P. courses just to protect their grade point average. Adds Christine Turner, a senior, "Pretty much the reason I am taking A.P. courses is to get into college, nothing more." Of course if A.P. courses aren't available at your high school, even that doesn't work.

The Colleges' Reaction

Most colleges recognize that the system is not perfect. As a result, community colleges are now offering A.P. courses to help make up for a high schools' deficiencies. These courses receive the same bonus points as A.P. and honors classes. Many four-year colleges are also reaching out through computers to prepare more high school students for college. Virtual high schools, on the World Wide Web, with help from colleges and universities, have sprung up as a way for college-bound students to take A.P. courses. Illinois, Maryland, Michigan, New Mexico, Utah, and West Virginia all have started virtual high schools. Florida, Indiana, Kentucky, Massachusetts, Nebraska and California also have programs in place.

Most schools have sought out alternatives. South Dakota participates in a program offering online A.P. courses through APEX Learning, a private company that provides online A.P. courses to states and schools. APEX Learning courses are standards-based curriculum that offer one-on-one instruction from teachers through interactive multimedia.[3] On average about 116 students in 31 schools across South Dakota participate in this program.

According to Jamey Fitzpatrick, vice president of development and education policy at the Michigan Virtual University, "I think it is just a matter of time before every state in the country deploys some sort of statewide virtual program in the K-12 arena." The Michigan program started in fall 2000 with 12 A.P. courses. While this is a step in the right direction, with the program dramatically increasing student access, in practice, neither the schools or the students find it a perfect solution. The high schools or the colleges still need to pay for the programs. Educators find that many high-school students lack the motivation and discipline to work through the self-paced courses and that some lack academic language proficiency to complete the courses, causing the dropout rate to be high in some courses.[4]

Lisa Hansen, the A.P. coordinator at Roosevelt High School in Sioux Falls, S.D., stresses: "We need to spend more time mentoring individual students. Two of the four students at Roosevelt who started the program ended up dropping the courses." According to Mary Gohring at Wessington Springs High School in South Dakota, "Only one of the three students who started taking an online Advanced Placement course is likely to finish that course."[5]

The other solution is for colleges to level the playing field by not giving an extra grade point for completing an A.P. course. Colleges are reluctant to do this. But civil rights organizations now complain the policy is unfair and probably unconstitutional. The ACLU in California filed suit against the University of California charging that white students are more likely to gain admission than African American, Filipino, Latino, and low-income students because the schools attended by minority students offer fewer A.P. courses. This suit was settled out of court, and the settlement requires that the University of California make public specified records regarding UC Berkeley's undergraduate admissions procedures and outcome.

In answer to this, the University of California Board of Regents considered cutting the bonus points offered for the completion of A.P. courses. The proposal was rejected. Regent Ward Connerly says "If you want to go big time, you're going to have to take these courses." Connerly believes that cutting the A.P. bonus point would indicate that the UC system was reducing the standards to make it easier for African American and Latino kids to get in. "What we want to say," explains Connerly, "is, here is the bar, and we know you can make it." Other schools across the country have expressed similar reactions.[6]

This is not the end of it. Until colleges solve the problem of the inequities created by the disparity of A.P. courses, it is difficult to say that the playing field is actually leveled. At the moment, students attending the more affluent high schools have a distinct advantage in gaining entry to the better schools. This is a problem that affirmative action had helped alleviate. Without it, there is still a problem.

Inferior Inner City Schools

Many African Americans, Latinos and Native Americans attend inner city schools— schools that are ill prepared to get them ready to go to college and compete with students from more affluent schools. Students in these inner-city schools have to make do with out-of-date textbooks, fewer resources and substandard school libraries. The schools offer fewer college preparation courses, less qualified and less effective teachers and fewer counselors than suburban schools. In addition, many inner-city schools are deteriorating, with leaky roofs, peeling walls and run-down grounds.[7]

Overall, few inner-city high school students are being prepared for college. Often the students who say they are headed to college are advised to take only two years of math when most colleges require three. Wendy Purham, formerly a student at Jean Baptiste Point DuSable High School in Chicago, almost gave up on herself when the principal discouraged her from trying to become valedictorian. Her guidance counselor, who wouldn't include her in trips to college campuses, did, too. But, on June 9, 2000, she read her valedictory poem to the DuSable graduates.

Dr. Lenzy Wallace, assistant dean for the School of Business at South Carolina State University, feels inner-city schools haven't changed much since he went to high school. As a high school student, Wallace was told not to take college preparation classes because he would only end up pushing a broom. While nobody says this anymore, the attitude of the teachers is often the same. In addition, often when the students take the required courses, the material on the placement exam hasn't been covered in the courses.

High schools in poor urban areas provide less access to college preparatory programs, making the college-going rate lowest for minority students. According to the Education Trust (2002), a Washington based research organization, 50 percent of white high school students are enrolled in the college prep track, while fewer than 30 percent of low-income high school students and just 35 percent of Latino and 43 percent of African American high school students are enrolled in college preparatory courses.

The problem is that many states provide less money to districts of high poverty and serving larger numbers of minority students. These districts have a greater need to provide the basics to a larger number of at-risk students and students with disabilities. The higher cost of special education services means they need additional funding to meet the same academic standards. An Education Trust (2003) report, using data from the U.S. Department of Education, found that nationwide, the top 25 percent of school districts with high poverty rates receive less funding than the bottom 25 percent.[8] The case was the same for school districts with high enrollments of underrepresented minority children. In 28 states the district with the largest number of minority students received less funding. This pattern was apparent nationwide. New York, California, and Texas, three of the largest states with some of the highest populations of underrepresented groups, are apart of the list of 28 states. For example, in California, funding for districts with fewer minority students is $6,233, and for districts with the highest number of minority students is $5,652, a difference of $581. In New York the funding gap is an egregious $2,073 with districts with the least number of minority students receiving $9,283 and those with the highest receiving $7,210.[9]

At Broad Acres Elementary School in Montgomery County, Maryland, English is a second language for most students. Teachers seldom talk to the children about attending college, and when teachers asked second-graders what they wanted to be when they grew up, the kids answered mechanic, pizza deliveryman and bus driver. At nearby Broad Acres Elementary School, almost all the students are low income. The test scores at this school have declined to where the state is about to take it over. Contrast these two schools with Burning Tree Elementary School in affluent Bethesda (also in Montgomery County). All third-graders have studied algebra and have discussed college and are exposed to classical music.

In the poverty-stricken schools in Montgomery County, however, students do not have access to classical music, and the discussions revolve around "Ricki Lake " or "Jerry Springer" shows.

There is another side to this, however. Every year, Thomas Jefferson High School for Science and Technology in Fairfax County, Virginia, boasts more National Merit Scholarship semifinalists than any school in the nation. The Ivy League offers admission to at least 25 percent of its graduates. Says School Superintendent Daniel A. Domenech: "We have a substantial minority community in Fairfax County, and many minority students are very bright and capable, they just are not taking advantage of the opportunity that a school like Jefferson has to offer." The problem seems to be that the teen culture in the county has created an anti-intellectual attitude that prevents middle-schoolers from wanting to leave their friends to attend an "egghead" school.

Inferior Teachers

Children with challenges like these need superior teachers. William Sanders, developer of the added-value assessment while at the University of Tennessee, stresses that of all the factors he studied, ethnicity, location and poverty, none is as important for a student as an effective teacher. Norm-referenced tests at Tennessee University show that a teacher's concern, their high expectations and role modeling are important to student learning. Sanders discovered students who are unlucky enough to have a succession of poor teachers are virtually doomed to the educational cellar.

Sanders also found that three consecutive years of the least effective teachers in grades three to five yielded math scores from the 35th to the 45th percentile. Conversely three straight years of the most–effective teachers resulted in scores at the 85th to 95th percentile.[10]

Stresses Peter Martinez of the John D. and Catherine T. MacArthur Foundation: "With notable exceptions, predominantly black and Latino schools produce valedictorians who don't do well on standardized tests because these schools are more likely to have 'low performing' teachers who do not challenge bright students and offer 'less rigorous' curricula."

Unfortunately, with some exceptions, the inner-city schools get the bottom of the barrel. This is because these schools, which serve poor and minority children, have such limited funds for teacher salaries. Urban schools tend to have higher teacher absenteeism, higher teacher turnover and a higher percentage of substitute teachers compared to other schools. These schools must function with more new and uncertified teachers than do the more affluent suburban schools.[11]

Research in Texas shows that in schools with large African American and Latino student enrollment, a high percentage of the teachers failed the state competency exams. In Chicago inner-city schools, more than 40 percent of the tested teachers failed the state exams. In addition, a large percentage of teachers in low-income secondary schools do not have a college major in the subject they are teaching in high school. In schools with the highest minority enrollment, only about 50 percent hold a credential or a degree in the subject matter they are teaching. Students taking math in these schools will more often than not be taught by a teacher with a home economics or English major rather than math. Physics students in these schools have a 56 percent chance of having a teacher who majored in some other subject. The same holds true in English. Often, teachers teaching out of their major have little interest in the subject taught. They are just there to get a paycheck. How in the world can students taught under these circumstances expect to compete for college admissions with students who have much better teachers fully qualified in their subject?[12]

Inner-city schools often are faced with a substitution problem. That is, the regular teacher can often be absent 35 to 50 percent of the time, requiring a substitute for the class. Some classes never have a permanent teacher. Imagine what chaos this causes when a class often has someone new every week or sometimes every day. There is no continuity in the subject matter and no consistency. Students often have difficulty understanding just what they are trying to study. At Northwest Middle School in Chicago, the school never found a permanent teacher the entire school year for a seventh-grade class. Eva, a sixth-grader, spent four months in a classroom with a succession of substitutes after the regular instructor quit in early December. Says Eva: "I was angry because we wasted a whole semester."[13]

Central city schools suffer from far greater teacher shortages than do suburban or rural districts. It is easy to see why students in these schools have an obstacle thrown in their way in their quest to get into college. In fact, the single greatest source of educational inequality is in the dispro-portionate exposure of poor and minority students— those students who fill inner-city schools— to less trained and experienced teachers.[14]

And under new federal regulations like that of No Child Left Behind, some states are not accurately reporting the number of qualified teachers. The problem is that federal law requires that all states have highly qualified teachers by 2005, but the law does not penalize states if they do not. Cou-pled with inconsistent reporting criteria from state to state, the outcome is a lack of functional data ripe with deception. With inaccurate data you cannot address the problem if you do not know it exists and at what level. Wiener (2003) says, "Yet many seem to have chosen to obfuscate and obscure the problem rather than address it, and the Department of Edu-cation has been complicit in this deception."[15]

Minority students in inferior schools are being penalized for cir-cumstances beyond their control. These are students with the least resources and the least access to opportunity and who are solely depen-dent upon teachers to provide them with the content they need. Then you give them the least qualified teacher and blame them and their families when the child scores low on tests. These students who start out in the educational race with no shoes are placed at unreasonable expectation lev-els and are dehumanized when they fail to finish the race at the same level and time as their counterparts. This is a deplorable experience for any child to encounter, yet this is exactly what many minority students face on a daily basis.

The Preference Question

Critics of affirmative action stress that college admissions must be color-blind and that students applying for college must have a level play-ing field. The problem is that colleges have been so used to offering pref-erences in admissions that many of these have become almost invisible to university officials and difficult to challenge. In addition, there has been a lot of hypocrisy. According to Harry P. Pachon, president of the Tomas Rivera Center, University of California regents who voted for a "level play-

ing field" then turned around and requested exceptions for their associates' children.

Colleges regularly offer preferences for children of alumni (called
legacies), children of wealthy families likely to donate generously to the
college, admission by exception (a back door access for students who do
not meet all the normal qualifications) and of course, the real sacred cow,
athletic admissions. All of this deadwood needs to be cleaned up before
we will have a fair and equal admission process.

Children of Alumni

Giving preference to legacies is a long-standing tradition. Schools like
Harvard, Yale, Princeton and Columbia have been doing it since the early
1900s. According to the Washington Monthly and the Daily Princetonian,
many Ivy League schools admit two to three times more legacies than regular applicants. For example, Harvard admits 35 percent (one in three) of
legacy applicants in contrast to 16 percent of all applicants. For Yale it was
45 percent of all legacy applicants, at Princeton 33 percent (one in three),
Dartmouth 27 percent, and Columbia 32 percent. The Washington Post
and Journal of Blacks in Higher Education revealed that legacy admissions
have a huge advantage over other applicants applying to elite institutions.
For example, 40 to 42 percent of legacy applicants are admitted to Georgetown University. At Haverford College, 75 percent of all legacy applicants
were admitted compared to 32.5 percent of all applicants. At Oberlin College 70 percent of legacy students gained admission in comparison to one-
third of all applicants admitted. With a fraction of the nation's minority
population as alumni of elite college and universities, there are very few
underrepresented students of color who benefit from this preference.[16]

At Harvard University where about 1 in 5 students are children of
alumni it sparked an investigation by the U.S. Department of Education's
Office of Civil Rights into the institution's admissions practices. The investigation found that legacy candidates admitted are less qualified than regular applicants, their SAT scores on average are 350 points lower and on
average they had a lower GPA than regular applicants admitted.

For instance, Steve, who had always dreamed of going to an Ivy League
school, set his sights on Harvard. However, he only had an SAT score of
1250. He was convinced that he didn't stand a real chance in competing
against a student with a 1400 SAT score and 4.0 GPA average for the freshmen class. But Steve's dad was a graduate of Harvard. When filling out the
application he noticed the legacy section on the form that asked where his
parents went to college. Steve received a letter of acceptance to Harvard.

Later, he learned that the fact that his father had graduated from the school increased his chances of getting admitted. About 12 percent of Harvard's freshmen class is comprised of children of alumni.

When questioning Ivy League admissions officers regarding their justification for this preference their response is that it is critical to the financial well-being of the university to build strong alumni relations.

According to Charles Deacon, undergraduate dean for Georgetown University, "It seems reasonable, as a tip factor in a close call, that it's in everybody's best interests that colleges show some exceptions for alumni children."[17]

Some institutions' response to the lower academic standards of legacy students is that they bring other qualities to the institutions beyond that of a test score. According to Marilyn McGrath Lewis, Harvard's director of admissions: "We owe them a great deal. But not to the degree of giving up quality of our student body."[18]

Actually, the Ivy League schools are just the tip of the iceberg. The CAF (common application form), designed to cut down on paper and accepted at over 600 universities, has a legacy question on it. According to the Journal of Blacks in Higher Education, many schools besides Harvard use this form, including Johns Hopkins, New York University, Swarthmore, Rice, Vassar, Williams, and Wesleyan. Schools like Stanford that do not use the CAF still ask the legacy question. Legacy preference is a universal practice that schools defend vigorously. Legacy preference puts white children at a huge advantage and penalizes underrepresented students of color whose parents are less likely to have attended college at the same rates. Some institutions have an entire office devoted to legacy admissions. At the University of Pennsylvania there is an office devoted to alumni and their children when they apply for admission. "The Alumni Council on Admissions interviewed 753 legacy applicants for the class of 2007, of which 447 applied for early admission to the university. Of those, 47 percent, were admitted to the school, as compared to a rate of 33.1 percent of the general early decision applicant pool."[19]

Actually a student doesn't always need a parent who attended the institution to achieve legacy status, but it helps if your brothers or sisters have attended. Says Indiana University admission counselor Larry Gonzalez: "We have a strong family tradition here, so if there's a family member related to IU, we give the student a second look. It really says something to us that a student has been on campus and knows a lot about it from relatives."[20]

Affluent Families

Students who come from affluent families are three times more likely to gain admission than regular applicants at the prestigious universities (Harvard, MIT, Yale, Stanford, and Columbia).

According to *The Cavalier Daily*, the student newspaper at the University of Virginia, the admissions office listed the prospects of future gifts and heirs to fortunes from students associated with companies like that of Boeing, Merck, and Smithfield. The offspring of the affluent families connected to these companies were all admitted even if they were not fully qualified.

According to the College Board, students from families with incomes of more than $200,000 were five times more likely to be accepted at an elite institution than regular applicants. As the cost of elite colleges and universities rises the opportunity for middle- and low-income students to attend decreases. According to the College Board, for the 1999–2000 academic year the average annual cost for residential students in private institutions was $30,000 to $40,000. This perpetuates a two-tier system in higher education at the elite colleges, one solely for the rich and one for all the others.

This makes their inheritance "educational property," giving them automatic access after graduation to professional and managerial work at the better companies. College admission based on family status perpetuates a cycle that those who are privileged by birth are given access.

Another term for affluent preferences is what most institutions call "development admits." These are students of wealthy families who have been rejected or wait-listed by their college of choice. The *Wall Street Journal* reports that to attract donations, college and universities are bending admission rules to make room for influential families in hopes of building long-lasting relationships with the institution. For example, there is the story of Caroline Diemar, daughter of an investment banker and a Duke University senior. She had an 1190 SAT score and a B average GPA, well below the 1320–1600 SAT score and 4.0 GPA that the university considers for most freshmen. When she applied she was wait-listed. Then, there is the story of Maude Bunn, who had a boarding school education but a low SAT score. Her family are well known in the coffee industry. Both of these students became development admits. Diemar received two letters of recommendation from family friends who are Duke donors, and Bunn's parents made a donation to the university. Both the families of these students have concealed how much money they gave the institution. Maude's mother told the newspaper, "My child was given a gift, she got in, and now I'm giving back." The Diemars and Bunns serve as co-chairpersons on the Duke fund-raising committee.[21]

Ivy League institutions like Duke admit about 3 to 5 percent of students in the wealthy family category, which equates to about 125 students annually. Duke University is in the top 10 of the nation's higher education institutions. It accepts about 23 percent of its applicants and rejects more than 70 percent of high school valedictorians. Duke received close to $3 million in unrestricted gifts from nonalumni parents in 2001–02. According to former Duke President Nan Keohane, preferences for children of alumni are "disproportionately favorable to white students. It seems odd to me to allow one sort of preference, but not the other."[22]

Admissions by Exception

Admissions by exception is a policy most universities employ in admitting students who do not meet all of the academic qualifications, meaning they are not eligible. The University of California says, "Because all students have not had the same opportunities to prepare for higher education, the university gives special consideration to a limited number of freshman and transfer applicants who show the potential to succeed even though they do not meet the minimum admission requirements." The university admits up to 6 percent of students under this policy. Some universities refer to this policy as "conditional," or "open" admission. Admissions offices at colleges and universities under the guide of alternative admission have allowed for policies of this nature to ensure that students who display other talents are given the opportunity to gain access.[23]

The University of South Florida admits up to 10 percent of new enrollees as exception to the minimum requirements. So does the University of Kansas, along with the state schools of Arizona, Missouri, and North Dakota. Colorado admits up to 20 percent of its incoming freshmen, Kentucky 5 percent, and Maryland, Montana, and Washington all allow 15 percent. Prior to 1995 the University of Massachusetts had exempted 22 percent of freshmen with 15.4 percent at the Amherst campus and up to 6.6 percent at the Boston campus. That has now changed. Realizing that the percentages varied widely among the universities, a state committee ordered public colleges in Massachusetts to exempt no more than 15 percent of new freshmen. Almost every state has a policy that exempts eligibility requirements.[24]

Says Daniel C. Walls, dean of admission at Emory College, "I feel we can take a flier on a student who may not have all the numbers exactly where we'd like them, but who has some kind of a hook that we think would be a great addition to the class. Jeremy Silver from Deerfield, Michigan, was one of these. Despite an average GPA and subpar ACT scores, he was admitted to highly selective USC because of his dramatic ability — he had been in a lot of high school musicals at Deerfield High School and almost every play. This was a "something extra" that won him an admission by exception.[25]

Early Decision Admissions

Some colleges' early decision plans are also a twist on admission by exception. Under early admissions, a high school senior applies to one college in the fall, hears in December and if admitted, promises to accept early. Today 330 institutions offer early decision plans. The chances for admission don't improve at all schools, but for some they do. At Wesleyan University in Middletown, Connecticut, 43 percent of early decision applicants get the thumbs-up, opposed to 25 percent of the regular applicant pool.

Says Nancy Hargrave Meislahn, dean of admission and financial aid at Wesleyan, "Early admission is to a student's advantage here." If a student doesn't quite have the average GPA or admission test scores, the early decision plan may help. "During early decision we may give more weight to things like community contributions and personal qualities."[26]

Yale University President Richard C. Levin believes that the elite colleges have unleashed a process that has gotten out of hand. "If we all got rid of it, it would be a good thing." As competition for admission to the most prestigious colleges and universities has increased in recent years, the number of early applicants has skyrocketed. Hunter R. Rawlings III, president of Cornell University, points out that early admissions has been an upper-middle-class white student from the Northeast phenomenon for the past decade.

Unfortunately, when a university fills its early decision slots with mostly white students or students from a certain part of the country, that makes it difficult for underrepresented students of color who often apply later. [27]

Athletic Admissions

Athletes gaining college admission has been a practice of institutions since colleges had teams. Yet the gap between test scores and academic achievements for athletes and nonathletes is greater than the gap between underrepresented students of color and white students. Unfortunately, few affirmative action critics extend their merit-based arguments to athletes.

Athletes in some cases are three times more likely to gain admission than most students. According to a study conducted by William Bowen, former president of Princeton, it is easier for athletes to gain admission to college than any other group. "If admissions were based solely on academic merit, it would affect even the best programs. Most of the Duke basketball team or the Notre Dame football team would be playing elsewhere." Athletes (male and female) who are recruited enjoy a tremendous advantage in gaining college admission. In 1976 a recruited athlete had a 23 percent greater chance of gaining admission at all colleges than a regular student seeking admission, in 1989 that number grew to 30 percent, and in 1999, 48 percent.[28]

At the University of Virginia, for instance, athletes get extra points because the university strives to compete at the highest level of college sports. Before the Supreme Court ruling invalidating the University of Michigan 150-point scale, recruited athletes received 20 points in the admission process. Something similar exists at most universities.

For example, David, a Minnesota high school student, starred on his football team and helped them win a championship. David has a 3.0 grade point average and a 1000 SAT score. Under ordinary circumstances he would have a challenging time gaining admittance to any elite university. But David was a football standout. He received inquiries from UCLA, Stanford, Northwestern and similar schools and now plays football for Stanford.

It is easy to see why schools like Notre Dame and the University of Florida would give preference to athletes. But it is hard to understand why the most elite universities, especially the Ivy League schools, give bigger preferences to athletes than they do other students. However, Ivy League schools and other elite schools feel obliged to be competitive in sports, even minor sports, because the alumni like seeing their alma mater perform well and good teams provide publicity.

At Princeton, for instance, athletes on average fall 100 SAT points below the admission standards used for everyone else. According to the groundbreaking study "The Game of Life: College Sports and Educational Values," in one institution male athletes recruited by the college had a 48 percent greater chance of being admitted than did the average male student applying to the same school. Recruited female athletes had a 53 percent greater chance than did other students with similar scores. The results are similar for the other academically selective colleges in the study, which included elite schools like Oberlin, Swarthmore, Williams, Yale, Smith and Wellesley and many others.[29]

Amherst College designates 75 out of the 450 places in each year's freshman class to athletes recruited by coaches in 27 varsity sports, and some of these students do not meet regular admission standards. At Middlebury College, the hockey coach asked the admissions office to admit Tom Skoglund, a star ice hockey player. Says Skoglund; "I probably wouldn't have gotten into Middlebury without hockey. Being a hockey player gave me access to a first-rate education."[30]

In 1972, congress enacted Title IX, a federal law barring all forms of educational discrimination on the basis of sex. The federal Office for Civil Rights then ruled that colleges must provide equal sports options for women and men and provide comparable facilities and scholarship assistance for women.

The recruitment of women athletes at these colleges has become aggressive and intense since that time. This is true of all sports, including the low-visibility sports such as tennis and swimming. As a result, colleges bestowed significant preferences in admissions.

Mount Holyoke College in South Hadley, Mass., has become increasingly aggressive in seeking out talented athletes. Says Laurie Priest, the director of athletics: "Athletics is important at all institutions. It allows us to cast a wider net for women who might be interested in a women's college."[31]

In 1989, women athletes at Ivy League schools had SAT scores 60 points below those of their classmates. In 1999 at one selective school, "recruited" women athletes enjoyed a 59 percent admissions advantage. Once enrolled, the school found female athletes earn lower grades than their nonathlete classmates.

A "jockocracy" has taken hold in the Ivy League schools as athletes are divided socially, academically, and culturally from the rest of the student body. "Recruited athletes earn far lower grades than both their fellow athletes who were walk-ons and other students. Eighty-one percent of recruited athletes, men playing football, basketball and hockey, ranked in the bottom third of their class. Forty-five percent of recruited female athletes also were in the lower tier academically. Similar trends exist in the New England schools, such as Williams, Amherst, Trinity and Tufts,"[32] asserted Bowen and Levin in their new study. Their research tracked 28,000 students who entered 33 selective colleges and universities in 1995.

Proponents of college sports stress that the current system offers opportunities for more minority youngsters to get out of the ghetto than they otherwise would. According to Harry Edwards at the University of California, Berkeley, that is not the case because only a tiny percentage of such youths win college athletic scholarships. The opportunity of African

American males to gain a scholarship are as likely as winning the lottery. According to National Collegiate Athletic Association statistics and USA Today reports, during the course of one year about 90,000 African American males are playing basketball in schools across the country and about 1,100 of them are offered "full-ride" athletic scholarships making their chance about 1 percent.[33]

The former admissions director at Williams College calls athletic recruiting "the biggest form of affirmative action" in higher education. Athletic preferences, of course, are so entrenched that it will be difficult to make any inroads. However, it all has to do with fairness. This is not a level playing field because more deserving candidates are shut out of an opportunity to attend the school of their choice. Yet, college officials and political policymakers don't seem ready to reform college sports. After all, people seem to like college athletics just as they are. Academic-merit becomes redefined when it comes to athletics, where special admissions take over and loopholes are created for these students who otherwise would not be eligible under the regular admission criteria.

The current structure of the system is completely out of balance and inequitable. It creates a huge irony, as advocates of merit-based admissions look the other way when it comes to athletics. They articulate the need for fairness and a level playing field in admissions when it applies to race but see no problem when exceptions are made to accommodate individuals with special talents who possess substandard grades and GPAs, even when these students displace large groups of underrepresented students of color and those in the dominant group who often have stronger academic qualifications and a greater potential for academic achievement. Those who advocate being anti-affirmative action for most admissions, but support special admissions for athletes, are not supporters of the level playing field but malevolent defenders of special-talent and economic preferences at any cost to equity.

Traditional Merit

For most of us, the word merit conjures up an image of a successful individual who excels in many of the things he does and is, in general, an outstanding person. To us, he or she is a person of merit.

If you expect merit to have the same meaning when applied to college admissions, you couldn't be more wrong. Most colleges, even the elite colleges (outside of test scores and grades), resist the idea of applying other criteria. "I accept the fact that we want well-rounded students, but we're

not the Rotary Cub," says University of California Regent Ward Connerly,"
we're trying to select scholars." To most Americans the concept of merit
is given to hard-working individuals as a consequence of their ability and
perseverance.

That's not quite the correct view of what's happening, as mentioned
in Chapter Two. UC Berkeley's grade-weighing scale provided merit and
points based on the former school the student attended. The University
of California advises that the higher a student's grade point average the
lower his SAT score can be, but it is mandatory that he take the exam.
Brandy Malone, a resident of Berkeley had always wanted to go to UC.
Brandy is an average student and is very bright, with a 3.25 grade point
average and an SAT score in the 900 range. While Brandy fulfilled all of
the admission requirements, she was not admitted. In 1998, the average
freshman admitted to UC, Berkeley, had a 4.2 grade point average and a
1400 SAT score.[34]

There has not been much change as in 2003 the average student admitted to UCLA, the flagship campus, had a 4.3 grade point average and a 1450
SAT score. And this is what schools think of as merit. Standardized tests
may reward a student's ability to guess, conformity or obedience. Test performance may not be a predicator of real-life merit such as talent, ability
to take on increased family responsibilities, or long commutes while maintaining good grades and working. An example of real-life merit is 16-year-
old Tanika. Tanika is the oldest of six from a single-parent family. While
she attends high school she also works part-time to assist with the finances,
takes care of her younger siblings and her grandmother. Tanika's daily life
starts at 5 A.M. and ends at 11 P.M. She maintains all of this with a 3.5 grade
point average. Tanika would like to go to college but does not feel her
chances are good because she does not test well and her family is poor.[35]

Legal scholars Strumm and Guinier (2003) believe that the idea of
ranking students based on test scores is not a fair and valid test of merit.
A Professor emeritus at UCLA says, "The SAT is a big fuzzball." It doesn't
give an accurate picture of the students who will do well in college. Factors
that determine student success, such as talent, ability and perseverance, are
not measured by standardized tests. Successful student performance,
Strumm and Guinier stress, needs to be interpreted broadly.[36]

Says Jane Brown, chief enrollment officer at Mount Holyoke College:
"The SAT is a very narrow measure of student ability. Frankly, I think GPA
is a very narrow predictor. I'd rather look at civic engagement." Some colleges have always used what they call comprehensive admissions. Applicants are accepted on the basis of grades, test scores and such factors as
special talents and experiences with adversity. According to Joyce Slayton

Mitchell, director of college advising at the Nightingale-Bamford School in New York, some of America's colleges are beginning to choose disciplined young people who have already notched achievements in filmmaking, church work, developing software programs, political contests, poetry, music, scientific experiments, theatrical sets and more. Admissions deans now want to find leaders for school publications, student government and other areas of student life, and this means students with special talents and those from underrepresented ethnic groups and geographical areas.

The Posse Foundation of New York provides a different form of admission. It yearly invites students from public high schools and some youth organizations and provides a unique college selection process. During a series of initial meetings, candidates participate in activities designed to expose leadership potential, ability to work in teams, creativity, problem-solving skills, willingness to listen to other points of view and openness to diversity.

One exercise challenges the students to build a duplicate of a robot made out of Lego blocks. Students are given 15 minutes to complete the task, and only one team member at a time may leave the group to look at the original robot. Under this pressure, fights often erupt. About one in four of the initial group makes it to the final round for a series of meetings with representatives of participating colleges. Each participating college agrees to accept (usually) 10 students. "The kids that survive this process," says Robert Innes, Director of the Human and Organizational Development program at Vanderbilt University, "have a lot of guts. They also survive when they get to campus."[37]

A study of three classes of Harvard alumni over three decades found a high correlation between successes defined by income, community involvement, and professional satisfaction and low SAT scores and a blue-collar background. When asked what predicts life success, college admissions officers at elite universities report that it is an above-minimum level of competence, initiative or drive.[38]

College campuses are the doorways to racial socialization. For some students, their first experience of diversity takes place on a college campus. In a diverse society, institutions of higher education have the opportunity to establish positive group interactions for students. An educational study comprised of researchers in support of affirmative action argued that colleges have an obligation to students to foster campuses built on diversity. Institutions of higher education have the opportunity to create positive intergroup climates within which diverse groups of students can interact, learn from one another, and develop positive attitudes toward one another. The benefits of diversity impact not only the individuals on college campuses but society as well. One of the fundamental goals of education is to prepare students to participate in the world that they will enter upon graduation, and in the United States that world is increasingly international and multicultural. With the diversity that exists in everyday interactions, increasing diversity in higher education should be a critical policy. In an anti-affirmative action climate the need for diversity as a critical policy is not the major criterion or a criterion at all for most colleges.[39]

Affirmative action is a modest and effective tool that universities need, and it is simply wrong to suggest that we have found any kind of simple nonracial alternative.

— Gary Orfield, Civil Rights Project,
Harvard University

6. Percentage Plans to the Rescue

The Supreme Court has now given colleges and universities limited tools to create diversity. The states that have a percentage plan policy are likely to keep those plans, and other states will probably add something similar. Taken in conjunction with affirmative action, most percentage plans can be useful in extending opportunities to lower-income students. Let's look at what's happening.

When Jovanny Salgado graduated in the top 5 percent of her class at Houston's Charles H. Milby High School, she had no idea she was already assured a place in the highly selective University of Texas at Austin. Today, Salgado, a psychology major, is a sophomore at the university with a grade point average of 3.7.

Her admission, however, was not voluntary: A court decision forced Texas, Louisiana and Mississippi to abandon their longstanding use of race or ethnicity as a factor in admissions at public colleges and universities. In the Hapwood case, the U.S. Fifth Circuit Court of Appeals ended affirmative action in Texas college admissions.

In the aftermath of the Hopwood decision, some in the education community felt that Texas' historical past of segregation would return to the university. State Senator Gonzalo Barrientos convened a group of education and policy makers from the University of Texas, University of Houston and the Mexican American Legal Defense Fund. Their charge was to analyze the impact of the Hopwood decision and to produce alternatives.

The result of the task force was a plan for an automatic admission process for students who ranked at a percentage in their graduating class from an accredited private or public high school and would be first-time freshmen. Then the Texas Legislature passed a law (HB 588) requiring public colleges and universities to admit any graduate of an accredited Texas high school whose grade point average placed him in the top 10 percent of his high school. In the wake of this, other colleges immediately turned to percentage plans as a way out of the racial dilemma. Since the introduction of the Texas 10 Percent Plan, states have sought ways to increase the number of underrepresented students of color without the use of race.

With the elimination of race-conscious affirmative action in college admissions, in some states, the new alternative became percentage plans. Percentage plans guarantee first-time college applicants who graduate from high school within a predetermined class rank automatic admission into a college or university. Currently, Texas, California and Florida are implementing some form of a percentage plan for college admission. Proponents praise the plans as a race-neutral alternative, whereas critics hail them as an inadequate approach to equal educational opportunity and a nonreplacement of affirmative action.

Pennsylvania and Colorado debated percentage plans. The Pennsylvania state system of higher education proposed automatic admissions at the 14 state institutions to Pennsylvania students graduating in the top 15 percent of their classes. Pennsylvania abandoned the idea and is researching the use of a standardized test to be used similar to a percentage plan. In Colorado, law makers introduced a bill that would provide automatic admission to any University of Colorado campus if students graduate in the top 20 percent of their high school class. However, the bill never fully developed.

Examples of Percentage Plans

The Texas Plan, instituted in 1998, entitles the top 10 percent of the graduating class of each accredited high school in Texas to attend the University of Texas at Austin, Texas A&M or any other state university. The 10 percent plan was not a new creation. Until 1993, UT had an automatic admission of 10 percent, and in 1994, the institution altered that practice to include more rigorous standards.

The Texas percentage plan law also requires institutions to review the academic records and other factors deemed appropriate of non-top 10 percent applicants to determine individual abilities to perform university-level work. This assessment also determines whether an applicant would benefit from a retention program. Universities may require academically deficient students to enroll in enrichment courses and orientation programs during their academic career. The University of Texas, Austin, has established guidelines that direct its retention officer to carefully review the files of top 10 percent students who have "weak high school preparation or ... extremely low SAT/ACT test scores to determine the appropriate academic support required for success."[1]

By fall semester 2000, there was more than a 27 percent increase in the number of high schools represented among UT freshmen. Many of those high schools feeding graduates to UT for the first time were inner-city minority schools in San Antonio, Dallas and Houston, as well as rural, predominantly white schools. Also in recent years, some racially mixed high schools from South Texas's Rio Grande Valley sent students to UT for the first time. At Texas A&M, enrollment is 8 percent Hispanic and 3 percent African American — again, comparable to five years ago.[2] "They're just now getting back to pre–Hopwood levels," says Jose Moreno, assistant professor of educational studies and research analyst at Claremont Graduate University.

The Texas Plan at UT-Austin resulted in increased diversity in 1999 among freshmen students admitted in comparison to 1998. Texas also had a new scholarship initiative that targets students in the top 10 percent. The number of minority freshmen admitted to UT-Austin continued to increase during the first three years of the plan. The largest increase in the number of minorities admitted occurred between 1998 and 1999, when 125 more African Americans and 177 more Latinos were admitted. Such increases are partially the result of an increase in the number of students applying because of new efforts that encourage minority high school students to attend UT-Austin. This increase is partially explained by a change in recruitment policy and the reassessment of recruitment, retention, and scholarship programs that occurred during that time. Historically, UT-Austin had admitted students from only about 50 of the same schools within the state. The new policy has resulted in the aggressive recruitment of students from Texas high schools that historically had sent few students to the University of Texas. As a result, recruiters began targeting students in ninth and 10th grades as prospects for the program. To draw students attending schools traditionally underrepresented to UT-Austin, the Longhorn Scholarship program, aimed at specific low-income high schools, was created and awarded 64 four-year need-based scholarships in its first year.

Four years after the passage of the 10 percent plan, David Montejano, an architect of the plan, reported on changes. The research indicated that 74 high schools in Texas contributed half of the freshman class to UT-Austin. There were 700 high schools that did not send any students to UT-Austin. The study did not offer any insight as to why 700 schools failed to send any students there, although Montejano said that some of the students could be taking advantage of the program at other universities since the 10 percent plan is statewide.

Texas A&M

Texas A&M University regents tentatively approved a plan that would permit the university to pursue the top 20 percent of students at approximately 250 Texas high schools that had been deemed low-performing or disadvantaged. The goal: to automatically admit to Texas A&M graduating seniors from these schools who ranked in the top 20 percent of their class, if they met the university's requirements for curriculum, grade point average, and standardized test scores

Dr. Ronald Douglas, executive vice president and provost of the A&M flagship campus northwest of Houston, says an expanded automatic admissions program would help A&M encourage students who are supposedly being told by high school counselors "not to bother" applying to top-notch colleges. "That's what we're hearing from our recruiters," Douglas says. "But we're a land-grant college. We are supposed to provide opportunities to those normally not thinking of college. This is the group that is either settling for community college or not going to college at all. These high schools are at the bottom of the heap."[3]

Of the current A&M students who came from these targeted high schools, retention runs 90 percent. "This is slightly higher than retention rates of others between their freshman and sophomore years," says Joe Estrada, assistant provost for enrollment. "The value of an education is intact in these students. We just don't get many applications from them, that's all."

A&M regent Dr. Dionel Aviles says: "Even though the board has not made a final decision, they don't believe the top 20 percent proposal is race-based. If it was, I would be the first one not to touch it. We just want to recruit more students who normally don't come from those high minority schools. There's no doubt about it. Let's be realistic." In March 2002, university officials proposed to temporarily halt the 20 percent plan.

The Texas 10 percent plan, however, has failed to achieve enrollment figures similar to pre–Hopwood numbers, but the plan makes it possible for some students to attend UT-Austin who, after Hopwood, might have been excluded. The biggest increase in admissions under the percentage plan has been among African American and Asian students says Dr. Gerald Torres, vice provost at UT-Austin. "The retention rates for African American students admitted to the university under the plan have increased. These students are maintaining higher grade point averages, managing their time better, mastering study skills and not hesitating to ask for help. The Texas plan seems to say even if you come from a crummy school, you can make it, which may mean these schools weren't that crummy."[4]

The Texas plan has come under scrutiny for its weighing of academic curriculum. There is no distinction between those who take honors courses versus those students who take the minimum to graduate. In addition, private schools that do not rank their students academically are unable to compete against other students in the 10 percent slots.

Access and Equity Plan 2000

When the Hopwood decision evolved, Texas was in the middle of a desegregation plan put forth by the U.S. Department of Education's Office of Civil Rights. According to the Texas Higher Education Coordinating Board, the state's Access and Equity 2000 study was designed to outline the process of implementing a six-year plan for college enrollment. This plan established institutional goals aimed at increasing minority enrollment to a level reflective of the population the institutions serve. What is ironic is that in 1997, the Office of Civil Rights ruled that racial disparities still existed in higher education institutions in Texas a year after a court ruling outlawed affirmative action.

While there is controversy regarding their effectiveness, these plans have wide appeal because they benefit some underrepresented students of color and whites. Percentage plans permit poor whites from poorer counties to benefit, but the plans do not help to create increased minority admission. In Florida's colleges and universities, whites make up 67 percent of the academic top 20 percent of high school seniors. Meanwhile, African Americans are 14 percent of the top 20 percent. In Texas, research shows that high schools in Dallas Fort Worth, Houston, and San Antonio, in which the student population is predominantly minority, the number of students admitted to UT increased significantly in 2000. These 37 high schools sent 89 students to UT-Austin along with students from East and Northeast Texas, which are rural and predominantly white. There are 59 high schools that fall into this category, and they sent 92 students to UT-Austin.

Dr. Mary Frances Berry, former chairwoman of the U.S. Commission on Civil Rights, says her biggest criticism of the Texas plan is that it does not apply to law schools and other graduate programs. Under HB 588 graduate programs are not included, making percentage plans inaccessible for graduate admissions. So far, none of them have boosted levels of underrepresented students to that proportion in the overall college age population. According to a Harvard study in Texas, for instance, Latinos and African Americans accounted for about 52 percent of all 15-to-19 year-olds in 2000 but only about 35 percent of the freshmen admitted to the state university system. The chart shows an increase for underrepresented stu-

TOP 10 PERCENT OF STUDENTS ADMITTED TO UT-AUSTIN BY RACE			
	White	*Latino*	*African American*
1997 (before percentage plan)	2,262	613	118
1998	2,561	734	143
1999	2,753	911	268
2000	3,182	1,020	291
2001	3,213	1,012	245
2002	3,527	1,177	278

Source: Bruce Walker and Gary M. Lavergne, Implementation and Results of the Texas Automatic Admissions Law HB 588, Report 5, p. 5, Native American data not available. Combined summer and fall numbers.

dents admitted under the top 10 percent plan. The increase the university reports is the result of combining summer and fall admissions.

California

California has its own 4 percent plan, which so far has accepted about 100 students who might not otherwise have been admitted. The University of California's Board of Regents approved a plan to automatically admit students from all California high schools who graduate in the top 4 percent of their classes. The plan is known as admission in the local context. Under UC rules, nonacademic factors, ranging from unusual athletic or artistic talent to overcoming adversity, could be taken into account in admitting a portion of the freshman class. The remainder had to be chosen on the basis of grades, test scores and course work alone. However, UC like most premiere institutions did not willingly decide to adopt a percentage plan. The 1995 UC Regent Referendum SP-1 banning race in admissions, Senate Constitutional Amendment 7 (SCA 7), the 1998 governor's race, and a drastic decline in admission of underrepresented students of color provided the university with needed motivation to follow Texas.

CALIFORNIA SENATE CONSTITUTIONAL AMENDMENT 7. Senate Constitutional Amendment 7 was authored by State Sen. Teresa Hughes (D-Inglewood). This legislation, while overlooked, was the beginning of the public awareness campaign that put UC in the spotlight to provide an alternative to SP-1. Hughes served as chair of the California State Senate Select Committee on Higher Education Admissions and Outreach. Hughes introduced SCA 7 in February 1997. SCA 7 provided that students who rank in the upper 12.5 percent of their high school graduating class would be eligible for and, subject to meeting reasonable eligibility requirements, would gain automatic entrance to the University of California. While the bill failed passage in the Senate, it kicked off a firestorm of controversy within the education community, the media and most importantly UC, which opposed the bill as unnecessary and restrictive. Hughes held several committee hearings on the issue across the state. The strategy was designed to hold UC accountable to the Legislature to ensure that underrepresented students of color would have access.

The 1998 gubernatorial race between Dan Lungren and Gray Davis was vital to the University of California Board of Regents. In California, the governor appoints the regents. Lungren, the Republican candidate, was a supporter of the regents' SP-1, and if he won, the regents would not have to contend with any appointments that ran counter to the political makeup of the board. Gray Davis, the Democratic candidate, supported SCA 7 and proposed during his campaign that all valedictorians gain automatic admission to UC. Davis won the election, becoming the first Democratic governor in the state in close to 20 years. Also, during that year SP-1 went into effect for undergraduate admissions and once again, like graduate admissions, underrepresented student admissions dropped dramatically, with the underrepresented admission at the flagship campuses declining by 40 to 50 percent. UC begin to feel the political pressure to move toward a percentage plan, and in May 1999, the UC Board of Regents adopted a 4 percent plan.

TIMELINE OF EVENTS OF UC ADMISSION CHANGES:

July 1995 UC Board of Regents approve referendum (SP-1) banning the institution from using, "race, religion, sex, color, ethnicity, or national origin as criteria for admission."

July 1996 UC's Office of the President revamped the institution's "admission by exception" policy. Beginning in 1998, up to 6 percent of first-time freshmen, including 4 percent from disadvantaged groups, would be admitted by exception to the university's eligibility requirements.

November 1996 California voters approved Proposition 209, eliminating any use of race, ethnicity or gender as criteria in education, government, and contracting.

Fall 1997 SP-1 (prohibition on race) took effect for graduate admissions.

Feb. 1997 SCA 7 introduced. This legislation allowed automatic admission of 12.5 percent of the top high school graduates to the University of California.

Fall 1998 SP-1 took effect for undergraduate admissions.

November 1998 Gray Davis elected as governor.

March 1999 UC Board of Regents adopt 4 Percent Plan Program; it took effect in 2001.

May 2001 UC Board of Regents Rescind SP-1. However, under Proposition 209, the admissions policy will remain the same.

Fall 2001 The 4 percent plan, also known as eligibility in the local context, took effect.

November 2001 UC Board of Regents approve a comprehensive review process to evaluate and admit applicants beyond quantifiable measures to UC campuses in fall 2002. Multiple measures applied to examine students in the context by which they demonstrate academic achievement.

Fall 2002 First students admitted to UC under the comprehensive review process.

Source: California Senate Select Committee on Higher Education Admissions and Outreach and the U.S. Commission on Civil Rights, report Beyond Percentage Plans, 2003.

Under existing percentage plans in California, students must be in the top 12.5 percent of students statewide to gain admission to UC. The 4 percent plan relaxes this criterion so that the best students in each high school would qualify even if they were not in the top 12.5 percent statewide.

While the 4 percent plan has been toutted by proponents as providing more access for underrepresented students of color since the ban on race, that is not entirely accurate. Recent figures show underrepresented students are still on the decline at UC, specifically at the flagship institutions. In addition, the so-called success of the new policies is often weighted upon the year 1997, before the race ban was implemented.[v] Yet, according to the U.S. Commission on Civil Rights, the proposed implementation had already led to the dismantling of affirmative action programs, and therefore, the proportion of underrepresented students is not as high as the 1995–96 level. For example, the flagship campuses of Los Angeles and Berkeley were at the height of diversity with a 26 to 30 percent African American, Latino and Native American populations in 1995–96. In 2000–01, it dropped to only 17 percent for all three groups combined.

Florida

Florida also has enacted a percentage plan Gov. Jeb Bush signed Executive Order 99-281 in November 1999 for the "One Florida" initiative, which eliminated race and ethnicity as an admissions factor in the State University System. According to Bush, minority representation in universities was adequate, therefore race- and ethnic-based admissions policies could be replaced with achievement-based policies. The Florida plan guarantees state university admissions to high school seniors in the top 20 percent of their graduating class without regard to SAT or ACT scores.

The One Florida Equity in Education Initiative was established as an alternative to affirmative action, and through the initiative, the governor proposed and the regents established the Talented 20 Program to take effect in 2000–01. The program guarantees high school seniors in the top 20 percent of their graduating class automatic admission to one of Florida's public institutions in the state university system. To be eligible students must complete a 19-unit academic high school curriculum, which consists of college preparatory courses.

ONE FLORIDA EQUITY IN EDUCATION INITIATIVE. The One Florida Equity in Education Initiative consists of two segments. The first is three pathways to enrollment in the Florida State University System, and the second is goals for improvement in public education. The three pathways to SUS are Talented 20 Program, traditional criteria, and profile assessment. The goals emphasize increasing opportunities for low-performing schools so that students from these districts can gain access to higher education later in their academic career. Bush has heralded the plan as a successful alternative. Bush said: "With my One Florida Initiative, we can increase opportunity and diversity in the state's universities without using policies that discriminate or that pit one racial group against another. The One Florida Initiative transcends traditional notions of affirmative action and increases opportunities for Floridians of all racial backgrounds in ways that unite us, not divide us."[6]

TALENTED 20 NUMBERS. In 2001–02, Talented 20 students made up 61.5 percent of first-time freshmen. Ten percent were Latinos, 5.7 percent African Americans, 0.2 percent Native American, and whites at 71 percent. The U.S. Commission on Civil Rights says that the racial make-up of Talented 20 first-time students in the state university system compared to the University of Florida shows that among the underrepresented students in the system, Latinos made up 13.9 percent, African Americans 11.9 percent and Native Americans 0.4 percent. In April 2002, University of Florida officials announced they would automatically admit the top 5 percent of high school graduates in the state. The university devised the plan to admit more eligible students and indicated that the plan would admit 300 additional students who otherwise would not have been accepted. The three pathways to admission did not alter the overall enrollment rate of underrepresented students of color to the state university system. What the numbers assert is that the Talented 20 program did not produce any better results than affirmative action programs in its place before 1999.[7]

Differences in Percentage Plans

There are specific differences in the percentage plans that operate in Texas, California, and Florida.

Participation

The types of schools that can participate vary state to state. Texas and California allow public and private schools to participate. In Florida, only public school students can participate. In California the percentage plan only applies to the University of California, not to colleges within the state university system.

Academic Requirement

In Texas, students need only to graduate with minimal criteria to participate in the 10 percent plan, whereas Florida and California have specific college curriculum course work requirements. For Texas, this standard may soon change.

Class Ranking Percentage

Texas is at 10 percent, California at 4 percent and Florida 20 percent.

First Choice

Texas is the only state that guarantees admission to its top institutions of choice. Florida and California allow automatic admission into the system, not a specific campus or academic program.

Eligibility

In California, schools must use college preparatory specified coursework and GPA in identifying students in their junior year who qualify to be considered for the 4 percent plan. In Texas and Florida, individual districts calculate GPA and time of completion of course work in establishing class rank.

Are Percentage Plans an Answer?

The American Educational Research Association and the Center for Comparative Studies in Race and Ethnicity assert that colleges need to keep affirmative action policies in order to respond to the consistent racial inequities in our society. Obviously, efforts to level the playing field must continue. In the current college admissions debate, the real question is, Can percentage plans provide an alternative to race and still maintain access for underrepresented students? With the changing demographics for states like California and Texas, as people of color are becoming the majority, this question is vital. Through the utilization of studies, published information on percentage plans, higher education data, newspaper, published interviews, and political contacts, this chapter will attempt to answer that question.

Percentage plans, and the expansion of college scholarships, while a start, may not be the right start, and the research will show that they won't do the entire job. The need is to increase access for underrepresented students of color. While percentage plans have been heralded as a way to achieve diversity, they are flawed. The U.S. Commission on Civil Rights said, "the three percentage plans in Texas, California and Florida fail to create diversity." While affirmative action is not a perfect policy, it is 10 times more likely to be effective in increasing minority admissions than percentage plans. In a 2003 report on race-neutral alternatives in postsecondary education, the U.S. Commission on Civil Rights noted, "The percentage plan approach, according to career consultants, fails to diversify college campuses. It is essentially a Band-Aid approach to a much larger wound. American colleges and universities are still largely predominantly white elitist. While percentage plans award top-class graduates admission to states' top-ranked colleges and universities, it leaves those who do not make the cut to choose other institutions." The percentage plans that currently exist are being applied solely at undergraduate levels and not to graduate and professional schools.

The Systems

The three states (California, Texas, and Florida) that utilize percentage plans have very different public postsecondary systems. California has a three-tiered system often referred to as the tripartite structure. Under the 1960 California Master Plan, the University of California, with nine campuses, was designated as the premiere state-supported research institution, and it provides the undergraduate, graduate and professional schools (medicine, law, business). UC is to select students from the top 12.5 percent statewide for admission to the system. California State University, with 23 campuses, provides undergraduate and graduate education up to the master's degree level and also specializes in teacher preparation. The CSU goal is to select high school graduates from the top third of students statewide for admission. What is unique about the CSU system is that unlike other state universities it does not provide degrees in professional schools or doctorates. California Community Colleges, with 109 colleges, were designed to serve individuals from the community. The schools offer classes in general education, job-related training, and offer transfer to a four-year college. The flagship campuses in California are within the UC system at Berkeley and Los Angeles. On average they receive 30,000 to 40,000 applications for 10,000 freshmen slots.

Texas has 35 public universities and 50 community college districts with 83 campuses, and the Texas Higher Education Coordinating Board works with these institutions in developing and maintaining higher education. Texas has two flagship campuses, the University of Texas at Austin and Texas Agricultural and Mechanical University. They are the most competitive within the state.[8]

The State University System in Florida consists of 11 public institutions and 28 community colleges. In 2001, the Legislature created a governing structure that combines all three education systems— public schools, community colleges and state universities— under a K-20 system. The commissioner of education and the State Board of Education work with the Florida Board of Education Divisions of Colleges and Universities in maintaining higher education. The board of trustees and the president of each university provide operational responsibility of the institutions. Of the 11 institutions, the flagship campus is the University of Florida.[9]

California, Texas and Florida have had histories of limited access for underrepresented students of color seeking higher education. Coupled with continued inequities at the primary and secondary school systems, elite colleges and universities had made use of affirmative action to improve underrepresented enrollments. If percentage plans are the wave of the future, then they must go beyond just admission. Percentage plans should be implemented with affirmative action and other supplemental recruitment, admission and academic support programs. Recruitment, financial aid, and academic support to attract and retain underrepresented students of color, according to Gary Orfield of the Harvard Civil Rights Project, is needed "if you have a percent plan. Without those, you don't have too much."[10]

The concern critics put forth regarding percentage plans is that they are not tailored narrowly enough to accomplish the goals and need for diversity. Percentage plans have resulted in the rejection of minority students who would have been admitted under affirmative action because they didn't fall within the percentages set by the state. This must be addressed. These plans are another form of numerical quotas.

A plan that focuses solely on class rank cannot achieve what affirmative action does by looking at qualified students in their totality and the schools they came from. According to the Leadership Conference on Civil Rights, percentage plans were not designed to maintain diversity. While proponents tout these plans as the new race-neutral answer to college admission, there is no evidence that these plans provide access or prepare leaders. While some percentage plans have seen an increase in the number of underrepresented students, the plans' success is not entirely credible. The results fail to include the growth of minority groups in the state population, specifically, states with the largest segregated minority groups.

Nationwide Perspective

Percentage plans will not work nationwide in selecting a diverse student body. When class rank is applied, it becomes increasingly difficult for institutions to measure leadership abilities, teacher recommendations, and extracurricular activities. Percentage plans remove the capability of institutions to examine students individually, to determine the benefits they will bring to the university. The ability to see the student as a whole person is removed, and the evaluation of his capability and potential contribution to the university is not measured. Percentage plans are rigid and do not allow for the flexibility of looking at a broader range of students. Colleges and universities only examine those students in a certain percentage of their class. Affirmative action gave and now gives again flexibility to look at students beyond the 4th, 10th and 20th percentile in reaching qualified applicants that fall within a broader range of the eligibility scale.

Percentage plans make it increasingly difficult for educators to judge a student's ability to perform academically at the college level. Depending on the school they attend, students may be unprepared to perform college-level work, increasing the need for remedial education. The University of Chicago found that valedictorians from low-performing schools were not well prepared for the rigors of college-level work and were unsuccessful in their first year at the university. For example, at 70 of Florida's high schools, several students with a C to C+ grade point average fell within the 20 percent of their graduating class, making them eligible under the Florida Plan. Class rank encourages students to avoid hard classes at competitive schools in order to improve their ranking. This eliminates an institution's ability to focus closely on the quality and challenge of the high school curriculum the student has completed.

Percentage plans are most successful in increasing the enrollment of underrepresented students when those students come from racially segregated schools. This may set a bad precedent in promoting increased segregation at high schools while pushing class rank in college admissions. According to Mary Sue Coleman, president of the University of Michigan: "It is wrong to endorse segregation as a formal system and to base our public policy upon it. On the contrary, we should be working to eradicate segregation from our school systems. Therefore, percentage plans motivated as race-neutral alternatives may themselves be touted as discriminatory because their success relies on educational and residential segregation. The concentration of population and groups centered in that population will impact the results so they cannot claim to be 'race-neutral.'"[11]

The demographics of each state play a role in the outcome of percentage plans. In Texas, California and Florida, with their large minority populations, the admission of underrepresented students has had mixed results but has not surpassed affirmative action figures. This could be telling for states with low minority populations. Native Americans, especially, who have numbers are so small, are almost entirely left out of the process. Depending on the state, Latinos and African Americans often also make up a very small percentage of the population. Percentage plans also increase the inequities between high schools. The class rank approach pits mediocre schools against elite schools, and the outcome is that students gain access to college based upon the competitive edge of earning a ranking at their school. Sylvia Hurtado, a professor at the University of Michigan, asserts that class rank ignores the fact that some high schools simply don't produce students who can be successful at some of these colleges. However, this argument does not carry too much weight if the student meets the eligibility requirements for entrance into the university. Students attending competitive schools may be inadvertently excluded from attending selective colleges under a class rank system.

Elsa Acevedo and Leah Burton attend schools in Miami. Elsa has a 2.9 GPA, 16 ACT score and no AP courses, but she is ranked 17th in her graduating class at Edison Senior High School. Leah Burton has a 3.9 GPA, 1150 SAT score, and five AP courses, and she is ranked 34th in her graduating class at Palmetto Senior High School. Under the Talented 20 program, Acevedo will be admitted and Burton will not; both are students of color.

In Texas, that was the case for Charlie Craig. At St. John's, a private elite school in Houston, he maintained a B average while taking AP courses that earned him a year of college credit. He is the son of UT alumni and also scored 1370 on his SAT. Since his high school does not rank academically, he was not considered for automatic admission. In a letter, UT-Austin indicated it would not accept him until he spent a year at one of the system's "less prestigious" campuses. Craig chose to attend the University of Colorado at Boulder.

Parents have expressed concern over these types of rejections. John Oberman, whose daughter was rejected by UT-Austin, says, "It has hurt some kids who are more qualified than the ones getting in." This reality has caused some students to transfer to other schools in order to increase their chances of acceptance.[12]

There are many similar examples. Christine Attia, for instance, a graduate of St. John's School in Houston with a GPA of 3.8 and a SAT of 1520, didn't get admitted to UT-Austin. Yet hundreds of others with lower SAT scores did. That was because these students met the eligibility requirements in addition to graduating in the top 10 percent of their class at their high schools. Stories like this are common in Texas.

Maria, for instance, graduated near the top of her class from a high school in southern Texas, where a majority of students are Latino. Her class rank was in the top 10 percent. Her SAT score was 940. Yet she was admitted to the University of Texas. At the end of her freshman year, she had managed a GPA of 2.39. Even with remedial classes and tutors, she had three D's. Some 10 percenters are doing well, but many are not.

Unfortunately, percentage plans lower the academic level of the entire student body at colleges and universities that fall within the plan. Since some high schools don't measure up to others, the colleges must lower their standard to meet their needs. The University of Texas had to come up with remedial classes for pre-med students with SAT scores as much as 200 points below the university average who graduated from lower-performing high schools. When this happens, good faculty go elsewhere. Research money follows, and graduates become less competitive. This is lowering the quality of first-rate state universities since these plans don't close the skills gaps between the races and may injure some of the major selective universities.

This gives universities accepting percentage plan students three choices. They can keep the classes relatively rigorous, causing fewer students to take them and pass. They can dumb the courses down. Or, as some universities are doing, they can set up special classes for students admitted under the percentage plan (Steele, 2000)[13]

The Texas Legislature is now getting involved; Sen. Jeff Wentworth (R-San Antonio) has proposed a law restricting automatic admission to students who complete a college-prep curriculum recommended by the state. Leaders in the Legislature have indicated they plan to revisit the issue and impose tougher restrictions on the Texas Ten Percent Plan.

Percentage plans are primarily designed for institutions that admit students on a statewide basis. Institutions that admit students from a national and international pool are not able to implement this model. For example, at the University of Michigan, one-third of the student body comes from outside the state, and most of the Latino students admitted are not from Michigan. Over half of the applicants of the freshmen class at Michigan are from out of state, while only 11 percent of applicants to UT-Austin are nonresidents.

Texas, Florida and California structure their plans on a statewide university system, so that students are eligible to enroll at a school within the system. For universities that are not apart of a statewide system, especially private schools, percentage plans will not work because they cannot guarantee admission of applicants if they exceed availability. For example, there is no way Stanford or the University of Michigan can admit a freshman if they run out of room. If some states were to adopt such plans, it would force their universities to reconstruct their process.

Percentage plans have not increased underrepresented enrollment at selective and elite colleges. California's 4 percent plan program has been most successful in increasing geographic diversity with an increase in students from rural areas of the state. In 2002, out of 11,000 students, 14 percent of them were rural students who were admitted under the plan. All groups except for African American and Native American students have gained a boost under the 4 percent plan. Latinos are at 17 percent compared to 15 percent of the traditional pool in admissions. However, African Americans made up only 2.8 percent of those admitted under the plan while the overall acceptance was 4.7 of the statewide pool.

The results indicate that the new admission policies, while increasing admission rates, did not always produce higher enrollment rates among underrepresented groups.

The University of California's response to this reality is its assertion that the plan was not designed specifically to increase the number of under-represented students but to offer another alternative route to admission. UC finds the plan most beneficial in including UC as a possibility at nearly every high school in the state. According to Hanan Eifenman, spokesperson for the system: "In our out-of-state schools or in our underfunded schools, students often feel that higher education is out of reach. This gets them to think about UC as a real option." The admissions office at Texas A&M targets its recruiting based upon geographic areas designed to highlight where underrepresented students reside.[14]

Percentage plans that only provide access by class rank do not address the total package of college admissions. Percentage plans need to address the need of financial aid of underrepresented students in order to be effective and successful in providing academic support for students. If students are guaranteed admission, but cannot afford to attend, the purpose is lost.

Do Percentage Plans Work?

This chapter examined three percent plans designed as alternatives to race-conscious admissions. While there is some increase in admission for students who otherwise would not be eligible, the research indicates diversity has not increased so much as geographic diversity. Percentage plans do not address the need for diversity in higher education. According to the U.S. Commission on Civil Rights, percentage plans in Texas, California and Florida designed in supplanting affirmative action admissions alone will not result in increased diversity in higher education or exceed inequities that exist in public education. Specifically, its study concludes that all three percentage plans fail to increase access for underrepresented students of color in postsecondary education admissions and college enrollment.

While affirmative action has made progress over the years in advancing equal access to education, disparities still exist. Underrepresented students of color are not admitted or enrolled in colleges and graduate programs in numbers that are equivalent to their population in society. These disparities will remain as long as states continue to replace this policy with race-neutral alternatives. At issue is while the number of undergraduate underrepresented students applying to the flagship campuses in Texas continues to increase since implementation of the Ten Percent Plan, the percentage of those admitted continues to decline. For example, the

U.S. Civil Rights Commission found that in Texas from 1996 to 2001, the number of African American applicants applying to UT-Austin increased 24 percent, but the proportion of African American applicants admitted decreased by 19 percent. During the same period Latino applicants increased 20 percent, but the proportion of Latinos admitted decreased by 15 percent. Currently, the enrollment of underrepresented students at UT-Austin is still lower today than before the Hopwood decision. In 2002, Latinos made up 14.3 percent of first-time freshmen, African Americans 3.4 percent and Native Americans 0.4 percent. The result is that acceptance rates for underrepresented students of color have not kept pace with the numbers applying to UT.

The result of the Ten Percent Plan is that it does not serve as an effective or sole alternative to affirmative action because it produces minimal increases to campus diversity. The 4 percent plan in California also resulted in declines for Latino, African American and Native American students. Like Texas, California experienced minimal increases in admission in the beginning; the preban rates have not restored numbers in enrollment. The UC system has shown an enrollment decline for all three groups enrolled every year since 1995–96. The UC system has experienced a decline of 4,000 Latinos, 1,600 African Americans and 675 Native Americans.

In examining the 2001–02 data for first-time students enrolled in the state university system in Florida, 17 percent are African American, 0.41 percent Native American, 14 percent Latinos and 60 percent whites. At the University of Florida, the flagship institution, African American enrollment is 7 percent, 11 percent for Latino, and 0.34 percent for Native American. According to the U.S. Commission on Civil Rights, since 1999, African American enrollments have declined by .25 percent and Native American enrollment by .16 percent, whereas Latinos made a .69 percent gain. In 2001, at UF underrepresented students suffered declines. Freshman enrollment for Latinos declined by 32 percent, from 377 to 260 students; 75 percent for Native Americans, from 36 to 9; and 51 percent for African Americans, from 528 to 259.[15]

Another challenge is that there is an inability to close the gap between underrepresented students gaining access and high school graduates. The K-12 system needs work. The pool of students eligible to participate in percentage plans must be able to successfully complete high school to take advantage of higher education. The demographics of high school graduating classes will have an impact on the demographics of students who are eligible.

While California, Texas and Florida are growing, there is increasingly less diversity. The population trend for whites is the exact opposite at selective college campuses. Percentage plans do not assist in maintaining proportionate levels of access in parity to population. According to the 2000 Census, Latinos make up 39 percent and whites make up 34 percent of the 15- to 19-year-old population in California, but whites are admitted at a larger rate into college than Latinos. The case is the same in Texas, where Latinos comprise 39 percent of 15- to-19-year-olds and whites make up 44 percent, yet the Latino college admittance rate is not close to their parity in the population.

The critical challenge to percentage plans is that unlike affirmative action, there is no guarantee the students admitted will be more diverse or adequately prepared. The risk of percentage plans is that they admit students based on one criterion: their rank.

Research is needed to examine additional analysis on holistic ways to develop effective admissions policies. In looking at the research, what is revealed is that three separate studies have been conducted on this issue. Two of them (Harvard Civil Rights Project and U.S. Commission on Civil Rights) take a nationwide look at all three percentage plans and the latter (Admissions & Enrollments at the Texas Public Flagships) looks at the Texas Top 10 Plan. Collectively, what these studies conclude is that percentage plans are not the complete or sole answer to affirmative action. On one hand, while they give a boost to underrepresented students of color, that boost is not only minimal, but exists in admissions and not enrollment. However, in looking at the institutions in which these plans are conducted, there is a contradiction because Texas, California and Florida state that their plans have all boosted access and therefore are successful. For example, at the flagship campus of UT-Austin the university released statements that enrollment of first-time underrepresented freshman students are now at levels that surpass affirmative action.

A report by the Office of Institutional Research says that 2002 figures for Latinos are 14.3 percent; African Americans, 3.4 percent; and Native Americans, 0.4 percent. In 1996, the count was Latinos, 14.3 percent; African Americans, 4.1 percent; and Native Americans, 0.4 percent. While there has not been much change, the university makes the assertion based upon raw numbers. Latino enrollment for fall/summer is 1,137 (942 in 1996), African Americans at 272 (266 in 1996), and Native Americans 175 (156 in 1996).

Enrollment numbers have not bounced back for the professional schools. According to the president of UT-Austin, Larry Faulkner, the Top 10 Percent law has allowed the school to diversify enrollment with talented students who succeed. Faulkner says that Top 10 Percent students earn grades that exceed those of non–Top 10 Percent students and have SAT scores that are 200 points higher.

Yet a report conducted by researchers at Princeton, UT-Austin, and the University of Iowa conclude that the Top 10 Percent law is not a substitute for affirmative action. African American and Latino students have a larger risk of rejection under the plan as the population grows increasingly diverse. Restoring diversity will require increasing the number of applicants from underrepresented groups. "The success of HB 588 in restoring campus diversity is minimal at best because the 1996 metric becomes more obsolete with every passing year."[16]

According to the Texas Higher Education Coordinating Board, the data is not complete for Texas as UT and A&M enroll 23 percent of the student body matriculating in public four-year universities. Once again as the population grows, more students will be discouraged by admissions decisions even if the admissions criteria remain the same.

The U.S. Commission on Civil Rights and the Civil Rights Project find that the ideal percentage plan should include outreach innovations like that of the University of California, allowing students to identify and enroll in their school of choice as identified in the Texas plan, focusing on K-12 education as stressed by the Florida plan, and resources to ensure financial aid is provided to students admitted. The commission's study states that the One Florida Equity in Education Initiative's second component, improving public education, has the potential to play a pivotal role in reducing the admissions gap and is well worth emulating by other states.

If states adopt percentage plans as an alternative to race-conscious admissions, they run the risk of undoing the progress made by affirmative action. In order for percentage plans to be successful they should be implemented in combination with other efforts. For example, overall assessment of first-time students, resources and support beyond admission are critical components that should comprise any percentage plan. Targeted outreach activities aimed at underrepresented students of color should be done in conjunction with the plans.

Most importantly, institutions need to consider the possibility of including graduate and professional schools in percentage plans. "Unless qualified minority students who are admitted to the public flagships actually enroll, both institutions will weaken their reach in educating a leadership class for the state's growing minority soon to be majority population." The reality is race or no race, colleges and universities will be increasingly challenged by the growing number of qualified applicants and the few slots available, making the need to evaluate students beyond their high school rank vital to establishing a diverse student body.

The future of percentage plans at this point is still in doubt, but because of the number of students applying, the plans will probably always have a place in some states.

*I believe in the color-blind society, but it has been and remains an aspi-
ration.*

— Justice Thurgood Marshall

7. To Be Color-blind or Not?

Exactly how have the color-blind policies practiced by a number of
universities fared? Not so well. For instance, the 1,500-student law school
at the University of Texas at Austin (after passing a percentage plan)
enrolled only four African American* students in the 1997–98 academic
year — down 29 from the year before. Other schools affected by the policies shows similar results. Says Reginald Wilson, a senior scholar at the
American Council on Education in Washington, "This country is made
up of 25 percent minorities, which are growing every day. What are we
going to do about our people?"

Supreme Court Justice Oliver Wendell Holmes stated long ago that
"the life of the law has not been logic; it has been experience." Race-neutral polices force college admissions officers to ignore the diverse experience of underrepresented students whose access to postsecondary
education will be drastically reduced.

In 1995, Ward Connerly, a University of California regent, pushed
through the UC board a vote that ended affirmative action at the university. A year later he became the main organizer of California's Proposition
209, the voter initiative that ended affirmative action for state-run government programs. Three years later, Connerly helped pass a similar voter
initiative in Washington state. He has now authored a racial privacy initiative which would eliminate California's practice of classifying and track-
ing individuals by race, ethnicity, color or national origin. Supporters of
Proposition 54 collected 980,283 signatures in just 130 days. The initiative, however, was defeated in an October 2003 vote. However, Connerly
still calls it a needed step toward a "truly color-blind society."[1]

Antonio Villaraigosa, former speaker emeritus of the California

Black also includes African American.

196

Assembly, says, "Ward Connerly and his supporters are playing a game of Russian roulette with California's public-health initiatives, public education and civil rights protections.[2]

"Today's Supreme Court decision only muddles the law on affirmative action," says Horace Cooper, a former member of the George Mason University board of trustees. Cooper is also a member of Project 21, established by the National Center for Public Policy Research to address the concerns of conservative African Americans who feel that their commitment to fanity has not been fully represented by the civil rights movement. Coopers says, "This approach to constitutional lawmaking will lead to further challenges and greater division in America. Letting skin color be the basis for admissions in law school, but not in undergraduate admissions, is nonsensical."[3]

Warrenville, Ohio, Mayor Marcia L. Fudge, who is also national president of Delta Sigma Theta, a sorority of African American women, says "It's time for blacks and whites to abandon questions of skin color. People who treat people decently, who work hard and who talk to people are going to do well no matter what their skin color."[4] What if the race question is banned? For some people it makes little difference. Sara Schoen filled out all the details of her college application, the Social Security number, her family's income, her work on the high school newspaper, her experience as an exchange student in Spain. But when she came to the question of race, she left it blank.

"I just feel like being a white, middle-class girl from the suburbs is a huge strike against me, and I don't want to further that effect," Schoen said. "I don't think skin color should have a lot to do with who you are as a person or whether you get into college."

On June 1, 2003, the *Washington Post* ("College Bound Students Often Skip Race Question") reported that more than 2,000 applicants at George Washington University had skipped the ethnicity question that year, a 45 percent increase from two years before. At the College of William & Mary, almost one applicant in five left the check box empty, and at the University of Maryland, nearly 1,500 of the 25,000 undergraduates enrolled did not disclose their race. Many of the students who avoid the racial check boxes say they are doing so for reasons rooted in frustration with the dynamics of race in college admissions.

"On the other hand," says Barmak Nassirian of the American Association of Collegiate Registrars and Admissions Officers, "good data drives so many planning decisions they can't make it up. They can't have people go out on campus to record actual ethnicities. We can only provide the data we happen to be in possession of."

Some minority students actually conceal their race on applications to prove to themselves, or their classmates, that they made into college on their own merits. Will Frankenstein, a graduating senior from a New York City public school who is half–Asian, half–Caucasian, decided not to tell the college admissions officials his race. "I don't want to be defined by ethnicity," said Frankenstein, who is headed to Stanford University. "I have friends from all over the world that don't judge me by my ethnicity. Why should someone else judge me that way?"

Race and skin color, however, remain one of the most highly charged issues at the University of California, Berkeley, provoking anxiety and conflict on a campus where the number of African American and Latino students has sharply declined.

One late February morning in 2003, the Berkeley College Republicans held a bake sale, charging passers-by different prices for chocolate-chip cookies based on their race. The action touched a nerve on campus. People glared, some argued and others flashed, "Way to go!" It snared the attention of a group of black upperclassman who, visibly agitated, later denounced the sale in a packed African American studies class. The Republican club countered that this sale was held to demonstrate the need to be color-blind, that everyone should be considered equally.[5]

Patricia J. Williams, professor of law at Columbia University, says: "You will not find quick solutions to the 'small aggressions of unconscious racism.' This does not mean that there are no solutions. There are not quick fixes."

Jonathan Coleman in "Long Way to Go: Black and White in America" asserts that whites must no longer make their acceptance of blacks conditional on their being "more like us" or "acting white"; they can no longer exploit blacks living in the same neighborhood or exploit the advantages that come to them just because they are white. LaRay M. Barna adds in her essay, "Stumbling Blocks in Intercultural Communication," that coming to terms with cultural uniqueness requires that we avoid the familiar impulse to say that deep down inside we all are the same."[6]

Glenn C. Loury, professor of economics and director of the Institute on Race and Social Division at Boston University, points out that "There is nothing in the history of affirmative-action abuses that requires us to tie our hands with color-blind formalism. Consider, for instance, in an army where African Americans are one-third of the enlisted personnel, but they are only 3 percent of the officer corps. This army is likely to function poorly. The U.S. Army cares about the number of African American captains because it needs to sustain cooperation among its personnel along racial lines. And the racial identities of captains and corporals sometimes matters. The color-blind principle is in my opinion neither morally nor politically coherent. If it was we would discontinue all racial classifications associated with the collection of statistics by government agencies. Yet monitoring the racial dimension of social and economic trends is a vital public function."[7]

Justice Powell, in the landmark 1978 case of *Regents of California v. Bakke*, embraced the idea of intellectual diversity. "I have never been persuaded that taking race into account to assure the presence of varying perspective in a classroom is a weightier justification than attempting to repair decades, indeed centuries, of racial and gender oppression."

The University of Virginia has long felt the need to stress the importance of race and diversity. For almost a decade, the percentage of African American freshmen enrolled at the University of Virginia has been at or near the top of the list of the 25 highest-ranked universities in the country. John Green, a top African American student, feels right at home at the school. "If there is one thing that I love about this university," Green says, "it's that everybody that's here truly deserves to be here. I feel comfortable." One reason is that there is a "critical mass of minority students on campus."

Today, about 23 percent of undergraduates are American-born minorities, including 9 percent African Americans. The school's meteoric rise in academic stature has come at the same time as the diversity on campus skyrocketed. John Blackburn, dean of admissions at the University of Virginia, says that the school gives underrepresented students of color* the same extra consideration in admissions accorded applicants who are athletes, or children of alumni, or wealthy donors. Such applications are tagged to denote a "plus factor. That plus can help if the student is borderline, but the academics still have to be there.[8]

Virginia Tech, a sister university, recently reinstated its affirmative action policy despite the fact that the state's attorney general thought that some of its diversity programs were still unconstitutional.

Corey Walker, an Afro American studies professor at the University of Virginia, feels that acceptance of the idea that affirmative action is reverse discrimination ignores reality. "You have the football team, mostly black, cheered on by an audience almost entirely white. Now what's wrong with that picture?"

What's wrong is that African Americans are still pigeonholed within society and academia, like athletes and entertainers, and is only slowly

---

*Underrepresented students of color are used to identify African American, Latino and Native American students.

breaking out of that box to be taken seriously. Even at the university, he says, faculty diversity lags far behind that of the student body.

Alfred Prettyman of Rockland Community College in New York says: "Seeming absent from the conversation is a critical mass of minds capable of absorbing multiple perspective with nonjudgmental but not uncritical intelligence. Also missing are the voices of those enmeshed in the mundane frustrations and joys of mingling with Americans of different colors and cultures, those who have replaced aversion or unfamiliarity with personal friendship, even intimacy. Dispelling one's ghosts through the recognition of present, real persons requires an arduous commitment to continuous self-education."

The Color-blind Perspective

Another myth of affirmative action is that America is a color-blind nation and that affirmative action has no place in this society. Critics believe the color-blind perspective will curtail discrimination if we did not socialize or see each other in terms of our race. This premise holds weight for critics in ascribing to the individual theory of success. We should not see color, just the individual. This is a noble goal, but America is nowhere close to that reality. For example, a Gallup poll noted that most whites do not believe that racial discrimination is still a problem today. Whites and underrepresented groups of color tend to view issues of equality quite differently. In the Gallup Survey on Race Relations, seven out of 10 whites believe that African Americans are treated equally in their communities. In addition, eight in 10 whites believe that underrepresented groups receive equal if not preferential treatment in education.

In a study conducted for the American Jewish Committee, Smith (2001) examined the ethnic images that people have toward certain groups. In researching if positive intergroup relations exist in diverse America, the study examined data from the 2000 Census and compiled a survey. Since the United States is characterized by groups of race, religion, and gender, intergroup relations become vital in the color-blind discussion. The survey examined the perceived contributions of various groups under the category of ethnic images.

While progress in race relations has been made, there are still challenges America faces. The results of the survey indicated that whites are still ranked as the most advantaged and accepted and African Americans ranked the lowest and less socially accepted. For example, 43 percent of respondents found blacks lazy and less hardworking than whites. Thirty-seven percent of respondents found Latinos lazy in comparison to whites. Forty percent found Latinos more prone to violence than whites, and 44 percent said Blacks were. Thirty-four percent of respondents found blacks less intelligent than whites, and 44 percent said Latinos were.

One exception that researchers found was college-educated respondents had a positive and more realistic image of underrepresented groups of color in regard to work ethic, violence and intelligence. Respondents with a high school diploma or less had negative images of underrepresented groups of color. The main results of the study find that underrepresented groups of color to be quite disadvantaged in comparison to whites and assert that they still experience overt racism and discrimination (Sikes and Feagin, 1994; Smith, 2000).

While the United States is a diverse society, our ability to reach equity and tolerance have not been fully realized and are still challenged. Fifty percent of respondents in suburban areas prefer all-white neighborhoods along with 54.2 percent of white respondents. The survey found that African Americans were the most negatively viewed. In the category of intelligence, African Americans and Latinos were seen as less intelligent than whites. In the category of wealth and class, Jews and whites were ranked favorably, and African Americans and Latinos were ranked below whites.

The ranking of people of color below that of whites is not surprising but can actually be the results of the isolation that exists between those from the dominant group and those in underrepresented groups. According to Wise (2001), the ignorance about the everyday lives of people of color should not be surprising for it is in large part the result of our isolation from underrepresented groups in daily life. "More than 80 percent of whites live in communities with less than 1 percent black populations. What's more, only 12 percent of whites in law school today say they had significant interaction with blacks while growing up. One can only expect this degree of isolation to lead to a skewed perception of what other people experience. After all, if one doesn't know many blacks, or personally witness discrimination, it is all the more likely that one will find the notion of widespread mistreatment hard to digest."[9]

Critics are quick to insist that highly competitive public colleges and universities have consistently admitted unqualified underrepresented students of color over qualified whites. This myth is at the heart of the controversy regarding race-conscious admissions.

The college-education gap narrowed slightly between 1997 and 2002 but generally has increased since the 1970s. There is also a gap between the words and actions of many elite colleges. Georgetown University eliminated a committee that gave a second reading to applications from minority candidates. Other colleges were careful not to even highlight a student's race when summarizing an application. Officials at The College of William and Mary had long considered an applicant's race, says Karen Cottrell, William and Mary's associate provost for enrollment. "But they never reduced it to numbers," she said. "Admissions staff would simply take mental note of ethnic background during a 'file' reading of a student's application along with factors such as personal initiative and unusual talents. It's all wrapped up for us in the personal side of the application."

The Supreme Court and the Color-blind Movement

In a 5–4 ruling for the University of Michigan law school, the Supreme Court upheld that race can be one of many factors that colleges consider when selecting students. At the same time, in a 6–3 ruling (*Gratz v. Michigan*), the high court struck down a point system used by the U of M in its undergraduate admission program.

The court's decisions also effectively overruled major portions of the 1996 ruling of the U.S. Court of Appeals for the Fifth Circuit in *Hopwood v. Texas* and will allow colleges and universities in Texas, Louisiana and Missouri to use race-conscious admissions policies designed to advance educational diversity.

Both sides have hailed the decisions as a partial victory. In a story of June 20, 2003 ("Supreme Court Upholds Affirmative Action Programs"), the *Black Voice News* quoted Wade Henderson, executive director of the Leadership Conference on Civil Rights, a leader in the fight to preserve affirmative action. Henderson said that the Supreme Court rejected arguments that would have turned the clock back 50 years. "If you don't take race into consideration, schools universities will primarily admit children from privileged backgrounds rather than children from disadvantaged backgrounds."

Julian Bond, speaking to the 94th annual convention of the National Association for the Advancement of Colored People, said, "The Supreme Court decision gave legal sanction to what we knew to be morally, socially and educationally correct." He urged states that have abandoned affirmative action policies to come back into the union. The court ruled against the use of a point-based system for enrollment decision.

For the vast majority of college admissions offices, the Supreme Court ruling is unlikely to have much effect on undergraduate admissions. That's because relatively few colleges had selective admissions before the decision.

Most colleges essentially accepted all qualified applicants regardless of race. And even among that exclusive group of public and private colleges that have considered race, many abandoned a racial point system several years ago.

The pressure to adopt a more wide-ranging set of admissions criteria will require admissions counselors to read all applications carefully when appropriations of many public colleges are being slashed by state lawmakers. The University of North Carolina at Chapel Hill and the University of Virginia hire temporary staff to read applications. These two universities together receive 32,000 applications annually. Officials at both institutions stress that taking essays and other written material into consideration is more subjective than using only grades and test scores, but they point out that each application is reviewed by two or more readers to ensure consistency.

By October 2003 the University of Michigan started to re-evaluate its procedure to reject the idea of being color-blind. "We continue to believe in gathering a group of students that are very bright but different from one another," said Michigan Provost Paul Courant, "students from all walks of life and backgrounds. We will now know more about these students than any other incoming class."[10]

At Michigan, a reader reviews the application and makes an initial recommendation based on the areas of academics, personal background and official recommendations. Separately a professional admissions counselor reviews the application. A manager in the admissions office reviews them and balances the ratings, then decides which rating best fits an applicant's experience. Screeners take note of students who overcame economic hurdles or whose parents didn't attend college.

The evaluation ratings are only to be used as guides by the faculty of each school and college. Initially the university hired 16 part-time readers and five new professional admissions counselors for a total of 22 full-time counselors.

Applicants will be given the option to identify their race, but the answer will be considered "holistically" with the rest of the application. How much it matters in any individual file will be determined by that file.

"The devil really is in the details," says Curt Levey, director of legal and public affairs for the Center for Individual Rights in Washington. " If it turns out that race is more of a decisive factor, the new system will be just as illegal as the point system."

"Unfortunately, the University of Michigan's new undergraduate admissions policy appears just as shameful and as belittling to all as its old admissions policy," said Justin Jones, director of policy and planning of the American Civil Rights Coalition in Sacramento.[11]

The University of Texas at Austin has said it was likely to bring back race-conscious admissions. Robert Hill, senior researcher at a Rockville, Maryland, research firm, says, "There has been a strong shift from Jim Crow — the overt manifestation of racial hatred by individuals in white society — to James Crow, Esquire — the maintenance of racial inequality through covert processes of structure and institutions."[12]

Rutgers Law School in Newark, New Jersey, has a unique approach to this. Applicants are asked to check one of two boxes. If they check the first, the school gives most consideration to their numbers — grade point averages and test scores. If they check the second, the school will give more weight to their experiences and accomplishments. This is how the Rutgers law school has been trying to maintain minority enrollment of about one-third without encountering the resentment of white applicants.

White applicants are also allowed to opt out for the experiences and accomplishments track. "I think my first reading was why?" said Oris Bryant, a 29-year-old who just completed his first semester. "But then it made sense to me. It gave everyone the same opportunity, as opposed to automatically being put in a pile based on other factors."[13]

Rutgers, however, doesn't claim to be color-blind. Despite the school's novel admissions system, Dean Stuart Deutsch said the school still needs to consider the applicants' race and ethnicity to maintain its diversity.

A report titled "Diversity and College Admission in 2003" conducted by the National Association for College Admission Counseling claims that race is not playing a large part in the process.

Roughly one-third of colleges consider race or ethnicity as an ingredient in admissions decisions. Such results suggest that despite the U.S. Supreme Court rulings on admissions procedures at the University of Michigan, race might still play a small part among numerous factors in admission decisions. Although the study found that only a relatively small number of colleges evaluates race in the admissions process, the survey nonetheless showed that nearly 74 percent of colleges pledge a commitment to diversity in their mission statements. About the same number of schools reported that they use a variety of recruiting tools, such as scholarships and college fairs, to attract a diverse student body.

The survey also found that universities look at race in a broad way, with consideration of such factors as religion and socioeconomic status. Of the institutions that reported factoring race into the admissions process, which were commonly highly selective institutions, 82 percent claimed that the race factor increased the number of minority students on campus.

The survey, which included 451 colleges and universities nationwide, was conducted in June 2003 before the Michigan ruling was finalized. Nearly 40 percent of the respondents were public universities, and the rest were private institutions.

Eleven percent of the university respondents said the law restricted the extent to which they could weigh a student's race, and 21 percent said they use a percentage plan, which admits students based on a certain percentage of their graduating high school class.

The University of Illinois, Chicago, has earned a national reputation for graduating significant numbers of African American and Latino physicians. At UIC's medical school, one of the largest in the nation, roughly 4,500 students apply for 300 spots annually. Twenty percent of the school's 1,200 students are estimated to be underrepresented students of color.

Students at UIC need 76 points for admission. The 60-point cutoff is determined by a formula based on grades, medical entrance exam scores, and the strength of a students' pre-med program. Students from underrepresented minority groups automatically get 13 points, along with points granted to students who agree to practice in a rural area.

Kent Barrett, news manager at the University of Wisconsin at Madison Communications, said the university makes a commitment to maintaining a diverse campus climate. "I can't speak for any other colleges, but diversity on campus is and has always been a major goal of the University of Wisconsin-Madison, and our admissions policies reflect that," he said. "UW's big goal is not only to admit a diverse student body, but to graduate a diverse student body."[14]

Clifton Conrad, a professor of higher education at UW, said he is skeptical of the survey's findings. "These findings both underestimate and overestimate the role of diversity in colleges and universities today. The results underestimate the number of colleges that use race in admissions and overestimate in the sense of how serious the consideration of race really is.

"The problem is many universities aren't thinking beyond recruitment and percentages," Conrad said. "This university, as well as other elite colleges, could be more hospitable and welcoming of diversity, from admissions all the way to higher learning."[15]

UW sophomore Jamie Silkey said she feels that race and ethnicity should not be a factor in admission policies. "Diversity should be based on the different experiences and personalities of potential students, not based solely on color," she said. Silkey added that she feels other factors guarantee campus diversity more strongly than race or ethnicity. "Socioeconomic status plays a greater role in making a person who they are rather than their color, because a student may have different opportunities at different levels."

However, UW sophomore Alex Means said he feels that race and ethnicity play an important role. "When UW admits more racially and ethnically diverse students, everyone ultimately benefits. Ensuring these factors in each incoming student body just makes for a better education, inside and outside the classroom," Means said. "That's what I came here to learn."

Rebecca Dixon, associate provost for university enrollment at Northwestern University, points out that self-segregation occurs at many universities. She reiterated that race is but one factor for Northwestern University admissions officers, who consider other characteristics such as the quality of an applicant's high school that improve economic diversity even without a class-based selection process.

Emily Calhoun, a University of Colorado law professor who served on the law school's admission committee, said that CU was in compliance. "The university has never admitted students solely on grades and test scores. The whole idea that somehow there is an entitlement to admissions because people score at a certain level on a test just doesn't fit the real world."[16]

Jim Morales, University of Connecticut admissions director, said his joy at the decision was quickly tempered by the reality. "No sooner did I sigh than my expression of relief became an expression of consternation," he said. He said the Supreme Court decision immediately raised more questions than it answered, by not defining many of its key findings, in effect leaving admissions officers to interpret the ruling in many different ways. The bottom line, he said, is that "there's no single approach that works for every institution, and that's probably just what the court had in mind."[17]

The University of Connecticut, which has a minority population of about 18 percent, does not use a point system for admission. Morales says applications to Connecticut are judged on many factors, including standardized test scores, class rankings, how rigorous the applicants' high school courses were, participation in extracurricular activities, an essay, and whether a particular applicant is the first person in his or her family to attend college.

Drastic Changes

The most drastic changes are likely to be felt in such states as Louisiana Mississippi, and Texas. Colleges in those states were prohibited from using race in admissions following a 1996 decision by the U.S. Court of Appeals for the Fifth Circuit in the Hopwood case.

The University of Texas, after the Hopwood decision, watched its minority student enrollment plummet. Minority enrollments rebounded to pre–Hopwood levels only after legislators passed a law that automatically admitted the top 10 percent from the state's high schools to the University of Texas and Texas A&M.

"Hopwood is no longer law," said Douglas Laycock, a professor and associate dean at the University of Texas School of law. "This completely supplants Hopwood."[18] The president of the Austin campus, Larry R. Faulkner, said the university would begin using race again to award final decisions.

One of the complications is that 70 percent of the fall 2003 freshman class of UT-Austin was automatically admitted under the 10 percent plan, so even if admissions counselors had been allowed to consider race, they would have been able to use it for only the remaining 30 percent of the class.

Within a few years, even if admissions counselors consider race, they may be able to admit only those students coming in under the 10 percent plan. Officials at Texas A&M said that the institutions would look to the state's attorney general's office to interpret the Supreme Court decisions.

Rice University, a private institution in Houston that eliminated the use of race will go back to considering it, president Malcom Gillis says.

The court's undergraduate decision is likely to be costly for a few colleges— particularly large, top-ranked public institutions. They will need to hire more admissions officers.

The Anti–Affirmative Action States

Officials in California and Washington were somewhat less enthusiastic because they will still have to abide by bans on affirmative action approved by voters. The University of California will continue to comply with the voter initiative, says the former UC president Richard C. Atkinson. "We will continue to work through other legal means to achieve excellence and diversity on our campuses," he says. "Most feel that these initiatives will be attacked in those states." But Ward Connerly says, "I don't believe the voters have changed their minds."

The current UC president, Robert Dyne, said that creativity, imagination, motivation and work ethic must be taken into account, along with traditional standards such as the SAT, in judging any student bound for the UC system.

"Diversity of students remains an extraordinarily important goal for a sprawling university system that represents one of the most varied places on the planet, saying we still have a long way to go," he said.[19] Dyne also said the university had not done enough to educate the public on the intricacies of the admissions system and explain the rationale for favoring a lower-scoring student over others who scored very high on the SAT.

In Florida, Gov. Jeb Bush, who signed an executive order in 1999 prohibiting the use of affirmative action, issued a statement saying that his policy would stand. "We are going to stay the course on race-neutral admissions and expand our programs to reach all Florida students who yearn for higher education," he said.[20]

Even with the Supreme Court decision, the future of affirmative action is not assured. Ballot measures in California and Washington outlawed affirmative action in university admissions.

The Gun Is Still Loaded

Colleges are not just up against a few rejected white applicants in the national debate over affirmative action on campuses. The forces aligned against them are much more formidable. President George W. Bush's administration, however, is still pushing race-neutral recruiting and enrollment ideas it says have shown promise in California, Texas and Florida. Officials still want to try to maintain diversity without using the racial preferences that Bush calls divisive and untenable.

Ward Connerly of the University of California's Board of Regents, speaking after the decisions were handed down, said, that "colleges should not view the Supreme Court decisions as 'open invitations to consider race in admissions.'"

"Since neither the judiciary nor the Congress are going to be disposed to solve this problem, then we will be looking at other states to carry the battle there and certainly the state of Michigan would be one that would be ripe for such an initiative. I'm not looking at a lawsuit, I'm looking at a ballot initiative."[21]

"Organizations drive the debate on both sides," Connerly says. "This is a war in the trenches between organizations and individuals trying to further their aims. That is reality. Despite the fact that the Supreme Court partially sided with Michigan, the groups plan to continue their attack by promoting legislation and ballot referendums to ban racial and ethnic preferences. Corporate America, however, is emphatically not interested in supporting the fight against racial preferences."

Luke Massie, a national leader for the Fight for Equality By Any Means

Necessary, said groups like his, which have organized students in support of affirmative action, will be closely monitoring the new system.

Four groups are at the forefront of the fight against affirmative action: the Center for Individual Rights, a Washington-based nonprofit legal organization; the American Civil Rights Institute, a Sacramento, California-based group that successfully led a ballot initiative to amend Washington state's constitution to ban racial and ethnic preferences; the Center for Equal Opportunity, based in Sterling VA; which is still pressuring institutions to drop race preference policies; and the 4,500-member National Association of Scholars, which encourages opposition to race-conscious policies.

These conservative organizations have not given up on more lawsuits to challenge college admissions policies. "A school that tries to make a piece by piece system work is inviting further litigation to which they will have to try to prove to a federal judge that they are not running a quota system," says Terry Pell, president of the Center for Individual Rights.

"No matter what the court did, this is going to be a hot issue. It is going to be with us a long time," added Curt Levey of the center.[22]

Lee Cokorinos, research director of the liberal New York-based Institute for Democracy Studies, who has extensively studied the groups opposing affirmative action, characterizes the various challenges to colleges' affirmative-action programs as "a project of the major foundations of the political right" carried out "by a well-funded nationally based network."[23]

We Are Not There Yet

A color-blind society is a noble goal America should strive toward every day. However, we are not close to that goal by any means, and eliminating the collection of data or banning the use of race-conscious policies does not create a color-blind society. One way we monitor and defend our civil liberties and work toward leveling the playing field of equality is based upon the collection of data. The reality is that racial and ethnic categories are socially significant constructs that shape human behavior. Data on race and ethnicity also aid understanding and address inequities in primary social institutions such as law enforcement, criminal justice, the workplace, health care and education.

Ward Connerly's obsession with race does not mean that a color-blind society eradicates discrimination, nor does elimination of data alone achieve the color-blind society he craves. Color-blindness under the conservative perspective enhances the ability to erode the rights of all Americans to defend themselves against discrimination by removing from public records the very empirical data to protect those rights. For example, under the banning of information as a constitutional provision, what would have been the outcome of the 1954 *Brown v. Board of Education*, the 1964 Civil Rights Act, or the 1971 *Serrano v. Priest*? What all of these cases had in common was their ability to show a pattern of discrimination based upon impartial research using factual data. Color-blindness in our society simply makes it easier for people of color to be overlooked, ignored and made invisible. In a democracy everyone has the ability to seek justice and equality — they are the fundamental principles upon which this country was founded. But we cannot have "liberty and justice for all" if there is no legal recourse for discrimination.

How can justice be blind if you make it impossible for those who discriminate to be held accountable? Under a color-blind agenda, Jennifer Gratz would not have had any data to sue the University of Michigan. If knowledge is power, we cannot remove policies designed to protect us nor data that will add to needed research, empower individuals and hold government accountable. So long as the color-blind perspective pushed by critics of affirmative action quashes the ability to collect and maintain data, the dream of eliminating discrimination will never be realized.

The answer to the question is that America has not reached the color-blind level. According to Rice (2003), we will know when race no longer matters. Rice listed specific changes that would need to take place before America could truly be a color-blind society, including "when real estate agents no longer ask me to leave and remove family pictures before showing my house…. When black Court of Appeals judges in suits no longer get mistaken for bellhops. When Tim McVeigh look-alikes — tall angry-looking white guys with buzz cuts — get profiled and rounded up like black suspects. When the projected date for full housing integration between blacks and whites ceases to be more than 100 years from now. Finally, when statistics like this are measurable because the disparities are gone."[24]

As long as you are convinced you have never done anything, you can never do anything.

— Malcolm X

8. Can We Fix the Problem?

Are race-conscious policies evil? That's what their opponents say. While the current race-blind policies deny access to many underrepresented students, there remains discomfort and even ignorance of the benefits of race-conscious policies. What is widely misunderstood is that affirmative action is used synonymously with the use of race. This is just not the case. Affirmative action does not really involve race, it allows access for historically underrepresented groups. Affirmative action is needed for men who wish to gain access to teacher credentialing programs and nursing schools because historically they have not been well represented in these fields.

Affirmative action assists women who wish to be firefighters or engineers in gaining access to programs from which they have historically been excluded. What makes affirmative action about race is the racial discrimination used for centuries to keep people of color excluded. This is where race comes into play for opportunities like education. Unfortunately, we still live in a separate and unequal society. To achieve equity we must eliminate institutionalized racism in all facets of life, primarily education. This is an enormous task for the country because what makes racism almost impossible to eradicate is that institutionalized racism is largely unseen, for it's an accepted everyday way of life within educational institutions. In order to reduce the need for racial affirmative action we must begin to find possible solutions to providing equitable access to quality education for all Americans. This chapter will propose recommended alternatives and possible solutions to address major issues impacting access to quality education for students of color. Here are recommendations.

For centuries education, specifically opportunities in accessing college, has been seen as the sole predictor in escaping poverty. However, what has become a major hurdle for underrepresented students is the transition from high school to college. Students of color and their families, more than their white counterparts, had little information about college or resources in preparing for college, therefore, more often than not these were the very students who had little preparation in doing college-level work and were found in high numbers in underperforming, inadequate schools. In the twenty-first century this is still the case. So what can we do about it?

Underperforming Schools

First, we need to improve underperforming schools so they can prepare more underrepresented students for college. Inequality in public schools relegates students of color to an inferior education. The Washington-based Education Trust estimated that over half of the persistent educational gap between white students and students of color could be closed if students of color were not exposed to substandard teachers.

According to government and education group research studies, teacher quality has become a vital component in education equity. Research shows that secondary teachers are the key to educational achievement for underrepresented students. Yet many secondary teachers are teaching in areas that are out of their field. Education reform is raising the bar on student achievement and expectations on what pupils need to know to advance to the next grade and graduate.

However, states have not passed on expectations to teachers about knowing their subject and having the ability to educate students. The numbers of teachers teaching out of their fields and lacking the minimal academic qualifications in the subject being taught is fairly high across the nation, especially in schools that are predominantly of color. Nationally, one out of four secondary classes in core academic subjects are assigned to a teacher lacking even a college minor in the subject being taught. Classes in majority nonwhite schools are over 40 percent more likely to be assigned to an out-of-field teacher than those in mostly white schools.[1] Poor students and students of color get the short end of the stick on this issue. According to the Education Trust, 21 percent of students of color are being educated by an inexperienced teacher compared to 10 percent of students in predominantly white schools. Students of color are educated by teachers who scored poorly on licensing exams, and they are twice as likely to be taught by a teacher on an emergency permit, at a nine percent, in comparison to 5 percent for students in predominantly white schools.

From 1993 to 2000, the problem has gotten worse for underrepresented students in middle and high schools. According to the Federal Schools and Staffing Survey, 28 percent of high school teachers in schools with a high percentage of students of color are lacking an undergraduate or graduate major in the field they teach. It is worse for the same students in middle school classes, where the percentage rises to 49 percent.

Georgia and Louisiana had the highest percentage of teachers teaching out of field, both at 42 percent and working in schools that teach predominantly students of color. These teachers teach in secondary classes and lack a minor in the field they are teaching. Delaware, Tennessee, New Mexico and Arizona also have over a third of all secondary classes with teachers in the same category as that of Georgia and Louisiana.

New York has outlawed the hiring of uncertified teachers for low-performing schools. Kentucky is the only state that prohibits all out-of-field teaching, so no teachers can be assigned to a classroom if they are not licensed in that area. Ten other states limit the practice within school sites and districts.

In California, 23 percent of teachers in the lowest-achieving schools lacked full credentials to teach in the 2000–01 school year, compared with only about 6 percent of teachers in the highest-achieving schools.[2] The conditions in California are so severe between the poor and affluent schools that a class-action lawsuit was filed against California (*Williams v. the State of California*). The suit claims that the state has failed to provide basic educational needs to the students most at risk and denying them qualified trained teachers.

The Achievement Council, a Los Angeles-based organization dedicated to reducing those differential achievements, summed up the situation well: "In education of poor and minority children, we put less of everything we believe makes a difference. Less experienced and well-trained teachers, less instructional time, less rich and well-balanced curriculum, and less well-equipped facilities. We also put in less of what may be most important of all: a belief that these youngsters can really learn. This situation is compounded by the fact that some communities have less, too. Most have less knowledge about how the educational system works. Less ability to help with homework and less money to finance educational extras."

Dr. Richard M. Ingersoll, a researcher with the University of Pennsylvania, found four key reasons why this epidemic continues: school district regulations concerning minimal education requirements for new hires, quality leadership by the principal, strategies schools use to cope with teacher recruitment and hiring, and average class size.[3]

Another factor that contributes to the problem is the teacher burnout rate. Teachers leaving the profession contribute to the vacancies in core academic areas of instruction. However, committed teachers working in low-achieving schools are not to blame for the gap in quality. The results may be related more to fragmented policies, political inconsistencies, and challenging working conditions.

The federal government needs to fund beginning teacher and induction programs that support new teachers nationwide. Sixteen states provide funding for these programs while five provide support beyond the first year. Beginning teacher programs should be mandatory for three years for new hires, and states should require mandatory mentoring of teachers in low-performing, high-needs schools.

Teacher Gap

According to David Haselkorn, dean of the National Education Programs and Policies at Lesley University in Cambridge, Massachusetts: "If you want to understand the root of the achievement gap, it's the teacher gap that exists between the affluent schools and the less affluent schools. It's scandalous."[4] However, the difference in achievement has been attributed to the number of years students have access to a qualified teacher. Research indicates that students taught by good teachers for three to four consecutive years can make a difference in student achievement. For example, high school science and math instructors who completed a major in their field will educate students who achieve more than students taught by teachers with less training in their subject.

If students of color are going to have an equitable chance to compete for college admission, schools and states need to take action. More funds need to be spent on staff development that moves away from workshops and focuses on teacher training that will help teachers develop and enhance better teaching strategies.

It should be a nationwide effort to implement incentives that encourage qualified teachers to teach in low-performing schools. Incentives could include tuition reimbursement, retirement credits for every year a teacher remains within the school, and housing bonuses.

Twenty-four states provide college scholarships and tuition assistance to teachers. Of those 24, only seven target those incentives toward applicants willing to teach in low-achieving, high-need schools. For example, Massachusetts and California are the only two states that offer signing bonuses to teachers who work in low-performing high-need schools. Five other states provide signing bonuses, but they are not targeted to the neediest schools. These incentives need to be distributed nationwide and not just fragmented across states.

States should offer retention bonuses to tenured and skilled teachers. Specifically, states need to offer these bonuses to those teachers who work within low-performing schools. Currently, 34 states offer retention bonuses, but those bonuses are not geared toward moving and retaining skilled teachers in low-performing, high-need schools.

Teacher licensing commissions and agencies should ensure that state standards are aligned with teacher preparation programs. Licensing commissions need to work directly with universities to design intensified middle-grade teaching programs. States need to align accountability systems with teacher preparation programs based on creating a multicultural dual language foundation with an emphasis in classroom management strategies. This should be an effort to make teachers better prepared to deal with the diverse study body they will encounter.

The education community needs to work to change the status perception of the teaching profession to recruit more of the best and the brightest into the profession with additional financial resources directed to assist with maintaining and recruiting quality individuals for low-performing schools.

States need to provide waivers for licensing fees and testing requirements to applicants who wish to teach in low-performing schools. In some states testing fees are close to $1,500 for applicants completing their licensing requirements. Most state efforts to recruit and retain teachers are not targeted at high-poverty, high-minority, or low-achieving schools, where well-qualified teachers are needed most.[5] The push has been to increase the number of teachers overall. This means that students of color who are most at risk are not always getting the benefit of a fully qualified teacher.

The World Wide Web can be a fundamental tool to disclose teacher quality for students and parents. Only 24 states provide district report cards that have information on teacher characteristics. Of that 24 only Tennessee, Kentucky, Louisiana, and California provide that information via the Web along with the credentials of every public school teacher. This should be a mandatory practice nationwide.

According to the National Research Council, only 1 percent of math and science Ph.D.s were employed in K-12 education. While, Ph.D.s may be struggling for jobs in their own fields, K-12 schools need to recruit them into filling the much-needed vacancies in math and science.[6] Recruitment should not be limited to those who have just graduated with a teaching background. Schools and school districts need to set up recruitment centers working not only with universities, but with the community to attract working professionals as new teachers looking to establish and begin other careers.

Teacher recruitment centers can contract with school districts, universities and "alternate route providers" who go out into the community to recruit talented individuals to teach in high-poverty schools to establish a range of qualified individuals. Last, school districts need to work hard to evenly distribute talented teachers throughout the district so they are not predominantly in the affluent schools but are also teaching in the high-poverty schools. This is an issue that should not be held at the bargaining table.

Implementation of these strategies can assist in helping students of color to become high-achieving learners who are better equipped to compete for college admissions.

We need to correct the inequitable structure of advanced placement (AP) courses. While affluent schools can offer numerous AP classes in several different subjects, high-poverty schools struggle to provide one or two classes. For example, Inglewood High School in California offers three to four AP courses, whereas Beverly Hills High School offers 13 to 14 AP courses. At elite and selective colleges, the average freshman admitted has a 4.3 GPA as a result of AP courses, and he gets an advantage. The top students at high-poverty or low-performing schools cannot reasonably compete. UC Berkeley's fall 2001 enrollment data showed that of the estimated 36,000-plus freshman applicants, over 16,000 of them held GPAs at 4.0 or higher. Of the freshmen admitted, more than 40 percent had a GPA higher than 4.0.[7]

College admission has become the main factor to status, mobility and earning potential in the United States. College is the doorway to the American Dream. According to the College Board, "AP is the de facto standard for academic programs that help students make the transition from high school to college" (College Board 2001). Most schools that do not offer AP courses are often in poor and urban areas with little to no resources, which establishes another barrier against access for students who attend these schools. The College Board and Educational Testing Services (ETS) should restructure college admissions exams that reflect high school preparatory curriculum.

In an effort to help students compete, institutions have established online AP courses. One such program at the University of California is the Advanced Placement Challenge Grant Program, which allows high school students the opportunity to gain access to four AP courses in core academic areas. The program targets disadvantaged students and provides high schools with textbooks and software needed at no cost for qualified students to participate. As long as institutions will give extra grade points for AP courses, this type of program should be provided nationwide.

Second, institutions should eliminate weighted GPA scale on AP courses, or students without access to AP courses should be given additional grade points for other college preparatory requirements, such as completion of all college preparatory courses, leadership involvement, extracurricular activities, class rank, and quality of the applicant's high school and teacher. Third, if a 4.0 GPA is viewed as the highest a student can go without AP courses, then a cap should be placed on all GPAs.

Fourth, students should be encouraged to take classes at community colleges during their junior and senior year. These completed courses should garner extra grade points similar to those offered for AP courses.

Fifth, schools should establish an information campaign by which students of color enrolled in AP courses inform middle school students and their parents about the benefits of these programs. High school principals and administrators should make announcements at open houses and present to elementary schools within their district to ensure appropriate and accurate information is available to parents and students who want to attend college.

Colleges and universities need to launch aggressive programs to look for students who have overcome adversity — this means targeted outreach that seeks students from challenging backgrounds. Public schools face an enormous task of educating an increasingly diverse student body. The task becomes exacerbated when helping these students make the transition to college, and one main way to tackle that challenge is through effective outreach programs. Outreach programs are a pathway to postsecondary educational opportunities for students of color, and they can assist students who have overcome adversity.

While several nationwide and local outreach initiatives are geared toward increasing student achievement and college participatory rates of underrepresented pupils, it is not clear in what capacity all of these programs are working. Therefore, a clearinghouse should be in place as a one-stop shop for all outreach programs being used in the public and private sector.

Targeted Outreach

The research is clear that early intervention programs are critical to increasing the chances that at-risk or underrepresented students of color will go on to higher education. In order to increase the participatory rates of underrepresented students attending college, support is critical to their success. Outreach programs should be all-encompassing to assist the student from middle school through high school in preparing them for college. One way to do that effectively is to start with dissemination of information. In my years with the California Senate Select Committee on Higher Education Admissions and Outreach, we found that the lack of appropriate and timely dissemination of information is a barrier to students going to college. Educational resources and the opportunities for students to benefit from them are inequitably distributed throughout schools. The culture is that if students are at a low-performing school, they are not encouraged and provided with information at the same level as those students attending affluent schools, where most are expected to attend college.

At every public high school a list of outreach or academic development programs should be posted in the counselor's office and school offices and on the school Web site along with their eligibility requirements, so that students can be aware and encouraged to participate. Information committees designed to disseminate information regarding postsecondary education should be established in every school district to educate students on the opportunities to attend college.

In order to ensure that underrepresented students of color have a range of postsecondary opportunities we must begin to change the culture of low-performing public schools. We need to assist students in making plans early in their elementary and secondary careers.

According to research, a student is 21 percent more likely to attend college if the student has begun forming college plans in the 10th grade, rather than in the senior year of high school.[8] Based upon years of research on college access, Patricia McDonough of the Higher Education and Organizational Change Division at UCLA has developed key principles that enhance the college-going rate for underrepresented students of color.

The first principle is the need to establish clear and constant communication on school sites as to the criteria to attend college. Expectations must be clear, as students need to know exactly what is expected of them in order to be prepared for college. If schools wish to be successful in preparing and encouraging students for college, a majority of counselors at high schools need to be college counselors.

Schools need to inform students of critical tests like the Pre-SAT, SAT I and II, and ACT and assist them in preparing for and registering to take them. Faculty plays a major role in maintaining a college-going culture, and they need to incorporate important college information into their classrooms.

Families and parents have to actively participate in their child's education and need to be aware of the college planning process and must work with the school to ensure students have accurate and timely information.[9] Going to college should be a constant message articulated throughout the students' primary and secondary academic career.

Students, parents and diverse communities value education, so all programs should be tailored around the student's culture of what they value. Use college students who have come from similar backgrounds and communities to reinforce the importance of college.

The focus on postsecondary education needs to be shifted from access to college to success in college geared toward helping students graduate with a degree. Students overcoming adversity need more other students they can relate to who have made it to college. Peer groups are very important and influential to students in high school and play a vital role in college aspirations for students of color. Include the peer groups in the college process and help the group as a whole see the importance.

Mentoring is a critical part of increasing college-going rates. Mentors can come in the form of teachers, program directors, parents, and counselors. The important thing is that mentors develop and provide long-term support to students and encourage them through information and resources to attend college. Since most of these programs are administered at the local level, while some are administered at the state and federal level, the decentralization makes it not possible to list all of the individual programs. Following is a summary of Student Academic Development Programs:

Student Opportunity and Access Program: designed to improve the flow of information and to increase student enrollment in postsecondary education.

Advancement Via Individual Determination: targets educationally disadvantaged students in college preparatory classes to help prepare them academically to make the transition to college.

California Academic Partnership Program: designed to foster partnerships between schools and colleges with the intent to improve academic preparation for middle and high school students seeking to earn baccalaureate degrees.

College Readiness Program: to increase the number of first-generation and low-income students enrolling in college. The program works to improve the academic preparation of middle school students so they are better prepared to complete college preparatory high school curriculum.

Early Academic Outreach Program: to increase the eligibility of groups with low college-going rates. The program assists students in completing college preparatory courses that lead to eligibility for the university.

Break the Cycle Program: UC-Berkeley students provide instruction in math to underrepresented and disadvantaged students.

Community Teaching Fellowships: recruits mathematics teachers for low-income and urban schools. In addition, it recruits college math majors to tutor K-12 pupils in these schools.

The Puente Project Training Institute: This program originates out of California. It provides support and training to teachers and counselors for ways to work effectively with students from families who have no college experience. One of the main methodologies is the integration of cultural literature into the core curriculum so that teachers can better communicate with their diverse classrooms.

Upward Bound College Prep Academy: an academic enrichment program that provides high school students of all cultural backgrounds with the motivation and academic skills necessary to successfully complete secondary education and to enter postsecondary education.

The Urban Community-School Collaborative: according to the University of California, this program creates collaborative university/school/community models for strengthening K-12 urban education to promote the educational achievement of educationally disadvantaged youth.

Initiative Programs: summer and intersession academic programs for middle and high school students, teachers and counselors geared toward college preparation.

Technology Initiative: digital programs designed to promote equity and access to quality education. These programs connect college and universities to K-12 projects that promote and develop effective uses of computers and Internet technologies in standards-based K-12 teaching with academic activities.

Professional Schools

Like undergraduate institutions, the professional schools of medicine and law struggle with attracting underrepresented students of color. Access to resources and support are two main components to attracting and retaining students of color. Let's discuss some possible solutions that may encourage students of color to attend selective and elite institutions. Selective and elite universities as well as the communities they serve need to develop programs that enhance economic opportunities, employment and awareness for underrepresented students of color to increase their participation in the legal and medical professions.

Special education workshops, mentoring, internships and externships serve to increase the number of underrepresented students of color in these fields.

First, internship programs should be established to provide access to the fields of law and medicine for students. These will provide students of color with an opportunity to learn more about the legal and medical professions through work experience and educational programs.

Internships can help students receive assistance in working collaboratively with the community they hope to serve upon completion of their education. All selective and elite institutions should work with local school districts and the communities they serve to provide internships to students in their third and final years of professional education.

Second, volunteer programs should be established nationwide. For example, volunteer programs that encourage attorneys and physicians to donate their time and experience to nonprofit organizations like the United Way. These programs serve inner-city kids and target underrepresented students of color enrolled in area schools.

Third, professional organizations like the American Bar Association and the Association of American Medical Colleges and the selective and elite institutions should establish newspapers and newsletters that target kids and current law and medical students. These publications can provide literature that conform to K-12 curriculum and spark the interest of young students along with encouraging their use by teachers inside the classroom, but also enhance discussion and debate about current issues for law and medical students.

Fourth, job shadow days should be a requirement of all selective and elite law and medical schools. Job shadow days should be coordinated with attorneys and physicians and also with area programs serving at-risk neighborhoods.

Fifth, training and summer camps need to be established nationwide to provide underrepresented students of color and disadvantaged students with comprehensive six- or eight-week program offering an introduction to the fields of medicine and law along with training students to tackle the first year of medical or law school. These camps should provide students with the opportunity to take programs that most students take in the first year of law or medical school.

Sixth, selective and elite institutions need to pull from their undergraduate students in their junior or senior year and encourage them to apply to the professional schools. This can increase the number of underrepresented students of color in the applicant pool.

Seventh, selective and elite institutions nationwide need to establish eligibility task forces for the different racial/ethnic groups admitted to the institutions. The goal of the task force would be to study issues related to eligibility and develop recommendations for increasing and enhancing the presence of this particular segment of the student population.

Eighth, selective institutions need to establish welcome committees or student welcome days as year-round orientation programs where first- and second-year law and medical students connect with upper-level students. Welcome committees should be comprised of students, faculty, administrators, staff and campus organizations. The committee can go out into the community to encourage underrepresented students of color to apply and serve as an advisory committee that can meet regularly to develop recruitment and retention ideas and share commonalities related to underrepresented student issues. Let's take a look at a few programs that encompass some of these ideas:

• St. Louis Internship Program: established by the St. Louis Bar Association, works with local school districts and other organizations and employs students at area law firms and law agencies.[10]

• Writing competition: an essay contest for law and medical students centered on the awareness of diversity in the profession. The contest should be geared toward students in law or medical school. Winners should receive scholarship or grant dollars for their education.

• Summer law programs: geared for undergraduates and designed to familiarize students with career options in law and medicine. The program helps students with the application process and requirements for admission. The program takes place on a college campus. Students have free room and board and the program is structured after the first year of law or medical school, and students take classes.

• PALS: Practicing Attorneys for Law Students program connects underrepresented law students with attorneys as mentors to assist with information and guidance in the legal profession.[11]

• Mock trials: programs for high school students that teach them about the law and encourage them to consider going into law as a profession. This program is designed to provide positive role models and increase understanding of the role of lawyers for youth in urban communities.

• Nashville High School Summer Intern Program: underrepresented students of color in their senior year of high school in good academic standing are exposed to legal workplace or corporate, private and governmental law offices. The program also provides students with a weekly educational component on opportunities in the legal profession.[12]

• The National Bar Association Summer Law Camp: a four-week program intended for students in high school. The camp offers students access to college level courses on university campuses across the country. Faculty and law students participate in instructing students through the summer camp.[13]

• Summer Institutes: the American Bar Association also runs summer camps throughout the country. These programs are geared toward underrepresented low-income and educationally disadvantaged students. Students get an insight into the first year of law school on college campuses. This should be expanded nationwide, and medical schools are encouraged to participate.[14]

• Corporate and School Partnerships: corporate business sponsor programs geared towards increasing the number of underrepresented students of color into law and medical schools. The Lucent Technologies is one such example they sponsor a summer internship program for students at Rutgers University.

• New York County Lawyers Association: has an internship program first and second year law students of color in New York County are eligible to participate. The program is a paid judicial internship in which students work directly with judges in the New York Supreme Court.[15]

There are numerous programs and foundations designed to target graduate outreach for underrepresented students of color. The Bureau of Health Professions, the U.S. Department of Health and Human Services and the California Endowment have programs designed with the goal of increasing opportunities for underrepresented students. These programs include:

Health Careers Opportunities Program: designed to increase access for disadvantaged individuals in the health fields.

Minority Faculty Fellowships Program: assists professional schools in enhancing faculty at their institution through training and preparation, which will better prepare them for the tenure process.

Centers of Excellence: designed to establish educational pipelines in the community with the goal of increasing the number of health professionals.

Minority Medical Education Program: summer program designed to assist underrepresented students of color obtain access to medical school.

Health Professions Partnerships Initiative: a grant provided by the Kellogg Foundation that allows students from all backgrounds to participate in early intervention programs in medicine.

Minority Student Medical Career Awareness Workshop: an annual career fair sponsored by the Association of American Medical Colleges. This program is offered to high school and college students, and they are teamed up with different admissions officers and financial aid representatives from colleges and universities throughout the country.

Medical Minority Applicant Registry: admissions opportunities to medical school for underrepresented students of color and economically disadvantaged groups. These students, upon taking the MCAT, register with the program, which distributes their biographies to college and university admissions offices that belong to the AAMC.

Minority Student Opportunities in United States Medical Schools: through AAMC, a database of information about program opportunities for underrepresented students of color for a career in medicine.

Area Health Education Centers take on the charge of improving the distribution, supply and health workforce in underserved communities. Health Education and Training Centers have a specific goal of training a diverse workforce along the U.S. and Mexican border and in Florida.[16]

The Office of Minority Health's goal is to improve access to quality health care in communities of color. The program targets the number of minority health professional through increased grants for underrepresented students of color working and attending Latino-serving institutions, Historically Black Colleges and Universities and tribal colleges. The National Institutes of Health provides financial and professional assistance to increase the number of underrepresented students of color in biomedical research. The Minority Access to Research Careers is a collection of programs designed to provide grants to institutions through undergraduate student training in academic research and postbaccalaureate education program. Universities provide funds to support internships for underrepresented students of color and encourage them to pursue careers in biomedical research.

The Association of American Medical Colleges created the 3,000 by 2000 initiative when it was established in 1991. The goal was to provide 3,000 underrepresented students in medical schools by the year 2000. Today, the 3,000 by 2000 project works in a collaborative effort with other professional schools to increase diversity in the field.[17] Lastly, the Kids in Health Careers Program raises awareness of the health profession by encouraging kids to think about and enter the health field. While these are federal programs, they are not accessible to all underrepresented students of color. Some programs are grants, and others provide support through research. All these programs need to be fully funded and provided to all students.

Outreach programs are vital to increasing opportunities for underrepresented students of color from disadvantaged backgrounds in achieving eligibility and enrolling at selective four-year institutions. These programs should be expanded nationwide, funded fully and provided to all students seeking to attend postsecondary education. All colleges and universities need to offer the programs mentioned for underrepresented students.

Public schools and universities must continue to establish effective ways to provide information and resources within the K-12 community. Information must be provided to ensure all high school students are enrolled in college preparatory courses. All public schools should be given resources to maintain at least two college counselors on campus. There are not enough counselors in public schools; nationally the average student-to-counselor ratio is 600-to-1 for students in high school. While counselors are usually bogged down with other responsibilities like course scheduling, schools need to establish a development program solely for counselors, to provide information on college testing requirements and admissions criteria for colleges and universities. These recommendations, if provided nationwide and fully funded, can increase opportunities for students of color to obtain access to college.

Dr. Winston Doby, vice president for educational outreach at the University of California, indicated that to be successful in locating students who have overcome adversity you need to secure certain learning conditions for all students. These conditions are grounded in opportunity to learn and serve as a framework for student development and school reform. Doby identified three key areas that all schools must take charge of if students are going to make the transition to college. He advises, "a rigorous standards-based curriculum beginning in the early grades and culminating in a full array of Advanced Placement and honors courses in high school; a multicultural college-going identity that allows all students to see a connection between their identities and going to college; and access to external learning resources through enabling technology that gives low-performing schools equal access to the Internet and other resources."[18]

Colleges and universities need to level the playing field, making all admission standards fair. Former Princeton president William G. Bowen and James Shulman, in their book, *The Game of Life*, found that male athletes had a 48 percent greater chance of being admitted and female athletes had 53 percent greater chance. Students of alumni (legacy students) and those from wealthy families should not receive a preference. Why?

Admissions officers should seek students from all spectrums of the eligibility scale and eliminate all hidden preferences. The hidden preferences of legacy and athlete admissions is one of money these groups bring to the institution. Is money the purpose of the university? Of course it needs money, but wouldn't the lower standards affect the prestige and the quality of the education students receive?

When colleges and universities began changing admission policies to prohibit the use of race, the term "merit" came to the forefront. Many university officials began using the term as a means of describing the restructuring of admissions. The term, although never operationally defined by most institutions, is used in a host of admissions documents. Many in the education community, including myself, had assumed theories of the new shift in terms. Miller (1996), Forbes (1996) and Smith (1998) assert that the use of "merit" became apparent when the assumption was made that students were gaining admission based solely on skin color. For example, during the anti-affirmative action initiative campaigns in California (Proposition 209) and Washington (Initiative-200), the term merit took on new significance in college admissions. For example, the texts of both initiatives stated, "end preferential treatment and to promote individual opportunity based on merit."

The dictionary defines merit as a level of superiority, making it highly subjective in the world of college admissions, but what does that mean? Because academic qualifications have always been the primary focus, why use the term merit instead of academic qualifications? With this assumption, the term merit emerged to the forefront of the admissions debate. According to researchers, the subjective use of merit with no definition has become biased in its interpretation and use regarding admissions.

The conclusion that more than academic merit is the determining factor in admissions is not a simple one. According to Dr. Cheryl Miller-Browne, an education researcher, "when closely examined, academic merit, which was meant to be an unbiased, purely objective measure of a student's qualifications and achievement, loses some of its supposed objectivity. Why, because merit itself is a subjectively contrived concept. For those persons whose mental ability is viewed as less adept, is doubted for any reason, or just maybe is limited due to prejudice, higher levels of education are quite frequently considered inappropriate, with the justification that these persons simply do not measure up academically. This is how access to education is restricted on the basis of academic merit."[19]

We need to redefine merit. GPA and SAT scores alone fail to describe students and their academic potential. Such comparisons are like comparing apples with onions. Affluent students tend to have the advantage of college-educated parents and comfortable high school experiences. Comparable low-income students often take on increased family responsibilities in unstable homes. They are also often forced to take on jobs, face long transportation commutes, lack quiet and safe places to study, and often face the threat of violence. If they can survive and perform in their current conditions they have demonstrated merit.

As University of California, Berkeley's Robert Berdahl asserts, "While affirmative action was intended to reward individual merit in college admissions, the effort to attain the overriding moral objective of racial justice through other means may have actually weakened the merit-based system of admissions."

The focus of merit by selective and elite institutions weighs heavy on quantitative means, focusing more on student outcomes. This approach presents a faulty assumption that all students are the same. All students are not the same, and admissions officials who use a limited means to examine students' accomplishments will never be able to view the total student from the context of his background and what he faces on a day-to-day basis. This approach historically tends not to favor students of color.

The reason it becomes a disadvantage for underrepresented students of color is the perception within American culture that students in poverty or matriculated through inferior education do not have merit. This is a myth supported by those who believe that access to quality education is equally accessible to all. As Oakes (2003) articulates, "Merit permeates how Americans make sense about schooling, emphasizing the role of the individual, and de-emphasizing the responsibilities of school or society."[20] Basically, many individuals see the problem as the student and not the economic, social, and educational situation that made the student less competitive.

In an effort to examine merit beyond quantifiable means, institutions need to conduct extensive reviews of student applicants. Extensive reviews, like the University of California's "comprehensive review," need to be in place to examine student potential that goes beyond academic accomplishments. However, this is also challenging, since elite and selective institutions use background characteristics like leadership, overcoming personal hardship, etc., that can make only a slight difference in admission decisions.

Elite and selective institutions should consider eliminating the SAT and ACT scores in admissions decisions. Numerous research reports have well-documented that underrepresented students of color have disparate outcomes on standardized exams and that they end up serving largely as gatekeepers to admission. Former president of the University of California

Richard Atkinson in 2001 proposed eliminating the SAT in admissions decisions because the scores fail to reflect high school curriculum knowledge. In determining merit, selective institutions should rely more on high school courses, GPA and student potential.

Merit should be used twofold: first as achievement of outcomes and second as an assessment of student potential or ability. Universities must operate with a definition of merit that is twofold, which evenly examines outcome and potential and takes into account the relative. Student potential will allow for elite and selective institutions to view a broader context of an applicant's merit for admission. Potential fits within the context of students who work full-time and provide for families while going to school, and more often than not these are students of color.

Selective and elite institutions should consider both the individual merit as well as the applicants' group membership. This can augment perceptions of equity and fairness. Civil rights organizations and law and medical associations should conduct workshops to educate admissions committees at undergraduate and professional schools on qualitative characteristics and personal accomplishments in assessing student applicants.

For example, the Association of American Medical Colleges established the Expanded Minority Admissions Exercise. This workshop assists admissions committees in the use of "noncognitive variables" for students admitted to medical school. According to AAMC, the goal of this program is "to increase the participants' knowledge and awareness of the importance of noncognitive strengths of applicants and help participants to select students with a high likelihood of success."[21]

This would be an equitable utilization of real merit. These recommendations are just the tip of the iceberg. Success of these programs is dependent upon full funding, support from the community and a buy-in from colleges and universities to utilize all avenues in recruiting and retaining underrepresented students of color.

In conclusion, in order for the United States to become a fully democratic society, all students must have access to a quality education and in order for that education to be of quality and to train students to be competitive, it must be diverse. According to Justice O'Connor, "in order to cultivate a set of leaders with legitimacy in the eyes of the citizenry, it is necessary that the path to leadership be visibly open to talented and qualified individuals of every race and ethnicity. All members of our heterogeneous society must have confidence in the openness and integrity of the educational institutions that provide this training."[22] While there is evidence that educational opportunity is inequitable along racial lines, selective and elite institutions must utilize policies like affirmative action to fully integrate their institutions.

The current structure of disparities within school districts cannot be allowed to continue to exist. Students who are not given all the tools to compete adequately cannot be judged at the same level as students who are. What we must ultimately embrace and understand is that the public education system was designed to provide students with the necessary skills and abilities to enter the workforce of tomorrow. If we want to adhere to this mission we must improve our educational system to ensure that all students, especially our underrepresented youth, are able to succeed. If the United States is to provide a strong social and economic future for its youth, then it must ensure that equitable educational opportunities are available for all students.

Universities that seek out diversity for all students in the community and in society can only be successful by integrating all facets of diversity along with students, administration, faculty, and a more inclusive curriculum.

As one letter writer in *Commentary* magazine put it: "Every major institution in American society churches, universities, courts, academies of science, governments, economies, newspapers, magazines, television, film and others attempted to exclude black people from the human family in the name of white supremacist ideology. This unrelenting assault on black humanity produced the fundamental condition of black culture — that of black invisibility and namelessness."[23] The United States has a long way to go on the road to equity. Most of us may want to believe in a color-blind society, but so long as there are inequities and discrimination along racial and ethnic lines, a color-blind society is but an aspiration. Unfortunately, the United States is not free from the vestiges of discrimination reinforced for centuries by law. The conclusions in the U.S. Supreme Court decisions on affirmative action in *Grutter v. Bollinger* and *Gratz v. Bollinger* acknowledge that we still have work to do.

That idea of equal opportunity for all is what we must strive toward every day. We should start with the dream of what was denied my ancestors, access to education. Access to an equitable education will open the door to full integration, which will place us on the road to racial integrity.

Affirmative action will remain controversial. It is a complex policy that most Americans do not understand, and its very presence is a reminder of an immoral stain on the fabric of America. Its existence is the reality that we are not all created equal, that we have a history of dehumanization, exclusion and division. In order to move beyond that we need to move beyond our perceptions and conditions of social behavior that encourage division and discrimination. Desegregation in America has proven to be the easy part. It is integration that is the real challenge to our society. Affirmative action is an appropriate and necessary policy that encourages integration through all levels of education. This policy is helping to build middle and affluent classes of underrepresented people of color.

Appendix: Affirmative Action Timeline

1866 **Civil Rights Act of 1866.** First anti-discrimination legislation passed in the United States.

1868 **Fourteenth Amendment to the Constitution.** Ratified and conferred citizenship to individuals born in the country and granted equal protection of law.

1877 **Compromise Act.** Eliminated Reconstruction; enacted by President Rutherford B. Hayes.

1883 The U.S. Supreme Court struck down the Civil Rights Act of 1875, and Jim Crow laws begin throughout the South.

1896 **Plessy v. Ferguson.** In this historic case, the Supreme Court upheld racial segregation under the doctrine of "separate but equal."

1909 W.E.B. DuBois along with others established the **National Association for the Advancement of Colored People** (NAACP).

1934 **Public Works Administration.** A federal order issued by Harold Ickes, secretary of the Interior to President Roosevelt, prohibited discrimination against people of color working on public works administration projects.

June 1941 Executive Order 8802. Issued by President Roosevelt, it required all federal defense programs to Eliminate discrimination based upon race, national origin and citizenship.

1950 **Sweatt v. Painter.** The U.S. Supreme Court prohibits racial segregation in public law schools.

1954 **Brown v. Board of Education.** The U.S. Supreme Court dismantled racial segregation in public schools.

1957 **U.S. Commission on Civil Rights.** The agency was established under the Civil Rights Act of 1957. Through investigation of violation of civil rights, the agency's goal is to eradicate discrimination.

March 1961 President Kennedy signed Executive Order 10925, creating the Equal Employment Opportunity Commission. Mandates that affirmative steps are taken to eradicate racial bias in employment and hiring. The mission of the committee is to promote and implement equal employment opportunity for all qualified persons seeking government employment.

July 1964 President Johnson signs **Civil Rights Act**, prohibiting discrimination of all kinds.

September 1965 President Johnson signs **Executive Order 11246** which implements affirmative action for the first time, reiterating executive order 10925.

1967 President Johnson signs **Executive Order 11375**, which amended Executive Order 11246 to include discrimination based upon gender.

1969 **Department of Labor creates the Philadelphia Order.** Established by President Nixon, the order was designed to guarantee equity in construction jobs. Under the plan, the construction industry in Philadelphia implemented affirmative action to increase access for minorities in the industry.

1971 **Griggs v. Duke Power Co.** The U.S. Supreme Court held that employers must show the necessity of aptitude tests for performing jobs after evidence was provided that industrial aptitude tests were being used as criteria to exclude people of color from jobs and were largely irrelevant to the required job.

June 1978 **Regents of the University of California v. Bakke.** U.S. Supreme Court decision that approved the consideration of race, so long as it is not the deciding factor in college admissions, but found quotas unconstitutional.

1979 **United Steelworkers of America v. Weber.** The U.S. Supreme Court requires the establishment of an in-house training program that reserved 50 percent of spaces for African Americans. The ruling asserted that Title VII does not prohibit race-conscious affirmative action. The program was set up through a permissible plan designed to eliminate existing patterns of racial segregation without adversely impacting white employees.

1979 EEOC issued guidelines on affirmative action programs consistent with Title VII.

July 1980 **Fillilove v. Klutznick.** The U.S. Supreme Court upholds a federal law that requires 15 percent of funds for public works is set aside for qualified minority contractors.

1984 **Firefighters Local Union v. Stotts.** The U.S. Supreme Court ruled that authorized affirmative action plans were appropriate under Title VII to provide reprieve to victims of discrimination.

1987 **Wygant v. Jackson Board of Education.** The U.S. Supreme Court struck down the layoff policy of the board and found it unconstitutional because it violated the equal rights for white teachers.

January 1989 **City of Richmond v. Croson.** This set aside 30 percent of city contracts in Richmond for women and minorities. The Supreme Court ruled that past discrimination in an industry does not justify the use of a "racial quota." The court ruled that affirmative action was unconstitutional unless racial discrimination could be proven.

December 1990 Michael Williams, assistant secretary of education for civil rights under the Bush administration, issues an opinion that scholarship set-asides for students of color violate civil rights laws.

1991 **Civil Rights Act of 1991.** Angry at the U.S. Supreme Court's reversal of the Griggs decision, Congress passes the act of 1991 that restored the disparate impact standards in the Griggs case.

1994 **Podberesky v. Kirwan.** The U.S. Supreme Court struck down the University of Maryland's Banneker Scholarship Program for high-achieving African American high school students as unconstitutional.

July 1995   Regents of the University of California pass resolution SP-1, which prohibits the use of race-conscious admissions at all UC campuses. The University of California became the first university since segregation was legal to implement such a ban.

1995   Adarand Constructos Inc. v. Pena. The U.S. Supreme Court ruled that federal, state, and local government affirmative action programs are subject to strict scrutiny, meaning they are legal only if necessary as a compelling interest.

July 1995   White House presents guidelines on affirmative action. In a speech President Bill Clinton confirmed the need for affirmative action and reaffirmed the continued existence of systematic discrimination. The guidelines required the elimination of any program which provided preferences for unqualified individuals, created reverse discrimination, created a quota, or continues after equity goals had been achieved.

November 1996   California Civil Rights Initiative Proposition 209. California voters pass an initiative that bans all forms of affirmative action in public education, employment, and contracting.

March 1996   Hopwood v. University of Texas Law School. The Fifth Circuit U.S. Court of Appeals eliminated the university's affirmative action program after Cheryl Hopwood and three other white applicants sued the university with claims that the program discriminated against white applicants.

January 1997   American Civil Rights Institute. The nonprofit organization's mission is to eliminate affirmative action nationwide.

October 1997   Center for Individual Rights. A conservative law firm files lawsuits against the University of Michigan's undergraduate and law school affirmative action programs. The suits claim the admission programs discriminate against whites (discussed in detail in Chapter Four).

1997   One America. A yearlong initiative on race established by President Clinton. The goal was to research the issue and provide a report to the administration with recommendations.

December 1998   Initiative 200. Washington state follows in the footsteps of California and eliminates all affirmative action programs.

January 1999   The University of Georgia's affirmative action admissions policies are ruled unconstitutional by a federal judge.

February 2000   Florida prohibits the use of race in college admissions with Gov. Jeb Bush's "One Florida Plan."

December 2002   The U.S. Supreme Court agrees to hear the Gratz and Grutter Michigan cases (discussed in detail in Chapter Four).

June 2003   The U.S. Supreme Court reaffirms the use of affirmative action in college admissions.

Sources: Journal of Blacks in Higher Education, www.infoplease.com, Bloch 1994, Edley 1996, and Americans United for Affirmative Action.

Notes

1. The Grim Reality

1. G. Orfield, and D. Whitla. "Diversity and Legal Education: Student Experiences in Leading Law Schools." In Gary Orfield and Michael Kurlaender (eds.), *Diversity Challenged*. The Civil Rights Project (Harvard University: Harvard Education Publishing Group, 2001).

2. www.jbhe.com.

3. President's Report 1993–95, "Evidentiary Framework for Diversity as a Compelling Interest in Higher Education," 109 *Harvard Law Review* 1357 (1996).

4. Stanford University.

5. John Dibiaggio, "What Leaders are Saying About Affirmative Action and Diversity." *American Council of Education*, www.acenet.edu.

6. University of Georgia: www.uga.edu.

7. Association of American Colleges and Universities, www.diversityweb.org.

8. Patricia Gurin, "The Benefits of Diversity in College and Beyond: An Empirical Analysis," University of Michigan, 1999.

9. H.F. Pitkin and S.M. Shumer, "On Participation," in Goodwyn (ed.), *Organizing Democracy*, 1982. Princeton, NJ: Princeton University Press.

10. J. Piaget, *The Equilibration of Cognitive Structures: The Central Problem of Intellectual Development*. (Chicago: University of Chicago Press, 1975).

11. Association of American Colleges and Universities, *American Pluralism and the College Curriculum: Higher Education in a Diverse Democracy*. (Washington, D.C.: Association of American Colleges and Universities, 1995).

12. Interviews with college students (who requested that real names not be used), California State University, Sacramento, April 1998.

13. Tim Simmons, "Race's Role in College Admissions," *The News and Observer*, Dec. 15, 2002.

14. Ibid.

15. Jennifer Day and Andrea Curry, "Educational Attainment in the United States: March 1998 (update)," Current Population Reports P20–513, Washington D.C.: U.S. Bureau of the Census, 1998, and California Department of Finance, *www.dof.ca.gov*.

16. W. Bowen and D. Bok, *The Shape of the River: Long-term Consequences of Considering Race in College and University Admissions*. Princeton, NJ: Princeton University Press, 1998.

17. G. Orfield, and D. Whitla. "Diversity and Legal Education: Student Experiences in Leading Law Schools." In Gary Orfield and Michael Kurlaender (eds.), *Diversity Challenged*. The Civil Rights Project (Harvard University: Harvard Education Publishing Group, 2001).

18. Ibid.

19. University of California Board of

Admissions and Relations with Schools, "A Preliminary Analysis of the University of California, Berkeley Admissions Process for 2002," Sept. 24, 2003, draft.

20. Sara Hebel. "Berkeley's Chancellor Attacks University Regents for Publicly Questioning Admissions Practices," *The Chronicle of Higher Education*, Oct. 20, 2003.

21. Rebecca Trounson, David Silverstein and Doug Smith. "Overall, Race No Factor for Low-Scoring UC." *The Los Angeles Times*, Nov. 3, 2003.

22. Carl Glickman, "Defining a Great University," University of Georgia News Bureau; *www.uga.edu/columns*, May 3, 1999.

23. Tim Simmons. "Race's role in college admissions," *The News and Observer*, Dec. 15, 2002.

24. Justice Frankfurter, *Sweezy v. New Hampshire*, 354 U.S. 234 (1957).

25. Bob Schaeffer, "New FairTest Analysis Finds: More than 700 4-Year Colleges Do Not Use SAT I or ACT Scores to Admit Substantial Numbers of Bachelor Degree Applicants," *www.fairtest.org*, Oct. 8, 2003.

26. Ibid.

27. J. Banks and C.M. Banks, *Multicultural Education: Issues and Perspectives*, third edition, Boston: Allyn and Bacon, 1997.

28. Bob Laird, "Bending Admissions to Political Ends," *The Chronicle of Higher Education*, May 17, 2002.

29. Piper Fogg, "University of California, for First Time, Admits More Minority Students Than It Did Under Affirmative Action," *The Chronicle of Higher Education*, April 8, 2002.

30. Peter Schmidt. "U. of California Ends Affirmative-Action Ban, State Law Still Bars Preferences," *The Chronicle of Higher Education*, May 25, 2001.

31. M.A. Barreto and H.P. Pachon, "Turning the Tide or Turning Them Away? The Reality of Race Neutral Admissions for Minority Students at the University of California," The Tomás Rivera Policy Institute, *www.trpi.org*, April 2003.

32. Texas Higher Education Coordinating Board.

33. Lee Shearer, "Regents Deny Charges of Race Bias." Online Athens, *www.onlineathens.com*, Aug. 14, 2000.

34. Ibid.

35. Sharon Hannon, "Staying the Course Becomes a Rallying Cry," *Georgia Magazine*, *www.uga.edu/gm*, Dec. 14, 1999.

36. Ibid.

37. Sharon Hannon. "Can Race Play a Role in the Admissions Process?", *Georgia Magazine*, *www.uga.edu/gm*, Sept. 14, 1999.

38. Joan Stroer, "Judge Lets UGA Continue Admissions Policy." Online Athens, *www.onlineathens.com*, February 12, 2000.

39. Lee Shearer, "Ruling Draws Mixed Reaction," Online Athens, *www.onlineathens.com*, July 25, 2000.

40. Michael Adams, "Statement by UGA President," University of Georgia, *www.uga.edu/news/*, Nov. 29, 2001.

41. Joan Stroer, "Judge Lets UGA Continue Admissions Policy," Online Athens, *www.onlineathens.com*, Feb. 12, 2000

42. The Associated Press, "Fewer Blacks Enrolling in Georgia's Top Schools," Online Athens, *www.onlineathens.com*, July 30, 2000.

43. "Drop in Freshmen Applications Surprises UW; Some Blame I-200," *University of Washington Alumni Magazine*, June 1999.

44. Ibid.

45. Patrick Healy and Liz McMillen. "Judge Affirms Validity of Bakke in U. of Washington Affirmative Action Lawsuit," *The Chronicle of Higher Education*, Feb. 26, 1999.

46. Susan Wierzbicki and Charles Hirschman, "The End of Affirmative Action in Washington State and Its Impact on the Transition from High School to College," Center for Studies in Demography and Ecology, University of Washington, July 20, 2001.

47. Ibid.

48. Jeffrey Selingo, "Florida Plan to

End Racial Preferences in Admissions Attracts Attention — and Criticism," *The Chronicle of Higher Education*, Nov. 26, 1999.

49. Ibid.

50. Matt Avery, "One Florida in Hands of Legislature," *The Alligator*, March 13, 2000.

51. Ibid.

52. W.B. Harvey, "Minorities in Higher Education Annual Status Report," *American Council on Education*, October 2003.

53. Ibid.

54. *Journal of Blacks in Higher Education*, Volume 29, Autumn 2000.

2. The Professional School Armageddon

1. American Bar Association, *www.abanet.org*.

2. Alexis de Tocqueville, "Democracy in America" 1835

3. American Bar Association, "Common Racial and Ethnic Diversity in the Profession," *Goal IX Report* 2000–01.

4. Report of the New York Judicial Commission on Minorities, *Urban Law Journal*, 181, 1992.

5. James Podgers, "Message Bearers Wanted: Judiciary Needs to Expand Effort to Explain and Bolster Public Perception of Justice System," *American Bar Association Journal*, April 1999.

6. David B. Rattman and Alan J. Tomkins, "Public Trust and Confidence in the Courts: What Public Opinion Surveys Mean to Judges," *Court Review*, Fall, 1999.

7. "Second Circuit Task Force on Gender, Racial and Ethnic Fairness in Courts Report of the Working Committees to the Second Circuit Task Force," Annual Survey American Legal, 117, 1997.

8. Minority Attorneys and underrepresented students of color are defined as Latinos, African Americans and Native American individuals.

9. "Miles to Go 2000: Progress of Minorities in the Legal Profession," American Bar Association Commission on Opportunities for Minorities in the Profession, 2000.

10. Law School Admission Council, "Minority Databook, Racial/Ethnic Representation of 2000 Graduates," 2002.

11. Blake Eskin, ed., *The Book of Political Lists*, (1998). Congressional Yellow Book, Leadership Directories, Inc, 2001.

12. "Miles to Go 2000: Progress of Minorities in the Legal Profession," American Bar Association Commission on Opportunities for Minorities in the Profession, 2000.

13. Senate Select Committee on Higher Education Admissions and Outreach, "Admissions and Access to the University: The Future of University Enrollment Providing Educational Equity for the Changing Population," hearing transcript, California State Senate Publications, 946-S, September 22, 1997.

14. Ibid.

15. 2003 data for Florida not available for this material.

16. Ibid.

17. Texas Higher Education Coordinating Board, "Projecting the Need for Medical Education in Texas: A Report on Efforts to Increase the Number of Underrepresented Students Enrolled at the State's Medical Schools," October 2002.

18. Association of American Medical Colleges, "Focus on Affirmative Action," *www.aamc.org/diversity*, 2003.

19. D. Libby, Z. Zhou and D. Kindig, "Will Minority Physician Supply Meet U.S. Needs?," *Health Affairs*, July/August 1997.

20. U.S. Department of Health and Human Services, "Issues of Health Disparity," Office of Minority Health, July 2001.

21. M. Komaromy, "The Role of Black and Hispanic Physicians in Providing Health Care for Underserved Populations," *New England Journal of Medicine*, 334, 1305, 1996.

22. David Wheeler, "Racial Disparity

Found in Lung-Cancer Care," *The Chronicle of Higher Education*, Nov. 5, 1999.

23. D. Libby, Z. Zhou and D. Kindig, "Will Minority Physician Supply Meet U.S. Needs?" *Health Affairs Journal*, July/August 1997.

24. S. Saha, "Patient-Physician Racial Concordance and the Perceived Quality and Use of Health Care," 159 ARCH International Medicine, 997, 1999.

25. J. Curtis, *Affirmative Action in Medicine: Improving Healthcare for Everyone.* Ann Arbor, Mich.: University of Michigan Press, 2003.

26. National Institutes of Health, "Strategic Research Plan to Reduce and Ultimately Eliminate Health Disparities," *www.nih.gov/about/hd/strategicplan.pdf.*

3. Historical Perspective

1. Interview with Tilly, former resident of Jackson, Miss. (August 2003).

2. Ibid.

3. Executive Order 8802, June 25, 1941.

4. *www.civilrights.org.*

5. Howard University, Commencement Address, June 4, 1965.

6. U.S. Equal Employment Opportunity Commission, Uniform Guidelines, 2000.

7. N. Glazer, "Society Needs Affirmative Action in Higher Education," In Bryan Grapes (eds.) *Affirmative Action*, Greenhaven Press, Inc. San Diego, CA, December 1999.

8. White House Memorandum, July 19, 1995.

9. *www.IMDIVERSITY.com*, 2002.

10. U.S. Department of Labor, Bureau of Labor Statistics data.

11. J.F. Dovidio and S.C. Baertner, "Affirmative Action, Unintentional Racial Biases, and Intergroup Relations," *Journal of Social Issues*, 1996.

12. J. F. Dovidio, K. Kawakami and S.L. Gaertner. "Reducing Contemporary Prejudice: Combating Explicit and Implicit Bias at the Individual and Intergroup Level," in *Reducing Prejudice and Discrimination*, Hillsdale, N.J.: Lawrence Erlbaurn Associates, 2000.

13. T. Wise, "Whites Swim in Radial Preferences," *www.Alternet.org* 2003.

14. M. Chang, D. Witt, J. Jones and K. Hakuta, eds., *Compelling Interest: Examining the Evidence on Racial Dynamics in Colleges and Universities*, Stanford, CA: Stanford University Press, 2003.

15. J. F. Dovidio, K. Kawakami and S.L. Gaertner. "Reducing Contemporary Prejudice: Combating Explicit and Implicit Bias at the Individual and Intergroup Level," in *Reducing Prejudice and Discrimination*, Hillsdale, N.J.: Lawrence Erlbaurn Associates, 2000.

16. National Opinion Research Center, 1991, 2000.

17. M. King, "Why We Can't Wait," New York: Harper & Row, 1964.

18. L. Chavez, "Admissions and statistics put to the test," *Washington Times*, Dec. 11, 2002.

19. "Graduation Rates of African American College Students," *Journal of Blacks in Higher Education*, Autumn 1994. "The Myth That Preferential College Admissions Creates High Black Student Dropout Rates." *Journal of Blacks in Higher Education*, Autumn 1993. "Searching for Good News on Black Student Graduation Rates," *Journal of Blacks in Higher Education*, Summer 2003.

20. D. Segal, "D.C. Public Interest Law Firm Puts Affirmative Action on Trial," *The Washington Post*, Feb. 20, 1998.

21. U.S. Department of Labor, 2001.

22. A. Hacker, "The Crackdown on African-Americans," The Nation, July 10. 1995.

23. Ford Foundation, *www.fordfound.org.*

24. Ibid.

25. Ibid.

26. Charles J. Ogletree, Jr., "The Case for Affirmative Action," *Stanford Magazine*, 1996.

27. W. Bowen and D. Bok, *The Shape of the River: Long-term Consequences of Considering Race in College and Univer-*

sity Admissions. Princeton, NJ: Princeton University Press, 1998.

28. T. Wise, "Little White Lies: The Truth About Affirmative Action and Reverse Discrimination," Twomey Center for Peace Through Justice, Loyola University, 1995.

4. The Courts and Affirmative Action

1. *Dred Scott v. Sandford*, 60 U.S. 19 HOW 393 (1857).

2. Eric Schnapper, "Affirmative Action and the Legislative History of the Fourteenth Amendment," Virginia Law Review, 71 Va. L. Rev. 753, 1985.

3. Ibid.

4. H.R. 63, Cong. Globe, 39th Congress, 1st Session. Constitutional Amendment XIV, 1866.

5. *Ward v. Flood*, 48 California (1874).

6. Missouri ex rel. Gaines v. Canada, 305 U.S. 337 (1938), p. 350.

7. Missouri ex rel. Gaines v. Canada, 305 U.S. 337 (1938), p. 10.

8. *Sweatt v. Painter*, 339 U.S. 629 (1950), p. 20.

9. *McLaurin v. Oklahoma State Regents for Higher Education* (1950).

10. Ibid., p. 25.

11. Ibid., p. 26.

12. *Brown v. Board of Education*, 347 U.S. 483 (1954).

13. Ibid.

14. P.G. Altbach, K. Lomotey, and C. Kerr, eds., "The Racial Crisis in American Higher Education," 1991. Suny Press, Albany, NY (1991).

15. *North Carolina State Board of Education et al. v. Swann et al.*, 402 U.S. 43; (1971).

16. Gary Orfield, *Schools More Separate: Consequences of a Decade of Resegregation*. The Civil Rights Project, Harvard University, July 17, 2001.

17. Manning Marable, *The Great Walls of Democracy: The Meaning of Race in American Life*, 2002. *www.BlackElectorate.com* (2002).

18. *F.S. Royster Guano Co. v. Commonwealth of Virginia*, 253 U.S. 412, 416 (1920).

19. *Hirabayahi v. U.S.*, 320 U.S. 81, 100 (1942).

20. *Korematsu v. United States*, 323 U.S. 214, 216 (1944).

21. Arthur Coleman, "The College Board, Diversity in Higher Education: A Strategic Planning and Policy Manual," 2001.

22. Dr. J. Owens Smith (1998) "Affirmative Action Measures Do Not Discriminate: The Nature of the Problem Is the U.S. Supreme Court's Violation of the International Human Rights Laws." Afro-Ethnic Studies: California State University: Fullerton, CA (Spring). Personal Interview.

23. *University of California Regents v. Bakke*, 438 U.S. 265 (1978).

24. Ibid.

25. Ibid.

26. Ibid.

27. *University of California Regents v. Roth*, 408 U.S. 564 (1973).

28. *University of California Regents v. Bakke*, 438 U.S. 265 (1978).

29. Dr. J. Owens Smith, "Affirmative Action Measures Do Not Discriminate," 1998.

30. *University of California Regents v. Bakke*, 438 U.S. 265 (1978).

31. *University of California Regents v. Bakke* (California Supreme Court, Nov. 25, 1974).

32. Goodwin Liu, "The Causation Fallacy: Bakke and the Basic Arithmetic of Selective Admissions," *Michigan Law Review*, Vol. 100: 1045, March 2002.

33. *University of California Regents v. Bakke* (California Supreme Court, August 1974) No. 31287.

34. Goodwin Liu, "The Causation Fallacy: Bakke and the Basic Arithmetic of Selective Admissions," *Michigan Law Review*, Vol. 100: 1045, March 2002.

35. Scott Jaschik, "High-Court Ruling Transforms Battles Over Desegregation at Colleges in 19 States," *The Chronicle of Higher Education*, July 1992.

36. *United States v. Fordice*, 505 U.S. 717 (1992).

37. Morton E. Winston, "Understanding Human Rights," in the *Philosophy of Human Rights*, Wadsworth, Thomson Learning, Florence, KY, 1989.

38. Dr. J. Owens Smith, Article 1(4) of the Convention for the Elimination of All Forms of Racial Discrimination in *Affirmative Action Measures Do Not Discriminate*, 1998.

39. Dr. J. Owens Smith, (1998) "Affirmative Action Measures Do Not Discriminate": The Nature of the Problem is the U.S. Supreme Courts Violation of the International Human Rights Laws. Afro-Ethnic Studies: California State University: Fullerton, CA (Spring). Personal Interview.

40. Adarand Constructors, Inc. v. Pena, 515 U.S. 200 (1995) 1.

41. Dr. J. Owens Smith, (1998) "Affirmative Action Measures Do Not Discriminate": The Nature of the Problem is the U.S. Supreme Courts Violation of the International Human Rights Laws. Afro-Ethnic Studies: California State University: Fullerton, CA (Spring). Personal Interview.

42. *Texas et al. v. Cheryl Hopwood*, 518 U.S. 1033; 116 S. Ct. 2581, 1996.

43. *Hopwood v. State of Texas*, 78 F. 3d 932 (5th Cir. 1996).

44. *Texas et al. v. Cheryl Hopwood*, 518 U.S. 1033; 116 S. Ct. 2581, 1996.

45. Ibid.

46. Ibid.

47. Ibid.

48. Ibid.

49. U.S. Department of Education Office for Civil Rights, Letter to Attorney General of Georgia (Michael Bowers) Regarding Affirmative Action and Public Colleges in Georgia, April 19, 1996.

50. Douglas Lederman, "Ga. Attorney General Urges Colleges to Curb Affirmative Action," *The Chronicle of Higher Education*, April 1996.

51. *Wooden v. Board of Regents of the University System of Georgia*, S.D. Court of Georgia, 1997.

52. Patrick Healy, "Lawsuit Attacks Race-Based Policies in U. System of Georgia," *The Chronicle of Higher Education*, March 14, 1997.

53. Ibid.

54. *Allen v. Wright*, 468 U.S. 737, 755 (1984), *Glenwood v. Intermountain Properties, Inc.*, 98 F. 3d 590, 593 (10th Cir. 1996).

55. *Green v. Board of Regents*, S.D. Ga. (1999).

56. Patrick Healy, "Dismissing Reverse-Bias Lawsuit, Judge Lashes Out at U. of Georgia Policies," The Chronicle of Higher Education, July 1999.

57. Matt Avery, *www.iwire.com*, "NAACP sues Regents over One Florida," April 2000.

58. Jeffrey Selingo, "Judge Upholds Florid Plan to End Affirmative Action," *The Chronicle of Higher Education*, July 2000.

59. Douglas Lederman, "Lawsuit Challenges Affirmative Action at U. of Washington," *The Chronicle of Higher Education*, March 1997.

60. *Smith v. University of Washington Law School*, 233 F 3d 1188 (9th Cir. 2000).

61. Ibid.

62. *University of California v. Bakke*, 438 U.S. 265 (1978).

63. *Grutter v. Bollinger*, 539 S. Ct. U.S. (2003).

64. *Gratz v. Bollinger*, 539 S. Ct., U.S. (2003)

65. *Grutter v. Bollinger*, 539 U.S. (2003).

66. Arthur Coleman and the College Board, *Diversity in Higher Education: A Strategic Planning and Policy Manual*, 2001.

67. *Grutter v. Bollinger*, 539 U.S., 2003.

68. *Gratz v. Bollinger*, 539, 123 U.S. Ct. (Ginsburg dissenting opinion), 2003.

69. *Grutter v. Bollinger*, 539 123 U.S. Ct. (Scalia dissenting opinion), 2003.

70. *Grutter v. Bollinger*, 539 U.S. (Thomas dissenting opinion) 2003.

71. *Grutter v. Bollinger*, 539 U.S. (2003).

72. Ibid.

73. Lewis Mumford Center for Comparative Urban and Regional Research, "Segregation in Neighborhoods and

Schools: Impacts on Minority Children in the Boston Region," Sept. 1, 2003.

74. Daniel Mark Fogel, "Opportunity: Expiration Date Is Set," *Chicago Tribune*, July 20, 2003.

5. Inequities in the System

1. Kenneth Ciongoli, "Discriminating Against Middle-Class Ethnic Americans (at the Country's Elite Colleges)." *USA Today Magazine*, November 1999.

2. Harry Pachon, Maya Federman and Laura Castillo, "An Analysis of Advanced Placement (AP) Courses in California High Schools," Tomás Rivera Policy Institute, *www.trpi.org*, 2000.

3. APEX Learning, *www.apexlearning.com*.

4. Jamey Fitzpatrick, Michigan Virtual University, *www.mivu.org*, 2001.

5. Sara Carr, "South Dakota Finds Mixed Results with Online AP Courses," *The Chronicle of Higher Education*, May 25, 2001.

6. "Ward Connerly: He Is America's Most Ardent Proponent of Colorblindness, a Successful Grassroots Political Leader, and a Bold Thinker on Questions of Race, Education and Government Policy." American Enterprise Institute for Public Policy: Gale Group, April–May 2003.

7. R. Corcoran, L.J. Walker and J.L. White, "Working in Urban Schools," Washington, D.C.: The Institute for Educational Leadership, (ED 299 356), 1988.

8. Kevin Carey, "Low-Income and Minority Students Still Receive Fewer Dollars in Many States," Education Trust, *www.edtrust.org*, Fall 2003.

9. Ibid.

10. Education Trust, "Good Teaching Matters: How Well-Qualified Teachers Can Close the Gap," Vol. 3:2, Summer, 1998.

11. J.E. Bruno and E. Negrete, "Analysis of Wage Incentive Programs for Promoting Staff Stability in a Large Urban

School District," *The Urban Review*, 15(3), 1988.

12. R. Rossi, B. Beaupre adn K. Grossman, "5,243 Illinois Teachers Failed Key Exams," *Chicago Sun-Times*, Sept. 6, 2001.

13. "Shortchanging the Neediest Students," (no author) *Chicago Sun-Times*, September 7, 2001.

14. L. Darling-Hammond, "Teacher Quality and Equality," unpublished paper prepared for the College Board's Project on Access to Learning, 1988.

15. Jeanne Brennan, and Kimberly Holmes, press release, "Getting Away with It: What Happens When No One's Minding the Store," Education Trust, *www.edtrust.org/edtrust*. December 2003.

16. Amy Argetsinger, "Legacy Students: A Counterpoint to Affirmative Action," *The Washington Post*, March 12, 2003. Also, *Journal of Blacks in Higher Education*, "Details on the Huge Advantage for Legacy Applicants," Jan. 3, 2004.

17. Amy Argetsinger, "Legacy Students: A Counterpoint to Affirmative Action," *The Washington Post*, March 12, 2003.

18. Jonathan Katz, "Legacy Keeping Preferential Treatment in the Family," Medill News Service, *journalism.medill.northwestern.edu*, March 2003.

19. Ibid.

20. Murray Sperber, "Affirmative Action for Athletes," *The Chronicle of Higher Education*, October 1995.

21. Daniel Golden, " Many Colleges Bend Rules to Admit Rich Applicants," *The Wall Street Journal*, Feb. 20, 2003.

22. Ibid.

23. Kit Lively, "Admissions Exemptions Prompt Concern in Massachusetts," *The Chronicle of Higher Education*, June 30, 1995.

24. Alene Russell, " Statewide College Admissions," State Higher Education Executive Officers, 1998. Also, Esther Rodriguez, "Diversity in Higher Education: An Action Plan Agenda for the States," State Higher Education Executive Officers, June 1999.

25. Careers and Colleges (no author) "How I Got Into College: 5 Students Share Their Secrets," September 2001. (monthly magazine)

26. Nancy Fitzgerald, "Considering Early Decision," Careers and Colleges, Sept. 1, 2000.

27. Jeffrey Young, "Yale Drops Early Decision," *The Chronicle of Higher Education*, Nov. 7, 2002.

28. William Bowen and James Shulman, *The Game of Life: College Sports and Educational Values.* Princeton, N.J.: Princeton University Press, 2002.

29. Ibid.

30. Chester Finn, Jr., "The Cost of College Sports," *Commentary Magazine*, Vol. 112: 3, October 2001.

31. William Bowen and James Shulman, *The Game of Life: College Sports and Educational Values.* Princeton, N.J.: Princeton University Press, 2002.

32. Milan Simonich, "'Jockocracy' Taking Hold Even at Many Elite Colleges," *Pittsburgh Post-Gazette*, Oct. 5, 2003.

33. Muaary Sperber, "Affirmative Action for Athletes," The Chronicle of Higher Education, Oct. 13, 1995.

34. Terri Hardy, "Write Stuff, Right UC Campus?," Sacramento Bee, Nov. 14, 2001.

35. Interview with Tanika who requested last name not be used, California high school student, April 2002.

36. Susan Sturm and Lani Guinier, "Lani Guinier and Susan Strum Respond," *Boston Review*, December 2000/January 200.

37. John Pulley, "How to Pick a 'Posse': A Foundation's Unusal Approach to Selecting Students," *The Chronicle of Higher Education*, April 28, 2000.

38. American Educational Research Association and Center for Comparative Studies in Race and Ethnicity, "Examining the Evidence on Racial Dynamics in Higher Education," May 21, 1999.

39. Ibid.

6. Percentage Plans to the Rescue

1. Catherine Horn, Stella Flores, Gary Orfield (2003). Percent Plans in College Admissions: A Comparative Analysis of Three States' Experiences. The Civil Rights Project, Harvard University.

2. Catherine Horn, Stella Flores, Gary Orfield (2003). Percent Plans in College Admissions: A Comparative Analysis of Three States' Experiences. The Civil Rights Project, Harvard University.

3. "Closing the Gap?: Admissions and Enrollments at the Texas Public Flagships Before and After Affirmative Action," Princeton, N.J.: Texas Top 10% Project, *www.texastop10.princeton.edu-publications.htm*, 2003.

4. Catherine Horn, Stella Flores, Gary Orfield (2003). Percent Plans in College Admissions: A Comparative Analysis of Three States' Experiences. The Civil Rights Project, Harvard University.

5. Ben Feller, AP Education writer, "Texas' Race-Neutral College Plan," *San Francisco Chronicle*, (June 20, 2003) *www.sfgate.com.*

6. Executive Order 99–281, *www.oneflorida.org*

7. "Government & Politics (no author). University of Florida to Open Its Doors to Top 5% of Each High School Graduating Class." *Chronicle of Higher Education*, March 22, 2002.

8. Texas Higher Education Facts 2003, *www.thecb.state.tx.us.*

9. Florida Board of Education, *www.fldcuorg/factbooks.*

10. Beyond Percentage Plans; *www.usccr.gov.*

11. "Reasons Why 'Percent Plans' won't work for college admissions nationwide *www.umich.edu/~newsinfo/releases/2003/Jan03/r012903.html.*

12. Facts & Figures (no author), "Using Class Rank: Who Makes It and

Who Doesn't." *Chronicle of Higher Education.* June 2, 2000.

13. Shelby Steele, *National Review,* Feb. 7, 2000.

14. Jeffrey Selingo. "What States Aren't Saying About the 'X-Percent Solution.'" *Chronicle of Higher Education,* June 2, 2000.

15. University of Florida, *One Florida,* Volume 26, Spring 2001 UF Student Affairs Update.

16. Closing the Gap: *www.texastop10.princeton.edu/publications.htm.*

7. To Be Color-Blind or Not?

1. "Ward Connerly: He Is America's Most Ardent Proponent of Colorblindness, a Successful Grassroots Political Leader, and a Bold Thinker on Questions of Race, Education and Government Policy." American Enterprise Institute for Public Policy: Gale Group. April–May 2003.

2. Hans S. Nichols, "Racial Tension Growing in California," Insight on The News: www.findarticles.com, May 20, 2002; Amy Aretsinger, "Reexamining Minority Admissions," *The Washington Post,* www.washingtonpost.com, March 12, 2003; Pete Williams, "Undergraduate Affirmative Action Program Struck Down," NBC, *www.nbc.com,* June 23, 2003.

3. David Almasi, "Supreme Court Affirmative Action Decision: Black Network Criticizes Muddled Ruling," National Center, *www.nationalcenter.org,* June 23, 2003.

4. Ibid.

5. Joy Bennett Kinnion, "Is Skin Color Still an Issue in Black America?" *Ebony Magazine.* April 2000.

6. Alfred E. Prettyman, "Seeing a Color-Blind Future: The Paradox of Race," *Cross Currents,* www.findarticles.com, Winter 1998.

7. Glenn C. Loury, "Is Affirmative Action on the Way Out: Should It Be?" *Commentary.* www.commentarymagazine.com, March 1998.

8. Andrea Psimer, "Virginia Tech Restores Affirmative Action," USA Today, April 6, 2003.

9. T. Wise, "Why Whites Think Blacks Have No Problems," *www.alternet.org,* July 2001.

10. "New University of Michigan Undergraduate Admissions Policy Modeled After Law School's Policy." *Black Issues in Higher Education,* September 25, 2003.

11. Oralander Brad-Williams, "U-M Policy Hailed," *Detroit News,* August 29, 2003.

12. "Urban League Warns Against Covert Racism," *www.cjcj.org,* July 28, 2003.

13. Amy Aretsinger, "Reexamining Minority Admissions," *The Washington Post,* March 12, 2003.

14. Brian Kladdko, Knight Ridder Business News. The Record, University Wire, Madison, Wis., Oct. 7, 2003.

15. This and the quotes in the following two paragraphs are from Stacy Waite, "Race May Not Have Large Effect on College Admissions, Raps at Shows," *The Mirror Online,* June 2003.

16. Adam Ewing, "Supreme Court to Rule on Affirmative Action," *Colorado Daily,* May 2003.

17. Richard Veileux, "Panel: Affirmative Action Battle Not Over Yet," *Advance* (*www.advance.uconn.edu*), October 27, 2003.

18. Jeffrey Selingo, "The Michigan Ratings: Decisions May Prompt Return of Race-Conscious Admissions at Some Colleges," *Chronicle of Higher Education,* July 4, 2003.

19. Eric Bailey, "UC Chief Defends Admissions Rules, Cites Diversity as Goal," *Los Angeles Times,* October 28, 2003.

20. CNN, "NAACP Leader Urges Affirmative Action Policies," All Politics, July 14, 2003.

21. "Ward Connerly: He Is America's Most Ardent Proponent of Colorblind-

ness, a Successful Grassroots Political Leader, and a Bold Thinker on Questions of Race, Education and Government Policy." American Enterprise Institute for Public Policy: Gale Group. April–May 2003.

22. Hazel Trice Edney, "Conservatives Seek to Circumvent Pro–Affirmative Action Ruling," *The Black Voice News*, July 26, 2003; Staff of Civilrights.org, "Connerly Announces Campaign to Ban Affirmative Action in Michigan," *www.civilrights.org*, July 8, 2003.

23. Peter Schmidt, "Behind the Fight Over Race-Conscious Admissions," *Chronicle of Higher Education*, April 4, 2003.

24. Connie Rice, "When Race No Longer Matters," National Public Radio, *www.npr.org*, Nov. 12, 2003.

8. Can We Fix the Problem?

1. The Education Trust, Inc., "All Talk, No Action," August 2002.

2. Lynn Olson, "The Great Divide (Report on the Teacher Gap)," *Education Week*, January 2003.

3. "Out-of-Field Teaching, Educational Inequality, and the Organization of Schools," University of Washington Center for the Study of Teaching and Policy, January 2002.

4. Lynn Olson, "The Great Divide (Report on the Teacher Gap)," *Education Week*, January 2003.

5. Education Week, "To Close the Gap, Quality Counts," January 2003.

6. The Education Trust, Inc., "All Talk, No Action," August 2002.

7. University of California, Berkeley Fall 2001 Undergraduate Admissions.

8. Patricia McDonough, "Creating a College-Going Culture in Increasing Access and Promoting Excellence: Diversity in California Public Higher Educa-

tion," State Senate Select Committee on College and University Admissions and Outreach, May 2002.

9. Patricia McDonough, *Choosing Colleges: How Social Class and Schools Structure Opportunity*, State University of New York Press, 1997.

10. Bar Association of Metropolitan St. Louis, St. Louis Internship Program, *www.bamsl.org*.

11. Practicing Attorneys for Law Students Program, Inc., (PALS), New York, *www.palsprogram.org*.

12. Nashville Bar Association, Nashville High School Summer Intern Program, *www.nashbar.org/*.

13. National Bar Association, American Bar Association Resource Guide, *www.abanet.org/*, 2002.

14. American Bar Association, Washington, D.C. *www.abanet.org*.

15. New York County Lawyers' Association, Minority Judicial Internship Program, New York, N.Y.

16. The California Endowment, "Strategies for Improving the Diversity of the Health Professions," August 2003.

17. Association of American Medical Colleges, 2003.

18. Dr. Winston Doby, "Toward a Level Playing Field," *UC Outlook*, *www.ucop.edu/outreach/outlook*, May 2002.

19. A. Miller-Browne, 1996. "Shameful Admissions: The Losing Battle to Serve Everyone in Our Universities." San Francisco, CA: Jossey-Bass, 1996.

20. J. Oakes and M. Lipton, *Teaching to Change the World*. McGraw Hill Higher Education: Columbus, Ohio, 2003.

21. Association of American Medical Colleges, Expanded Minority Admissions Exercise (EMAE), *www.aamc.org/*.

22. *Grutter v. Bollinger*, 539 S. Ct. U.S. (2003).

23. Jeff Zorn, "Affirmative Action" (letter to the editor), *Commentary Magazine*, January 2004.

Bibliography

"The Abolition of Race-Based Preferential Admissions Should Make Its Deepest Cuts at California's Medical Schools." *Journal of Blacks in Higher Education*, 9: 18, 1995.

Adams, F. Michael. "Statement by UGA President." The University of Georgia: *www.uga.edu/news/*, Nov. 29, 2001.

Adams, William. "Race Has a Place in College Admissions." *Los Angeles Times*, Dec. 30, 2002.

Affirmative Action Watch. "New University of Michigan Undergrad Admissions Policy Modeled after Law Schools." *www.blackissues.com*, Sept. 25, 2003.

"African-American Student First Year Enrollments at the Nation's Highest-Ranked Colleges and Universities." *Journal of Blacks in Higher Education*, 33: 6–14, 2001.

Almasi, David. "Supreme Court Affirmative Action Decision: Black Network Criticizes Muddle Ruling." Project 21: *www.nationalcenter.org*, June 23, 2003.

American Council on Education. "Percentage Plans for College Admissions." *www.acenet.edu/resources*, January 2001.

_____. "Students of Color Make Enrollment and Graduation Gains in Postsecondary Education." Washington, D.C.: *www.acenet.edu*, 2002.

Arenson, Karen. "As Early Admissions Rise, Colleges Debate Practice." *The New York Times*, December 23, 2002.

Argetsinger, Amy. "College-Bound Students Often Skip Race Question," 2003.

_____. "Where Early Decision Is Won and Lost." *The Washington Post*, Dec. 16, 2002.

Ascher, Carol. "Retaining Good Teachers in Urban Schools." ERIC/CUE Digest No. 77. ERIC Clearing House on Urban Education. New York, N.Y. (ED341762), 1991.

The Associated Press. "Admission Policies Not Leading to More Diversity, Report Says." *Los Angeles Times*, Nov. 20, 2002.

_____. "Fewer Blacks Enrolling in Georgia's Top Schools." Online Athens: *www.onlineathens.com*, July 30, 2000.

_____. "Maintenance of Racial Inequality Through Covert Processes of Structures and Institutions. July 28, 2003.

_____. "Michigan Students, Faculty Weigh In on Rulings." June 23, 2003.

_____. "Minority Levels Rebound at UC." *Los Angeles Times*, April 5, 2002.

_____. "Nation's Oldest Women's College Drops SAT Requirement." June 3, 2000.

_____. "State Attorney General Blocks Ohio State's Plans to Back U-M." *The Detroit News*, Feb. 22, 2003.

Bailey, Eric. "UC Chief Defends Admissions Rules, Cites Diversity as Goal." *Los Angeles Times*, www.latimes.com, Oct. 24, 2003.

Bauza, Margarita. "Both Sides in Case Vow to Monitor Minorities." *The Detroit News*, www.detnews.com, Aug. 29, 2003.

_____. "College Legacy Rules Lock Out Minorities, Critics Say." *The Detroit News*, March 10, 2003.

Bendick, Marc, Charles Jackson and Victor Reinoso, "Measuring Employment Discrimination Through Controlled Experiments." *Review of Black Political Economics*. 23: 1, pp. 25-48, 1994.

"Black Enrollments at the Nation's Highest-Ranked Colleges and Universities." *Journal of Blacks in Higher Education*, 37: 8–14, 2002.

Black Issues in Higher Education. "College Board-Sponsored Study Claims SAT Is Good Predictor of Grades," 2001.

Bloch, Farrell. *Antidiscrimination Law and Minority Employment*. Chicago: University of Chicago Press, 1994.

Blum, Edward and Roger Clegg, "Percentage Plans Admissions of Failure." *Chronicle of Higher Education*, March 21, 2003.

Bollinger, Lee, C. "A Resounding Victory for Diversity on Campus." *The Washington Post*, www.washingtonpost.com, June 23, 2003.

Bowen, William G. and Bok Derek. *Shape of the River*. Princeton, NJ: Princeton University Press, 1998.

_____ and _____. *The Shape of the River: Long-Term Consequences of Considering Race in College and University Admissions*. Princeton, N.J.: Princeton University Press, 1998.

_____ and Sarah Levin. *Reclaiming the Game: College Sports and Educational Values*. Princeton, N.J.: Princeton University Press, 2003.

Brand-Williams, Orlander. "U-M Policy Hailed, Assailed." *The Detroit News*, www.detnews.com, Aug. 28, 2003.

Brunner, Borgna. "Timeline of Affirmative Action Milestones." Infoplease.com: www.infoplease.com/, 2002.

Bunzel, John. "Affirmative Action: Where's the Line?" *The San Jose Mercury News*. Feb. 3, 2003.

Burdman, Pamela. "Advanced Placement Online AP Courses." National Cross Talk — Vol. 18: 3, National Center for Public Policy and Higher Education, Summer, 2003.

Burdris, John, "In Gatekeepers, a Real-Life Peek Behind Closed Doors of College Admissions Offices." *The Christian Science Monitor*, Dec. 10, 2002.

Campbell, Duane. *Choosing Democracy: A Practical Guide to Multicultural Education*. Pearson: New Jersey, 2004.

Carter, Terry. "Divided Justice." *American Bar Association Journal* 85, 42, February 1999.

Chafe, William. "Providing Guarantees of Equal Opportunity." *The Chronicle of Higher Education*, June 30, 1995.

Chang, Mitchell. "Assessing Affirmative Action at Selective Colleges and Universities." *Change*, July–Aug. 1998.

Chang, M.J., Witt, D., Jones, J., and Hakutta, K. *Compelling Interest: Examining the Evidence on Racial Dynamics in Colleges and Universities*. Stanford, CA: Stanford University Press, 2003.

Chenoweth, Karin. "Our Education Obligations Extend Far Beyond Affirmative Action." *The Washington Post*, www.Washingtonpost.com, April 24, 2003.

"Clarity in Admissions Rules Will Be Welcome Regardless of Decision." *Athens (Ga.) Banner-Herald*, Dec. 2, 2002.

Clayton, Mark. "On University's Case for Race." *The Christian Science Monitor*, www.csmonitor.com, April 1, 2003.

Cohen, Jodi. "Lott Clouds U-M Lawsuit." *The Detroit News*, Dec. 24, 2002.

_____. "U-M Takes Case to High Court." *The Detroit News.* Feb. 19, 2003.

Coleman, L. Arthur. *Diversity in Higher Education.* Sacramento, Calif. The College Board, 2001.

Cooper, Kenneth J. "'A Certain Distance' from 1960s in Georgia." *The Washington Post.* Jan. 3, 2001.

_____. "Deciding Who Gets in and Who Doesn't." *The Washington Post*, April 2, 2000.

Cross, Theodore. "Suppose There Was No Affirmative Action at the Most Prestigious Colleges and Graduate Schools." *Journal of Blacks in Higher Education* 3: 44–51, 1994.

_____. "Why Hopwood Ruling Would Remove Most African Americans from the Nation's Most Selective Universities." *Journal of Blacks in Higher Education* 11: 66–70, 1996.

Dalmage, M. Heather. "Tripping on the Color Line: Black-Write Multiracial Families in a Racially Divided World." Western Michigan School of Social Work, March 2002.

Day, Jennifer C. and Andrea E. Curry. "Educational Attainment in the United States: March 1998 (update)." Current Population Reports P20-513, Washington, D.C. : U.S. Bureau of the Census, 1998.

Delgado, Ray. "*Group Helping Kids to College Draws an Elite Crowd of Role Models.*" San Francisco Chronicle, www.sfgate.com, Feb. 21, 2003.

Edley, Christopher Jr. *Not All Black and White.* New York: Hill and Wang, 1996.

Edney, Hazel Trice. "Conservatives Seek to Circumvent Pro-Affirmative Action Ruling," The Black Voice News, *www.blackvoicenews.com*, July 26, 2003.

Education Trust. "New Frontiers for a New Century: A National Overview." Vol. 5:2, Spring, 2001.

Feagin, J.R. and P.S. Melvin. *Living with Racism: The Black Middle Class Experience.* Boston: Beacon Press, 1994.

Feller, Ben (AP Education Writer). "Bush Administration Promotes 'Race-Neutral' College Idea, Department of Education Guide." *The Detroit News*, March 29, 2003.

Fletcher, Michael. "Universities Alter Recruiting." *The Washington Post.* Dec. 3, 2002.

_____. "Use of Race in Admissions Upheld." *The Washington Post*, Dec. 14, 2002.

Fogg, Piper. "U. of California, for First Time, Admits More Minority Students Than It Did Under Affirmative Action." *The Chronicle of Higher Education.* April 8, 2002.

Frankenberg, Erica, Chungmei Lee and Gary Orfield. "*A Multiracial Society with Segregated Schools: Are We Losing the Dream?*" Cambridge, Massachusetts: The Civil Rights Project, Harvard University, January 2003.

Garibaldi, M. Antoine. "After Initiative 200, Applications Down for Minorities at U. of Washington." *Black Issues in Higher Education*, May 11, 2000.

Glazer, Nathan. "Society Needs Affirmative Action in Higher Education." In Bryan Grapes, ed., *Affirmative Action*, pp. 14–22. San Diego, Calif: Greenhaven Press, Inc, 2000.

Glickman, Carl. "Defining a Great University." University of Georgia News Bureau, *www.uga.edu/columns*, May 3, 1999.

Gose, Ben. "Former Wisconsin Chancellor Named Head of American Council on Education." *The Chronicle of Higher Education*, April 13, 2001.

Government & Politics. "Airlines Donate Tickets to Help 25 Black Applicants Visit U. of Texas Law School." *The Chronicle of Higher Education*, April 28, 2000.

Grapes, Bryan J., ed. *Affirmative Action*. San Diego, Calif.: Greenhaven Press, Inc., 2000.

Guernsey, Lisa and Patrick Healy. "Judge Rules that U. of Georgia Gave Unconstitutional Preferences to Black Applicants." *The Chronicle of Higher Education*, Jan. 22, 1999.

Guinier, Lani. "Colleges Should Take 'Confirmative Action' in Admissions." *The Chronicle of Higher Education*, Dec. 14, 2001.

Hannon, Sharron. "Can Race Play a Role in the Admissions Process?" *Georgia Magazine*: *www.uga.edu/gm*, Sept. 14, 1999.

_____. "Staying the Course." Online Athens: *www.onlineathens.com*, Oct. 4, 1999.

_____. "Staying the Course Becomes a Rallying Cry." *Georgia Magazine*, *www.uga.edu/gm*, Dec. 14, 1999.

Haynes, V. Dion. "College Admissions Rules in Four States Face New Challenge in Wake of Ruling." *Chicago Tribune*: Knight Ridder/Tribune Business News, *www.chicagotribune.com*, June 25, 2003.

Headlam, Bruce. "Nothing Personal." *The New York Times*, Feb. 17, 2002.

Healy, Patrick. "Lawsuit Attacks Race-Based Policies in U. System of Georgia." *The Chronicle of Higher Education*, March 14, 1997.

_____, and Liz McMillen. "Judge Affirms Validity of 'Bakke' in U. of Washington Affirmative Action Lawsuit." *The Chronicle of Higher Education*, Feb. 26, 1999.

Hebel, Sara. "Class-Rank Plans Found Lacking." *The Chronicle of Higher Education*, Feb. 28, 2003.

_____. "Court Ruling Could End Outreach to Minority Students in California." *The Chronicle of Higher Education*, Dec. 15, 2000.

_____. "Minority Students Sue Berkeley, Charging Bias in Admissions." *The Chronicle of Higher Education*, Feb. 12, 1999.

"High School Completion Rates." Washington, D.C.: National Center for Education Statistics (*www.nces.ed.gov/pubs 2002/droppub_2001*), 2001.

Hill, Karen. "Desegregation Plan Supported." *The Atlanta Journal-Constitution*, Feb. 24, 2002.

_____. "Parents Unite to Integrate Schools." *The Atlanta Journal-Constitution*. Feb. 22, 2003.

Holland, Robert. "How to Build a Better Teacher." *USA Today Magazine*, September 2001.

Holzer, Harry and David Neumark. "Assessing Affirmative Action." *The Journal of Economic Literature*, Vol. 38: 3, pp. 483–568, 2000.

Jackson, Derrick. "Trying to Negate Affirmative Action." *Boston Globe*, Dec. 4, 2002.

Jenkins, Wilbert. "Why We Must Retain Affirmative Action." *USA Today Magazine* (Society for the Advancement of Education), September 1999.

Johnson, Miki. "Faculty, Students Weigh Sides of Factoring Race in Admissions Policies at Schools Across U.S." *The Daily Northwestern, www.dailynorthwestern.com*, May 20, 2003.

Jones-Gutierrez, Carl. "Friends of Affirmative Action." *The Hartford Courant, www.ctnow.com*, Feb. 19, 2003.

Kaye, J. Harvey. "One Professor's Dialectic of Mentoring." *The Chronicle of Higher Education*, April 21, 2000.

Kenney, Genevieve and Douglas Wissoker. "An Analysis of the Correlates of Discrimination Facing Young Hispanic Jobseekers." *American Economic Review.* 84: 3, pp. 674–83, 1994.

Kiernan, Vincent. "Minority Enrollment in Florida Remains Unchanged." *The Chronicle of Higher Education*, Sept. 20, 2002.

Kinnen, Joy. "Is Skin Color Still an Issue in Black America?" *Ebony, www.ebony.com*, April 2000.

Kladko, Brian. "Rutgers Law School Aims to Achieve Race-Blind Affirmative Admissions." Knight Ridder/Tribune Business News, *http://ask.elibrary.com*, 2003.

Kozol, J. *Savage Inequalities: Children in America's Schools.* New York: Crown Publishers, 1991.

Laird, Bob. "Bending Admissions to Political Ends." *The Chronicle of Higher Education*, May 17, 2002.

Lane, Charles. "College Admission on Review: Justices to Decide If Affirmative Action Treats Whites Unfairly." *The Washington Post*, Dec. 3, 2002.

_____. "High Court Dismisses Affirmative Action Case." *The Washington Post*, Nov. 28, 2001.

"Law School Council Suggests De-emphasizing Test Scores to Encourage Diversity." *The Chronicle of Higher Education*, January 7, 2000.

Leatherman, Courtney. "A Nasty Gander at Michigan." *The Chronicle of Higher Education*, Sept. 15, 2000.

Loury, C. Glenn. "Is Affirmative Action on the Way Out? Should it Be?" Commentary, *www.commentary.com*, March 1998.

Lurie, Thea. "Americans See Many Benefits to Diversity in Higher Education, Finds First-Ever National Poll on Topic." The Ford Foundation, Oct. 6, 1998.

MacDonald, Christine. "Applicants Now Required to Write Essay on Diversity." *The Detroit News, www.detnews.com*, Aug. 29, 2003.

Mangan, Katerine. "White Students Do Better on LSAT Than Minority Classmates with Similar GPA's, Report Says." *The Chronicle of Higher Education.* Aug. 30, 2001.

Marin, P. and E. Lee. "Appearance and Reality in the Sunshine State: The Talented 20 Program in Florida." Cambridge, Mass.: The Civil Rights Project at Harvard University, *www.civilrightsprojectharvard.edu*, 2003.

Mathews, Jay. "Colleges' Admissions Policies to Be Studied," *The Washington Post, www.washingpost.com*, Sept. 6, 2003.

_____. "Yale, Stanford Abolish Early Decision Process." *The Chronicle of Higher Education*, Nov. 7, 2002.

Maxwell, Bill. "Times Have Changed for Black Students." *St. Petersburg Times*, Dec. 11, 2002.

McIntosh, Peggy. *Understanding Privilege.* Wellesley College Center for Research on Women: Wellesley College, 1984.

Morson, Berry. "Colorado University Debate Tackles Race, Admissions." *Rocky Mountain News: www.rockymountainnews.com*, Oct. 15, 2003.

"NAACP Leader Urges Affirmative Action Policies." All Politics, *www.cnn.com*, July 14, 2003.

Neumark, David and Michelle McLennan. "Sex Discrimination and Women's Labor Market Outcomes." *Journal of Human Research*. 30: 4, pp. 713–40, 1995.

O'Neil, James. "Colleges Ponder Diversity's Future." *The Philadelphia Inquirer*, Feb. 19, 2003.

Oppenheimer, David. "Understanding Affirmative Action." *Hastings Constitutional Law Quarterly* 23: 4, Summer 1996.

Orfield, Gary and Dean Whitla. "Diversity and Legal Education: Student Experiences in Leading Law Schools." In Gary Orfield and Michal Kurlaender (eds.), *Diversity Challenged: Evidence on the Impact of Affirmative Action*, pp. 143–173. Cambridge, Mass.: The Civil Rights Project, Harvard University: Harvard Education Publishing Group, 2001.

Parettyman, E. Alfred. "Seeing a Color-Blind Future: The Paradox of Race" (review). *Cross Currents*, *www.aril.org*, Winter 1998.

"The Progress of Admissions of Black Students at the Nation's Highest-Ranked Colleges and Universities." *Journal of Blacks in Higher Education*, 13: 6–11, 1996.

"The Progress of Black Student Matriculations at the Nation's Highest-Ranked Colleges and Universities." *Journal of Blacks in Higher Education*, 21: 8–14, 1998.

"The Progress of Black Student Matriculations at the Nation's Highest-Ranked Colleges and Universities." *Journal of Blacks in Higher Education*, 29: 16–21, 2000.

"Public School District Finance Peer Search." Washington, D.C.: National Center for Education Statistics, 1998–99.

"Racial Preferences in Higher Education: Whites Overreacting to a Minor Incursion on Their Historical Privileges." *Journal of Blacks in Higher Education*, 9: 19, 1995.

Reich, Robert. "How Selective Colleges Heighten Inequality." *The Chronicle of Higher Education*, Sept. 15, 2000.

Rivas-Perez, Manuel. "Silver Spring School Overhaul." *The Washington Post*, March 30, 2001.

Roberts, Beth. "Of Flagships, Admissions and Affirmative Action." University of Georgia Columns, *www.uga.edu/columns/*, Oct. 27, 1997.

Russell Sage Foundation, *www.russellsage.org/*.

Sacks, Peter. "How Admissions Tests Hinder Access to Graduate and Professional Schools." *The Chronicle of Higher Education*, June 8, 2001.

Schmidt, Peter. "Report Urges Colleges to Keep Affirmative Action." *The Chronicle of Higher Education*, June 4, 1999.

_____. "U. of California Ends Affirmative-Action Ban, State Law Still Bars Preferences." *The Chronicle of Higher Education*, May 25, 2001.

_____. "U.S. Supreme Court Agrees to Hear 2 Key Affirmative-Action Cases from Michigan." *The Chronicle of Higher Education*, Dec. 2, 2002.

Schrag, Peter. "Ethnic Diversity Without Race Preferences?" *Sacramento Bee*, Feb. 5, 2003.

Selingo, Jeffrey. "Broader Admissions Criteria Near Approval at U. of California." *The Chronicle of Higher Education*. Nov. 23, 2001.

_____. "Decisions May Prompt Return of Race-Conscious Admissions at Some Colleges." *The Chronicle of Higher Education*. July 4, 2003.

_____. "Michigan Law School's Admissions Policies Found to Be Unconstitutional." *The Chronicle of Higher Education*. April 6, 2001.

_____. "Small Number of High Schools Produces Half of Students at U of Texas at Austin." *The Chronicle of Higher Education*, April 13, 2001.

_____. "U. of California Regents Adopt Admissions Plan." *The Chronicle of Higher Education*, Aug. 3, 2001.

_____. "U. of California's 4 Percent Plan Helps Hispanic and Rural Applicants Most," *The Chronicle of Higher Education*. May 14, 2002.

_____. "What States Aren't Saying About the 'X-Percent Solution,'" *The Chronicle of Higher Education*, June 2, 2000.

Shearer, Lee. "Adams Addresses UGA." Online Athens, *www.onlineathens.com*, January 13, 2000.

_____. "Regents Deny Charges of Race Bias." Online Athens, *www.onlineathens.com*, Aug. 14, 2000.

_____. "Ruling Draws Mixed Reaction." Online Athens, *www.onlineathens.com*, July 25, 2000.

_____. "Summary Judgment Sought in Admission Case." *The Augusta Chronicle*, April 27, 2000.

_____. "UGA Drops Race Preference." Online Athens, *www.onlineathens.com*, Aug. 15, 2000.

Shelton, Hilary. "Society Needs Affirmative Action." In Bryan Grapes (ed.) *Affirmative Action*, pp. 9–13. San Diego, Calif.: Greenhaven Press, Inc., 2000.

"The Short History of Race-Based Affirmative Action at Rice University." *Journal of Blacks in Higher Education*, 13: 36–38, 1996.

Simmons, Tim. "Race's Role in College Admissions." *The News and Observer*, Dec. 15, 2002.

Slivka, Judd. "Universities Branch Out to Add Students, Diversity." *The Arizona Republic*, *www.arizonarepublic.com*, Nov. 6, 2003.

Smith, T.W. "Intergroup Relations in a Diverse America." The American Jewish Committee, 2001.

Sperber, Murray. *Shake Down the Thunder: The Creation of Notre Dame Football*. New York, NY: Henry Holt & Co., 1995.

Steinberg, Jacques. "3 See College Suit as a Way to Show They Belonged." *The New York Times*, Feb. 23, 2003.

_____. "Using Synonyms for Race, College Strives for Diversity." *The New York Times*, Dec. 8, 2002.

Stephanopoulos, George and Christopher Edley, Jr. "Affirmative Action Review Report to the President." July 19, 1995. *http://clinton2.nora.gov/WH/EOP/OP/html/aa/aa-index.html*.

Street, Scott. "Attacking George Bush, Affirmative Action Baby." *The Chronicle of Higher Education*, Sept. 22, 2000.

Stroer, Joan. "Judge Lets UGA Continue Admissions Policy." Online Athens, *www.onlineathens.com*, Feb. 12, 2000.

_____. "UGA Likely to Appeal Admissions Ruling." Online Athens, *www.onlineathens.com*, July 25, 2000.

"Taking Stock, Resuming Course: Court's Endorsement of Race Has Colleges Affirming Admissions Practices and Revamping Policies." Panel discussion, *Black Issues in Higher Education*, *www.blackissues.com*, July 2003.

Thernstrom, Stephan. *America in Black and White*. New York: Simon & Schuster, 1997.

Tobin, Thomas. "Will Choice Segregate Schools?" *St. Petersburg Times*. Feb. 27, 2003.

"U. of Florida to Open Its Doors to Top 5% of Each High-School Graduating Class." *The Chronicle of Higher Education,* March 22, 2002.

"U. of Texas to Put Race Factor Back into Admissions." *www.cnn.com,* June 26, 2003.

"U-M Readies New Admissions Plan." *The Detroit News, www.detnews.com,* Aug. 27, 2003.

U.S. Commission on Civil Rights. "Statement on Affirmative Action." No. 54, October 1977.

U.S. Commission on Civil Rights. "Toward Equal Educational Opportunity: Affirmative Admissions Programs at Law and Medical Schools." No. 55, June 1978.

University of Michigan Application Guide. "The Admission Review Procedure." University of Michigan Admissions: *www.admissions.umich.edu/process/review/procedures.* September 2003.

University of Michigan News Service. "New U-M Undergraduate Admissions Process to Involve More Information, Individual Review." University of Michigan News Service, *www.umich.edu/news,* Aug. 3, 2003.

University of Texas at Austin News Release. "University's Admission Policy to Include Consideration of Race." *www.utexas.edu.* Aug. 28, 2003.

"Ward Connerly: He Is America's Most Ardent Proponent of Color-blindness," interview. *American Enterprise, www.detnews.com,* April–May 2003.

Williams, John. *Race Discrimination in Public Higher Education: Interpreting Federal Civil Rights Enforcement, 1964–1996.* Westport, CT.: Praeger Publishers, 1997.

Williams, Pete. "Law School Affirmative Action Program Upheld." MSNBC: *www.msnbc.msn.com/* June 23, 2003.

Williams, Walter. "How Affirmative Action Hurts Minorities." *The News and Observer: www.newsobserver.com,* April 13, 2003.

Winters, Greg. "U. of Michigan Alters Admissions Use of Race." *The New York Times, www.newyorktimes.com,* Aug. 29, 2003.

Wolfe, Alan. "What Scholarships Reveal About Politics and Religion." *The Chronicle of Higher Education,* Sept. 8, 2000.

Young, Cathy. "Campus Diversity Without Dogma." *Boston Globe,* Dec. 9, 2002.

Zeman, David. "Admission Policy in Line with Supreme Court Ruling, Experts Say." *The Detroit Free Press, www.freepress.com,* June 23, 2003.

Zinsmeister, Karl. "Unchain Our Schools." American Enterprise, *www.blackenterprise.com,* April–May 2003.

Index

253